Battle over the Bench

Constitutionalism and Democracy

GREGG IVERS AND
KEVIN T. MCGUIRE,
EDITORS

Battle over the Bench

SENATORS, INTEREST GROUPS, AND

LOWER COURT CONFIRMATIONS

Amy Steigerwalt

UNIVERSITY OF VIRGINIA PRESS   CHARLOTTESVILLE AND LONDON

University of Virginia Press
© 2010 by the Rector and Visitors of the University of Virginia
All rights reserved
Printed in the United States of America on acid-free paper

First published 2010

9 8 7 6 5 4 3 2 1

LIBRARY OF CONGRESS CATALOGING-IN-PUBLICATION DATA
Steigerwalt, Amy, 1976–
    Battle over the bench : senators, interest groups, and lower court confirmations /
Amy Steigerwalt.
        p.   cm. — (Constitutionalism and democracy)
    Includes bibliographical references and index.
    ISBN 978-0-8139-2994-1 (cloth : alk. paper) — ISBN 978-0-8139-2998-9 (e-book)
    1. Judges—Selection and appointment—United States. 2. Political questions and
judicial power—United States. I. Title.
    KF8776.S74 2010
    347.73'14—dc22

                                                                            2009047757

To Greg

In memory of
Nelson Polsby

CONTENTS

TABLES AND FIGURES

FIGURES

ACKNOWLEDGMENTS

As with many projects, the list of those who have helped this book become a reality is numerous. The book is based on work begun at the University of California, Berkeley, and many professors and fellow graduate students provided excellent advice, feedback, and support; it is highly likely that any good ideas are theirs. Robert A. Kagan, my dissertation adviser, and Malcolm M. Feeley both supported this project from the beginning, and have been fantastic mentors and friends. Nelson W. Polsby, who is deeply missed, offered constant advice and guidance. I would not be the scholar I am today without the three of them. Many thanks are due to Lori A. Johnson, who first helped me conceive this study and shape it into a doable and successful project. The members of GWAP—Casey B. K. Dominguez, Justin Buchler, Matthew G. Jarvis, Keith W. Smith, and John E. McNulty—provided the feedback, critiques, stability, and encouragement that only fellow graduate students (and great friends) can.

I conducted the interviews for this project with the aid of a 2002 Dirksen Congressional Center Congressional Research Grant. Some of the interviews with interest group leaders were conducted with the help of Nancy Scherer. A list of opposed nominations, similar to that appearing in appendix C, was previously published in Nancy Scherer, Brandon L. Bartels, and Amy Steigerwalt, "Sounding the Fire Alarm: The Role of Interest Groups in the Lower Federal Court Confirmation Process," *Journal of Politics* 70 (2008): 1026–39. That article also quoted material from some of the same interviews featured in this book; these interviews were originally conducted for the dissertation project that led to this book.

I am extremely grateful for the enormous amount of advice, feedback, and support I have received from many colleagues since leaving Berkeley. I specifically want to thank Brandon L. Bartels, Lawrence Baum, Sara C.

Benesh, Sarah A. Binder, Eileen Braman, Paul M. Collins Jr., Pamela C. Corley, Jolly Emery, Alison Gash, Micheal W. Giles, Sheldon Goldman, Roger E. Hartley, Marcus E. Hendershot, Lisa M. Holmes, Robert M. Howard, Robert J. Hume, Tonja Jacobi, Forrest Maltzman, Amy McKay, Nancy Scherer, Jeffrey A. Segal, Elliot E. Slotnick, Susan Navarro Smelcer, Harold J. Spaeth, Richard L. Vining, Thomas G. Walker, and Stephen L. Wasby; to those whom I am positive I have inadvertently left off this list, thank you. I am thrilled to be part of a subfield in which support and collaboration are the norm rather than the exception. I especially thank Artemus Ward, Christine L. Nemachek, and Wendy L. Martinek, who offered hours of help and advice above and beyond the call of either professional collegiality or friendship. Thank you to my colleagues at Georgia State University for making my working days such a delight, and to my department for providing me with research assistants; I thank Clarissa Dias and Lindsey Herbel for their able assistance. I especially thank Jessica Burke, whose assistance on numerous tasks was invaluable. I am also indebted to my former colleagues at the University of New Orleans.

My editor at the University of Virginia Press, Richard K. Holway, and the two series editors, Kevin T. McGuire and Gregg Ivers, provided help and support as this book wound its way through the publication process. Two anonymous reviewers provided comments and suggestions that made this book all the better.

Finally, thank you to my friends and family who have encouraged me through the years, some all the way back to middle school. You are particularly lucky when your family and friends make even difficult events tolerable. The Steigerwalt and Smith families have all supported me in ways both big and small, and for that I am exceedingly grateful; I can only hope that I will be as great a parent as Ronna and Arnold Steigerwalt have been to me. Last but not least, to my husband Greg, who has stood beside me even as I've dragged him around the country, canceled plans to work, shoved chapters at him and asked him to please edit them in the next ten minutes, and needed him to wait on me hand and foot while I recovered from ankle surgery. I could not have done this without you, love.

Battle over the Bench

INTRODUCTION

The Changing Tone of Lower Federal Court Confirmations

On May 9, 2001, President George W. Bush sent his first set of nominations for the lower federal courts to the Senate. This list included Texas Supreme Court justice Priscilla Owen, who was nominated to the Fifth Circuit Court of Appeals. Almost immediately, battle cries were heard from liberal judicial watchdog groups, pro-choice groups, and Senate Democrats. Owen's offense? She had voted consistently to uphold restrictive abortion laws while on the Texas Supreme Court and had voted against every petition by a pregnant minor for a judicial bypass.[1]

By the end of the 107th Congress, more than one hundred groups had voiced opposition to Owen's nomination, and it was defeated in the Senate Judiciary Committee on a fractious, party-line vote. However, the story does not end there. As soon as the Republicans regained majority control of the Senate in 2003 (the start of the 108th Congress), President Bush promptly renominated Owen for the same vacancy. Not surprisingly, Democratic senators and liberal interest groups vehemently objected to this action by Bush, as never before had a defeated nominee been renominated. This time, with a Republican-controlled Judiciary Committee, her nomination was favorably passed out of committee, again on a strict party-line vote. The minority Democrats responded by filibustering her nomination on the Senate floor. By the end of the 108th Congress, nine other circuit court nominees would be filibustered as well.

This filibuster was not the only thing that stood in Owen's way, however. While she waited for the final Senate floor vote on her nomination, her path to confirmation was also delayed by three different holds placed on her nomination by three different senators. In all three cases, Owen's nomination was captured merely by accident—the holds were placed on *all* pending judicial nominations awaiting Senate floor votes, and they delayed Owen's progress (and others') for many months. Each of these holds was the by-product of an unrelated fight between senators placing the hold and the president rather than an expression of opposition to the blocked nominations.

Why have lower court confirmations—and especially those to the circuit courts of appeals—become so contentious? Why do presidents, senators, outside interest groups, and concerned citizens care so much about who gets seated on the federal bench? Simply put, the lower federal courts have increasingly become the final arbiters of the most important issues of the day. On important issues such as abortion, congressional redistricting, affirmative action, and religious displays on public property, the federal courts almost always have the final say. Since these issues all have a constitutional component, and since the courts have the power to review the constitutionality of both state and federal laws (referred to as the power of judicial review), the final determination of what is permissible is many times in the hands of the federal courts.

Furthermore, as the Supreme Court has slowly reduced its caseload in the past few decades, the circuit courts have increasingly become the last word on these key issues. As a result, appointments to the lower federal courts, and especially the circuit courts, have taken on enormous importance. Each presidential term brings the chance to make literally dozens of appointments to the lower federal courts, giving presidents the ability to shape the partisan and ideological makeup of the federal courts for decades to come. Not surprisingly, senators, interest groups, and concerned citizens also want to see the federal bench staffed with judges who reflect their views. This book is thus a story about presidents, senators, and interest groups, and how they all seek to influence the third—and most frequently forgotten—branch of government, the judiciary.

However, this is not merely a story of fights over whether nominees possess the "correct" judicial philosophy. As the case of Priscilla Owen illustrates, nominees awaiting Senate floor votes are often caught in holds. A parliamentary procedure relatively hidden from the public eye, holds allow senators to delay votes on nominations and bills indefinitely. Often the nominations and bills trapped by these holds are simply in the wrong place at the wrong time: they are blocked because they are convenient bargaining chips in unrelated disputes between senators or between senators and the current administration. Nominees may be delayed for months while disagreements completely unconnected to their nominations are resolved. This is therefore also a story of how judicial nominations have become a central feature of the tit-for-tat game of bargaining and compromise that defines the modern-day legislative process.

This book focuses on explaining the lower federal court confirmation process since 1985. Lower federal court nominations were traditionally patronage-rewarding, rather than policymaking, opportunities for presidents and home-state senators. Such nominations were given great deference by the Senate, and these nominees were usually confirmed quickly and easily. By 1985, however, important changes had begun taking place. Most notably, presidents started selecting judicial nominees, especially to the circuit courts, based primarily on the nominees' judicial philosophy or perceived ideological positions rather than as a reward for political service. In turn, senators, outside interest groups, and concerned citizens began to vet nominees more closely and to voice objections to potentially objectionable nominees. By the Clinton administration, and most decidedly by the George W. Bush administration, partisan and ideological tensions over the staffing of the federal bench had grown to a fever pitch.[2]

Even with this increased contentiousness, however, the reality is that the vast majority of lower court nominees are still confirmed easily and without opposition. The question thus becomes, why are some nominations contested while others are confirmed easily? What makes a nomination controversial, and who makes it become so? This book aims to answer these important questions. It does so by examining the lower court confirmation process itself, and the multiple stages a nomination must successfully pass through on its path to confirmation, to discover *how* nominations may be impeded, *when* nominations are stalled, and, most important, *who* stalls them and *why*. This introduction begins our examination of the lower federal court confirmation process by assessing the historical change from patronage-based to policy-based appointments and the implications of this change. It then briefly summarizes the central theoretical contribution of the book, the four tracks framework, and concludes by reviewing the arguments advanced in the rest of the book.

The Increased Politicization of the Lower Federal Court Confirmation Process

The federal judicial system is comprised of three levels of courts.[2] Article III, Section 1, of the Constitution established the U.S. Supreme Court and authorized Congress to create inferior courts as needed. The First Congress passed the Judiciary Act of 1789 to create these inferior courts—thirteen district courts and three circuit courts. These courts were arranged geographically: each original colony contained at least one district court, while groups of colonies composed each circuit. Today, at least one district court is located within each state, while geographically proximate groups of states make up a circuit. The district courts are the federal trial courts, and they conduct trials in criminal and civil cases involving questions of federal statutory or constitutional law, as well as trials in other cases where the federal courts have been granted jurisdiction. The district courts, like all trial courts, answer questions of fact, such as whether a person is guilty of murder or whether a company discriminated against its employees.

The circuit courts are the federal intermediate appellate courts. They hear appeals of decisions rendered by district courts located in states within their circuit, and they may also hear appeals of state court decisions that involve a question of federal law. The circuit courts are mandatory jurisdiction courts, meaning they must render a decision in all cases properly appealed to them. As appeals courts, the circuit courts answer questions of law, such as whether evidence gathered by law enforcement was properly admitted or excluded under the Fourth Amendment's protections against unreasonable searches and seizures.

The third and highest level of the federal judicial system is the U.S. Supreme Court. The highest court in the land, the Supreme Court has the final word on questions of federal statutory and constitutional law. The Supreme Court is also an appeals court, but it differs from the circuit courts in that its docket is almost entirely discretionary, and so the Court has the authority to choose which cases it will decide. In recent decades, even as the number of lawsuits filed in federal courts has increased, the Supreme Court has reduced its caseload; it currently decides approximately seventy-five cases a year. The Supreme Court's ability to select the cases it hears means it also sets its own agenda, and the Supreme Court's docket generally reflects the most important statutory and constitutional law issues of the day.

As stipulated by Article II, Section 2, of the Constitution, each of these so-called Article III judges is nominated by the president, "by and with the advice and consent of the Senate."[3] They serve for life terms and are removable only through retirement, death, or impeachment.

Many argue that the selection and appointment of U.S. Supreme Court justices has always been politicized (Abraham 1999; Maltese 1995; Silverstein 1994). George Washington's nominee to be the Supreme Court's third chief justice, John Rutledge, was defeated in 1795 because of his opposition to the Jay Treaty (Abraham 1999; Gerhardt 2003; Maltese 1995). Supreme Court nominees since Rutledge have also run into opposition as a result of their positions on controversial issues of the day. As leading scholars note, "Nominations to the Supreme Court in the 18th and 19th centuries were expected to be subject to politically motivated attacks" (Grossman and Wasby 1972, 560).

Fights over Supreme Court seats reached a fever pitch in 1987 with the nomination of Robert Bork. Senator Edward Kennedy famously began the attack on Bork's nomination forty-five minutes after it was announced with a speech on the Senate floor denouncing "Robert Bork's America." Kennedy argued that Bork's version of American legal jurisprudence would lead to "a land in which women would be forced into back-alley abortions, blacks would sit at segregated lunch counters, [and] rogue police could break down citizens' doors in midnight raids."[4] Bork's nomination was defeated in the Senate Judiciary Committee but allowed to progress to the Senate floor for a vote by the full Senate. His journey ended in defeat when the Senate voted 58–42 against his nomination. Since Bork, every Supreme Court nomination has been intensely scrutinized in terms of the nominee's potential voting record once on the Court.

In contrast, the lower federal court confirmation process is generally trouble-free. Traditionally, home-state senators on both sides of the aisle possessed large amounts of power during the nominating process with regard to lower court judges, and especially district court judges. Beginning with George Washington, presidents deferred to senators in selecting nominees for lower court vacancies that occurred in their home state because they feared reprisal: if the home-state senators backed another candidate, they would call upon their fellow senators to support them in rejecting the nomination, a custom that became known as senatorial courtesy (Maltese 1995).[5] The norm of collegiality in the Senate meant that senators supported their fellow senators' choices, and expected the same courtesy in return.

Lower federal court appointments also traditionally served as rewards for political patronage (Goldman 1997; Hall 1979). Presidents and senators rewarded supporters with seats on the federal bench, and in turn, senators deferred to the choices of their colleagues. Howard (1981) argues that circuit court judges serving during the late 1960s and early 1970s received their appointments based on four major factors: "Political participation, professional competence, personal ambition, plus an oft-mentioned pinch of luck. . . . Judgeships normally are rewards for political service. . . . To the politically active as well as the party faithful go the prizes" (90).

Over time, however, presidents began appointing lower court judges who were known to support the president's policy agenda, though not consistently until the Reagan administration (Goldman 1997). Presidents increasingly recognized that appointments to the federal bench represented another important method by which to influence the national policymaking process. A number of scholars have documented this change from patronage to political appointments at the lower court level (Bell 2002b; Goldman 1997; Scherer 2005). As the federal courts decide literally thousands of cases each year involving important constitutional and statutory determinations, federal judicial decisions greatly impact the development of national and state policy. Since lower court judges, like Supreme Court justices, serve for life, judicial appointments allow presidents to create a lasting policy legacy that may continue long after they leave office.

This shift from patronage-based to policy-based lower court appointments ebbed and flowed over time but was firmly ensconced by the Reagan administration. Goldman (1997) argues President Franklin Roosevelt utilized lower court appointments to further his policy agenda by selecting judges who would uphold and defend his New Deal legislation, while Harry Truman continued the practice of using appointments to reward fellow partisans. Presidents Richard Nixon and Lyndon Johnson both recognized the possibility of appointing like-minded judges to the lower courts, with the intention of furthering their agendas on civil rights and the issue of "law and order" (Goldman 1997; Scherer 2005). Carp and Rowland (1983) argue Johnson and Nixon "placed an inordinate emphasis on the ideological purity of their judicial nominees" (166). And, beginning with judges appointed by Johnson and Nixon, lower court appointees' votes began to be aligned with the appointing president's views on highly politicized cases (see, e.g., Scherer 2005). Even though a highly formalized selection process had yet to be instituted, presidents were increasingly more concerned with lower court judicial selection and the promise of appointing ideologically compatible judges.

The use of lower court appointments to reward political activists and supporters—as well as the power of senators to propose such candidates—was further diluted by President Jimmy Carter's decision in 1977 to establish the Circuit Court Nominating Commission (Goldman 1997; Maltese 1995).[6] The White House appointed the commission members and tasked the commission with suggesting circuit court nominees to the president. Carter additionally asked senators to voluntarily set up nominating commissions in their home states to select district court judges.[7] Carter's intent was to rely on merit, rather than on a spoils system, when selecting lower court judges; he also wanted to expand the number of minority and female judges on the federal courts. By transferring the power of selection to these nominating commissions, Carter decreased the ability of senators to reward political supporters. Carter therefore did not pursue a straightforward policymaking agenda when selecting his lower court nominees. However, his success in increasing the number of minority and female judges necessarily resulted in more liberal appointments and thus greater policy consistency (Scherer 2005).

Ronald Reagan continued to transfer the decision-making power over lower court selection away from home-state senators to the administration, especially for openings on the courts of appeals. Reagan abolished Carter's commission system and created the President's Committee on Federal Judicial Selection, which was staffed by members of the White House and the Department of Justice. The creation of this committee "concentrated power within—and institutionalized the role of—the White House" in selecting lower court judges (O'Brien 1988, 61).

The Reagan administration, led by Attorney General Edwin Meese, consciously sought out young, conservative nominees, with the goal of tilting the balance of the lower federal courts in a more conservative direction. As Goldman (1989) contends, "Arguably, the Reagan administration was engaged in the most systematic judicial philosophical screening of candidates ever seen in the nation's history" (320). In particular, the Reagan administration sought judges who engaged in "a jurisprudence of original intent" (Maltese 1995, 122).[8] Attorney General Meese candidly admitted that Reagan's judicial appointments were intended to "institutionalize the Reagan revolution so it can't be set aside, no matter what happens in future presidential elections" (O'Brien 1988, 23–24). While President Bill Clinton was not as policy-driven as his Republican predecessors, his nominees similarly reflected the more liberal mind-set of his administration. And these attempts to appoint ideologically like-minded judges worked: studies find that federal judges appointed by Republicans are usually more conservative in their rulings than those appointed by Democrats, and vice versa (Carp and Rowland 1983; Goldman 1966, 1975; Haire, Humphries, and Songer 2001; Rowland, Carp, and Stidham 1984; Scherer 2000, 2005).

These changes in how presidents approached the selection of lower court nominees subsequently led to a transformation in how the Senate processed these nominations. Senators grew dismayed at the reduction in their power to select nominees, as well as concerned by the increasing political and ideological tenor of the resulting appointments, and they began to screen nominations to the federal bench more carefully. As a result, each stage of the process became more significant: no longer would nominees quickly pass through the Judiciary Committee and the full Senate. When Edward Kennedy became chair in 1979, he determined that the Judiciary Committee would not rely merely on outside reports from the White House and Federal Bureau of Investigation (FBI) about judicial nominees; rather, the majority and minority staffs would independently investigate nominee backgrounds (Slotnick and Goldman 1998, 202). Strom Thurmond continued this practice when he gained the chairmanship in 1981. In 1986, Judiciary Committee Democrats assigned Senator Paul Simon the task of overseeing judicial nominations; part of his job was to increase the amount of scrutiny given to each nominee. Then, when the Democrats regained control of the Senate in 1987 at the start of the 100th Congress, newly enshrined Judiciary Committee chair Joseph Biden assigned Senators Patrick Leahy, Howell Heflin, and Howard Metzenbaum to work with Simon on a nominations task force charged with thoroughly investigating Reagan's nominees to the federal bench. In addition, Biden hired three new committee staff members specifically to help vet lower court nominees (Moran 1987). Committee Democrats thus took the lead in the attempt to increase the Democrats' power over judicial selection and the related effort to stop Reagan from, in their view, tilting the federal bench too far to the right. This practice of thoroughly vetting nominees at the committee stage, especially nominees to the circuit courts, continues today.

These changes in the process of selecting lower court nominees by different administrations also caught the attention of many outside activists. While senators have always played a central role in the judicial confirmation process, the consistent participation of interest groups is a much more recent development. Outside interest groups have historically participated in the Supreme Court confirmation process, though only "sporadically" until recent years (Maltese 1995, 52). The successful defeat of Stanley Matthews's nomination to the Court in 1881 with substantial help from populist and farmers' groups signaled the increasing power of outside interests in the process (Abraham 1999, 102). Labor groups subsequently failed in their attempts to defeat William Howard Taft's nominees Horace Lurton in 1909 and Mahlon Pitney in 1912, but the ratification of the Seventeenth Amendment in 1913 measurably altered the dynamics of the confirmation process by making senators publicly accountable for their votes on Supreme Court nominees (Maltese 1995). Gerhardt (2003) argues that the "watershed event signaling the importance of interest groups in influencing federal appointments" occurred with the confirmation battle over Woodrow Wilson's nomination of Louis Brandeis to the Supreme Court in 1916 (69). Though Brandeis was eventually confirmed, the fight over his confirmation showcased the power and effort groups were willing to exert in order to influence judicial appointments. Throughout the twentieth century, and especially after the Senate made its floor deliberations public in 1929, nominees such as Clement Haynsworth and John J. Parker were defeated in part due to concerted interest group campaigns against their nominations (Maltese 1995; see also Abraham 1999; Frank 1991; Gerhardt 2003; Goings 1990; Watson 1963).

Why were outside interest groups interested in Supreme Court appointments during the late 1800s and early 1900s? The increased interest came about because activists recognized that the decisions of the Supreme Court had important policy implications. Historically in the United States, citizens and groups who feel marginalized by those in power have turned to the courts for relief. Early on, labor activists who wanted increased protections for workers sought legal relief. Later, groups seeking rights and protections for women and minorities turned to the courts as well.

After the Civil War, numerous laws were passed, especially in the South, that restricted the rights and activities of African Americans; many of these laws mandated the separation of the races. In 1896, in *Plessy v. Ferguson* (163 U.S. 537), the Supreme Court declared that the legally mandated separation of blacks and whites was constitutional as long as the treatment of these two groups was "equal," creating the doctrine of "separate but equal." By the early 1900s, most states had laws requiring segregation in public places, including public schools, and racially restrictive voting laws. While *Plessy* technically mandated "separate but equal" accommodations, the reality was anything but equal. The executives and legislatures of these states were unresponsive to calls to change these laws to provide equal treatment for African Americans. Consequently, motivated citizens began to challenge these laws in the courts.

Led by the National Association for the Advancement of Colored People (NAACP), and later the NAACP Legal Defense Fund, groups filed cases that challenged the constitutionality of segregation laws and other racially restrictive laws under the equal protection clause of the Fourteenth Amendment of the U.S. Constitution. Soon after *Plessy*, the NAACP filed numerous suits alleging that states were not upholding the "equal" part of the bargain established by *Plessy*. This strategy worked well, as a series of legal victories began to chip away at the doctrine of separate but equal by revealing that most separate facilities for African Americans were starkly unequal to those for whites. While none of these early cases directly challenged the separate but equal doctrine, the NAACP's legal strategists believed that states would find it difficult to maintain separate *and* equal facilities, especially separate *and* equal schools. And they succeeded: the Supreme Court ruled that African Americans had to be admitted to all-white colleges and graduate schools if an equal, separate alternative was not provided by the state (see *Missouri ex rel. Gaines v. Canada*, 305 U.S. 337 [1938], and *Sweatt v. Painter*, 339 U.S. 629 [1950]).

In 1954, their ultimate legal goal was realized: the Supreme Court declared in *Brown v. Board of Education* (347 U.S. 483) that the doctrine of separate but equal was itself "inherently unequal." The Court's decision in *Brown* led to fundamental changes in how American society was structured as segregated schools and public facilities, as well as laws that treated citizens differently based solely on their race, would no longer be condoned by the U.S. Supreme Court.

Spurred on by these substantial legal victories, other disenfranchised groups began to turn to the courts for relief. Criminal defendants sought to see the Fourth, Fifth, Sixth, and Eighth Amendments incorporated and the due process protections required by these amendments applied to the states. Women began to challenge laws that treated men and women differently solely because of their sex. Once again, groups that had failed to achieve their goals in the elected branches of government began to realize victories in the courts. Protections for criminal defendants increased substantially,[9] sex-based laws began to be struck down,[10] and in 1973 the Supreme Court declared women possessed the constitutional right to choose whether to have an abortion without state interference as part of the Fourteenth Amendment's right to privacy (*Roe v. Wade*, 410 U.S. 113 [1973]). American society was rapidly transforming, and, notably, the source of many of these changes was the courts.

Not everyone was happy with these changes. *Brown* was met with considerable opposition, and the Supreme Court's decisions in the areas of the separation of church and state (e.g., banning school prayer), abortion, and the rights of criminal defendants faced backlashes as well.[11] While certain groups were actively pursuing social change through court decisions, other groups were arguing just as vigorously that questions about important policy issues were better left to the people and their elected representatives. Richard Nixon campaigned in 1968 and 1972 on the theme of appointing "law-and-order" judges to the federal bench (Scherer 2005), and by the early 1980s the issue of abortion politics had created a decisive split between the Democratic and Republican parties (Sanbonmatsu 2002).

Most important, elected officials and the American public began to recognize that judges' decisions may at times reflect their political beliefs, and that this was especially true with respect to contentious issues of rights and liberties (Segal and Spaeth 1993, 2002). With civil rights and liberties, passions run high, and the Constitution may provide insufficient guidance (Bailey and Maltzman 2008; Bartels 2009; Corley, Steigerwalt, and Ward 2008). Presidents began to consider how future Supreme Court justices would rule on issues of importance to them, and, not surprisingly, the Supreme Court confirmation process became heavily contested as the fate of the nation was seen to hang in the balance. While the first fight over a Supreme Court nomination took place in 1795, the Robert Bork confirmation fight in 1987 illuminated the fact that *who* gets seated on the Supreme Court matters greatly to presidents, senators, outside interest groups, and concerned citizens alike.

By the 1950s, interest groups had conclusively proved that they were a key player in the Supreme Court appointment process and that their concerns would have to be taken into consideration at both the nomination and confirmation stages. After witnessing the presidential shift from patronage to political appointments and the move by Reagan to nominate bright young conservatives to the federal bench in his first term, groups transferred their attention to lower court confirmations as well. Given the sheer number of lower court appointments made each congressional term, groups recognized the need to continually monitor these appointments.[12]

Liberal activists concerned about civil rights, women's rights, and other civil liberties issues feared the direction the Reagan administration would push the ideological balance of the federal courts. They formed judicial watchdog groups to monitor federal judicial selection and to try to prevent conservative ideologues from gaining seats on the federal bench. The leading liberal group, the Alliance for Justice, initiated its Judicial Selection Project in 1985.

Nan Aron, president of the Alliance for Justice, explained in a 2002 interview why liberal activists became so interested in appointments to the federal courts:

The way our democracy works is that poor people, people of color, disenfranchised people, women, have very little recourse to the executive branch. They don't make contributions to the Republican or Democratic presidential campaigns. They tend not to know the people in power. And, therefore, they have very little access to the executives or the Donna Shalalas [secretary of health and human services under President Clinton] of the world. They have almost no access to members of Congress because they clearly don't contribute to congressional or Senate races. The only recourse they have is to the judiciary. It's the only branch of government that is designed by the way our democracy is set up to hear cases brought by people without power, individuals, aggrieved parties. And therefore, it is critically important that the kinds of people that hear cases filed by unrepresented people are people that have an open mind. People who are well qualified in the law, but also people, I would say, who have a respect for the kinds of advances that America has made in terms of civil and women's rights, who have a respect for the rights that courts have granted consumers and environmentalists. And are people who have a demonstrated commitment to equal justice, because this is the only branch whereby a disenfranchised person or group has any ability to have redress for grievances. It's the only branch.

She further explicated why the Judicial Selection Project was created during the Reagan administration and decided to focus specifically on the issue of lower federal court selection:

We targeted courts of appeals and district court judges because we knew how important they were then to the administration, but secondly, we knew how important it was to begin to build an infrastructure that could engage the larger community around the issue of judicial selection. . . . By the time [William] Rehnquist was being elevated in 1986 [to the post of chief justice of the United States], we had kind of developed the infrastructure that allowed us to conduct research, put together a lobbying operation, engage a grassroots effort, and work the press. So we had kind of put together the elements of a campaign which to a large extent has become the model or template for today's work.

By the end of the Reagan administration, senators, interest groups, and concerned citizens were all clamoring to have a say in who should staff the federal bench. The failed Supreme Court nomination of Robert Bork played an especially crucial role in rallying these players (Bronner 1989a; Caldeira and Wright 1998; Gerhardt 2003; Lichtman 1990). By demonstrating that opponents could derail a judicial nomination, even one of a judge with superb qualifications who many had originally assumed would be easily confirmed, the Bork nomination defeat revealed the power of concerted interest group campaigns to sway public opinion and senators' votes. It also opened the door to the idea of using ideologically based objections to defeat judicial nominees.Bolstered by this win, liberal groups began paying more attention to federal selection at all levels, while conservative groups, such as the Free Congress Foundation[13] and Coalitions for America, formed to help promote ideologically conservative candidates to these different courts.[14] These groups squared off during the Reagan and Bush (41) administrations,[15] and the attention directed at federal judicial selection reached new heights by the time of the Clinton and Bush (43) administrations (Goldman and Slotnick 1999; Goldman et al. 2001, 2003, 2005).

The heightened amount of debate and contentiousness surrounding the Supreme Court and lower federal court judicial confirmation processes has been extensively documented in recent years by scholars, reporters, pundits, and participants alike (Bell 2002a; Carter 1994; Goldman 1997; Goldman and Slotnick 1999; Goldman et al. 2001, 2003, 2005; Maltese 1995; Silverstein 1994; Vieira and Gross 1998; Watson and Stookey 1995). In particular, nominees are taking longer and longer to move through the process (Allison 1996; Bell 2002b; Binder and Maltzman 2002; Hartley and Holmes 1997, 2002; Martinek, Kemper, and Van Winkle 2002; McCarty and Razaghian 1999; Nixon and Goss 2001; Renzin 1999; Scherer 2005). For example, President Carter's nominees were confirmed fairly quickly: on average, circuit court nominees were confirmed in 50.9 days (Martinek, Kemper, and Van Winkle 2002, 340). Comparatively, lower court nominees during the Clinton administration faced extensive waits: Clinton's circuit court nominees were confirmed, on average, in 100.3 days, and a record number of nominations were allowed to expire at the end of Clinton's second term (Goldman et al. 2001).

During the Bush (43) administration, this contentiousness reached new heights as ten circuit court nominees were successfully filibustered. In comparison, between 1968 and 2000, only thirteen judicial nominees had cloture motions even filed in relation to their nominations; all were eventually confirmed, with the exception of Abe Fortas in 1968 (Beth and Palmer 2005, 7–8).[16] The Senate arrived at a climactic showdown in 2005 over whether to engage the "nuclear option." The so-called nuclear option would allow the majority to alter the Senate rules concerning filibusters of judicial nominations and to do so by circumventing the pre-scribed Senate procedures for changing these rules; the end result would be the ability to confirm judicial nominations by a simple majority vote (Palmer 2005). The Senate rules remained intact, but this face-off has the possibility of arising once again if a determined minority attempts to stifle a future president's ability to seat his or her nominees on the federal bench. Challenges to lower court nominees, especially relating to controversial prior rulings or specific issue positions promoted in their public lives, have thus increased dramatically in recent years (Bell 2002a; Gerhardt 2003; Hartley and Holmes 1997, 2002).

Finally, the informal role of interest groups in the lower court confir-mation process has grown dramatically. Those interest groups that formed in the 1980s and 1990s are now consistent players in the confirmation process. While in recent years groups have been denied the chance to participate formally by testifying at confirmation hearings, they have routinely influenced the decisions of key players through numerous in-formal activities (Bell 2002a; Goldman and Slotnick 1999; Goldman et al. 2001, 2003, 2005; Maltese 1995; Scherer, Bartels, and Steigerwalt 2008). When interest groups publicly oppose a judicial nominee, the nominee is less likely to be confirmed, and, if confirmed, will take much longer to move through the process (Scherer, Bartels, and Steigerwalt 2008).

These changes make it hard to argue that the contemporary lower court judicial confirmation process is anything but political (see also Kahn 1995). This book therefore begins with the assumption that today's lower court confirmation process is a highly political process reflecting the myriad beliefs held by the central players and offering a public arena for debates over civil rights, women's rights, the criminal justice system, and other controversial topics of the day. Some recent developments have also specifically increased the importance of circuit court opinions, and hence appointments to these courts. First, circuit court decisions are many times the final word on questions of federal statutory, administra-tive, and constitutional law. In the early days of the Republic, the Su-preme Court was required to hear almost every case that was appealed to it, as well as those cases in which the Court had original jurisdiction.[17] In 1925 the aptly named Judges' Bill greatly expanded the Supreme Court's control over its own docket. This bill gave the Court the ability to select which cases appealed from the lower federal courts or state high courts it would hear. In 1988 the last remaining categories of mandatory jurisdic-tion cases were removed. As a result, the Supreme Court can now pick and choose which cases it wishes to hear. This power allows the Supreme Court to set its own agenda and to determine which cases—and which issues—the justices will consider (see, e.g., Baum 1977; Caldeira and Wright 1988, 1990; Murphy 1964; Provine 1980). This agenda-setting power is critical, as it means the Court can decide to tackle controversial topics, such as the decision to hear *Brown v. Board of Education*, or it can decide to stay quiet on certain issues, such as the Court's refusal to consider any cases involving the Second Amendment between 1939 and 2008, when it decided *District of Columbia v. Heller* (554 U.S. 290 [2008]).

The fact that the Supreme Court's docket is almost entirely discretionary also leads to important implications for the lower federal courts, and especially the circuit courts. Put simply, if the Supreme Court decides not to hear an appeal, or if the case is not appealed at all, the lower court's decision stands. Why does this matter? It matters because the circuit courts currently render the final decision in almost all cases filed in the federal courts. For example, in 2006, 66,618 cases were filed in the U.S. circuit courts, and each of these cases has to be heard and a decision rendered.[18] In comparison, 10,250 cases were appealed to the U.S. Supreme Court in 2006, of which the Supreme Court granted review to only seventy-seven, or 0.8 percent of all appealed cases and a mere 0.1 percent of cases decided by the circuit courts.[19] In other words, 99.9 percent of federal cases are ultimately decided by the circuit courts. While the Supreme Court uses its discretion to hear those cases it believes present the most important legal issues requiring a final, national decision, it leaves to the circuit courts scores of cases that also address important constitutional and statutory questions. The reality of our current federal legal system is that the circuit courts have become the final arbiters on the key questions of the day.

Second, the lack of a Supreme Court vacancy between 1994 and 2005, the second longest period in history, prompted senators and interest groups to transfer their attention (and resources) to circuit court confirmations. Third, the circuit courts are seen by many as the "farm team" for the Supreme Court. As of January 2009, all nine of the current Supreme Court justices had previously served as a circuit court judge.[20] Thus, many fear allowing potential Supreme Court nominees to argue that they were easily confirmed to the second most important courts in the land.

Even as the amount of contentiousness and partisanship has increased, however, the reality is that the vast majority of lower court nominees, including those to the circuit courts, are still confirmed quickly and easily. Even during the 108th Congress, when tensions reached their peak, eight circuit court nominees were confirmed unanimously, and three others were confirmed with only one negative vote on the Senate floor.[21] This study therefore seeks to explain why some lower court nominations run into trouble—as well as *how* they become encumbered—while most nominees are easily confirmed.

Studying the Lower Federal Court Confirmation Process

The study of federal judicial confirmations began with in-depth case studies of different controversial nominations; almost all of these studies focus on Supreme Court nominations (Abraham 1999; Bork 1990; Bronner 1989a; Frank 1991; Massaro 1990; Vieira and Gross 1998; Watson 1963). Early empirical research questioned why nominees were confirmed or rejected, with Supreme Court nominees again at the center of interest (Cameron, Cover, and Segal 1990; Guliuzza, Reagan, and Barrett 1994; Segal 1987; Segal, Cameron, and Cover 1992; Segal, Cover, and Cameron 1989). More recent studies have turned their attention to lower court confirmations. Since almost all lower court nominees are eventually confirmed, but the time it takes for lower court nominees to move through the process has increased significantly in recent decades, these studies analyze the causes of delay in the confirmation process (Allison 1996; Bell 2002b; Binder and Maltzman 2002; Hartley and Holmes 1997, 2002; Martinek, Kemper, and Van Winkle 2002; McCarty and Razaghian 1999; Renzin 1999; Nixon and Goss 2001; Scherer, Bartels, and Steigerwalt 2008). These macro-level duration studies find that institutional, political, and nominee-based factors may affect the length of time it takes for a nominee to move through the confirmation process. However, most existing studies do not address exactly how nominations are delayed or where in the process the delay occurs. The one exception is the use of senatorial courtesy by home-state senators, which has been addressed in a small number of studies (e.g., Abraham 1999; Binder 2007; Denning 2001; Massey 1991; Slotnick 1980a).

Even though interest groups garner substantial popular and media attention, few studies examine the role of these groups in lower court confirmations. Existing studies mainly analyze either formal modes of group participation or broad group strategies in a limited number of lower court confirmations (Bell 2002a; Caldeira, Hojnacki, and Wright 2000; Cohen 1998; Flemming, MacLeod, and Talbert 1998). Some recent studies address the direct impact of informal interest group activity.

Scherer's (2003, 2005) work begins with the assumption that outside groups are a powerful force in judicial selection politics and considers why groups play such an important role in the lower court confirmation process. Scherer offers a theory of elite mobilization according to which the groups active in judicial confirmation politics represent the most mobilized and active of citizen voters, and so presidents and senators must heed their calls or face electoral repercussions. In turn, presidents are more likely to choose ideologically like-minded candidates and senators are more likely to evaluate nominees based on their views as a way to appease elite party activists.

Scherer, Bartels, and Steigerwalt (2008) add interest group objections to a model of confirmation delay and find that group objections significantly influence whether and when a nominee will be confirmed.[22] According to Scherer, Bartels, and Steigerwalt, groups raise "fire alarms" and alert senators to problematic nominees; without such fire alarms, nominees are all but certain to be confirmed. The broader implication of the elite mobilization and fire alarm theories—namely, that senators listen and respond to group cues by voting against objectionable nominees—is tested in chapter 6.

Although these previous studies have greatly increased our understanding of the judicial confirmation process, they do not address systematically how and why lower court nominations may run into trouble and how, when, and why these nominations may be impeded. In particular, we do not know when in the process nominations are delayed, what (or who) delays them, and whether this delay is correctly attributed to the heightened partisanship surrounding the lower court confirmation process.

I propose that the key to understanding the dynamics of the lower court confirmation process is to analyze the process itself. By examining how the process works, we can discover when and how certain actors are able to exert influence over confirmation outcomes, as well as determine the degree of influence they possess. The central contribution of this book, then, is the development of a new analytic framework for conceiving of the lower court confirmation process, which I call the four tracks framework. The four tracks framework identifies the four main confirmation "tracks" a lower court nomination may follow on its path through the Senate confirmation process, as well as the characteristics that define each of these tracks. The four confirmation tracks differ as to the amount of contentiousness facing the nomination, which actors can influence the nomination's fate, and the options open to these actors to delay, or even defeat, the nomination. This framework illuminates the facts that the federal lower court confirmation process is a complicated one that is composed of multiple stages and multiple veto points, and that the actors with the greatest effect on confirmation outcomes are in part determined by where in the process the nomination is. By identifying the stages through which a nomination progresses and the Senate rules and norms governing each step of the process, the four tracks framework clarifies when and how two sets of key actors, senators and interest groups, may influence confirmation outcomes. This framework also recognizes that the lower court confirmation process is not simply a zero-sum game whereby nominees are either confirmed or defeated by the entire Senate; rather, nominees may experience several different confirmation environments as their nominations progress through the entire process. Most important, the four tracks framework foregrounds the different ways in which nominations may be impeded. This book examines each confirmation track in detail and empirically assesses each one by analyzing all nominations made to the circuit courts between 1985 and 2006—the 99th through 109th Congresses.

The second major contribution of this book is an analysis of the parliamentary tools senators may use to obstruct lower court nominations. The four tracks framework reveals how nominations may be impeded not by public confirmation fights but rather through the use of relatively hidden, out-of-the-public-eye Senate parliamentary procedures. Through the use of these tactics, individual senators can wield enormous power over the fate of nominations and legislation alike. My investigation shows that senators use these tactics because judicial nominations have become convenient bargaining chips in the tit-for-tat game that characterizes the modern legislative process. This analysis thus adds not only to our knowledge of lower court confirmation politics but also to our understanding of how and when senators use powerful parliamentary procedures to attain their policy goals.

Plan of the Book

Chapter 1 describes the four tracks framework. This framework specifically recognizes the different stages and veto points a nomination must successfully pass through on the way to confirmation. The four tracks framework conceives of the judicial confirmation process as a set of interconnected train "tracks" and each nomination as a "train" that must follow some combination of tracks from nomination to confirmation. Nominations begin on the *noncontroversial* track, as the default position of senators is to confirm swiftly and easily all lower court nominees (Scherer, Bartels, and Steigerwalt 2008). However, at each stage of the process—or train track "switch point"—nominations may be turned onto a different track by the actions of key actors. Senators may send nominations down the *senatorial courtesy* or *private political* tracks, and interest groups may act to push nominations onto the *public partisan* track. Most notably, this framework recognizes that nominees may have to travel multiple different tracks, and thus face different confirmation environments, on their path to confirmation.

Chapter 1 examines in detail each of the four different confirmation tracks: the noncontroversial track, the senatorial courtesy track, the private political track, and the public partisan track. By distinguishing among these different confirmation tracks, we can better understand not only which nominations become contested but also who affects each nominee's chances of being confirmed and how they are able to do so.

The following chapters then assess each track in turn, focusing on all nominations made to the thirteen circuit courts between 1985 and 2006. A number of different methodologies are utilized to thoroughly investigate the different confirmation tracks and the fate of nominees sent down these tracks.

Chapter 2 addresses the senatorial courtesy track. The custom of senatorial courtesy affords a mechanism by which home-state senators can effectively "kill" a nomination. The discussion in this chapter builds on previous studies by examining all instances of senatorial courtesy between 1985 and 2006 and the motivations behind each use of this tactic. I propose three distinct reasons senators may turn a nomination down the senatorial courtesy track: institutional disagreements, retaliation for past abuses, and ideological objections. Overall, I find senators utilize senatorial courtesy to sanction presidents and to gain retribution for the treatment of past judicial nominees. Studying senatorial courtesy also highlights the ongoing dispute between the president and the Senate over the power to select judicial nominees. Presidents and senators have long fought over what the Senate's constitutional "advice and consent" role actually entails, and the use of senatorial courtesy frequently reflects this institutional tug-of-war over senators' role in the selection process.

Chapter 3 explores the private political track. Nominations sent down the private political track are delayed, and sometimes defeated, through the use of different parliamentary procedures. This chapter begins by discussing the numerous mechanisms senators may use to delay nominations and assesses their use and impact. It then turns to an in-depth investigation of the use of holds once nominations reach the Senate floor. Holds are a powerful tool of obstruction, but their use is relatively unstudied. I identify two overarching reasons why senators place holds on nominees: to object to a particular nominee or for strategic purposes. I then investigate how often each of these types of holds was applied to circuit court nominees between 1985 and 2006. Contrary to conventional wisdom, I find senators primarily use holds to gain leverage or to exact retribution. Rather than using holds to obstruct ideologically objectionable nominees, senators routinely block nominees they support in order to gain leverage in unrelated legislative disputes. Holds temporarily reroute nominations onto the private partisan track, and the accepted use of holds as a negotiation device means nominations may be forced to visit this track more than once on their path to confirmation. Judicial nominations thus act as convenient bargaining chips in the modern Senate.

While the private political and senatorial courtesy tracks highlight the more hidden powers senators possess over judicial nominations, the public partisan track introduces another important actor into the process—outside interest groups. By drawing public attention to problematic nominees, interest groups play a central role in influencing confirmation outcomes by turning nominations down the public partisan track. The remaining chapters assess the public partisan track and the various roles interest groups play in the lower court confirmation process.

Chapter 4 begins this examination by investigating the different roles interest groups play in the lower court confirmation process. Through exclusive, in-depth interviews conducted with current and former Senate staff, I explore interest groups' role in transmitting information, other functions they play in the judicial confirmation process, and the extent of partisan differences in group activity. I find that outside groups play a central role in the lower court confirmation process by filling the sizable information gap on nominees. Senators and their staff rely on groups to thoroughly investigate nominees and identify which nominees require more scrutiny and which nominees can be swiftly confirmed. I also find important differences between conservative and liberal group activity on judicial confirmations, and that group lobbying tactics depend heavily on whether a senator serves on the Senate Judiciary Committee.

Once a nominee begins to move through the confirmation process, groups may decide to publicly object to the nominee and wage a campaign to defeat her nomination, sending the nominee down the public partisan track. However, given resource constraints and political realities, groups must choose their battles carefully. Chapter 5 addresses what factors groups consider when deciding whether to oppose a particular nominee. Through interviews with leaders of the most influential interest groups engaged currently in judicial confirmation politics, I examine the costs and benefits of waging confirmation fights and illuminate the major factors groups weigh when determining how to use their precious resources.

Chapter 6 ends my consideration of the public partisan track by asking what impact interest group objections, in comparison to other factors, have on Senate Judiciary Committee votes. Put simply, do nominations opposed by interest groups face senatorial opposition as well? Quantitative analysis reveals interest group opposition is by far the single most determinative influence on whether a nomination will receive negative votes from the Judiciary Committee. More broadly, opposed nominees face lengthy confirmation delays, as well as senatorial opposition in committee and on the Senate floor, while their unopposed counterparts are likely to be confirmed swiftly and easily. However, while senators usually listen to interest groups, other factors, such as whether the nominee has a Judiciary Committee patron, may trump group objections. Overall, interest group objections ensure the nominee (and president) will face a difficult and bruising political fight, even if the nominee is ultimately confirmed. This chapter ends by examining the most recent instances of public partisan fights, when Senate Democrats filibustered ten nominations during the 108th and 109th Congresses.

The conclusion returns to the question of why some nominees face a rocky road to confirmation while others are easily and swiftly confirmed. I argue that an examination of the lower court confirmation process yields important insights into who can exert influence on judicial nominations, how they do so, and, most important, why. I then discuss the implications of these findings for the future of the lower court confirmation process.

WHAT MAKES A NOMINATION RUN INTO TROUBLE?
Senators, Interest Groups, and the Four Tracks to Confirmation

The staffing of the federal judiciary has taken on enormous importance in recent decades as more and more people have realized the reach and consequences of judicial decisions. Especially with regard to the federal appeals courts—the thirteen circuit courts and the Supreme Court—the appointment of new judges can influence the formation of public policy for decades to come. These judges are increasingly called upon to decide the major policy and constitutional issues of the day. And, given their life tenure, these judges may put into law their views (and most likely the views of the appointing president) for decades after the appointing president has left office. For example, as of August 2008, the chief judges of eight of the thirteen circuit courts were appointed by President Reagan, whose administration had ended twenty years earlier.

While we know quite a lot about Supreme Court confirmations, we know comparatively little about how the lower court confirmation process works. We know that over time, presidents have begun using lower court appointments to further their policy agendas rather than as a way to reward patronage (Goldman 1997; Scherer 2005). We also know that nominations are taking increasingly longer to be confirmed (Hartley and Holmes 1997, 2002; Martinek, Kemper, and Van Winkle 2002). However, there is still much to learn. For example, despite the fact that the vast majority of contemporary lower court nominations are confirmed easily and without opposition, some nominees experience long waits and numerous obstacles. Why are some nominations contested while most are easily confirmed? What are the different ways in which nominations may be impeded? And what role do two key groups of actors, senators and interest groups, play in making certain nominations face a rockier road to confirmation, and in possibly blocking confirmation altogether? We currently lack the answers to these questions. Most important, we lack a coherent framework for understanding how the lower court confirmation process works in its entirety.

I therefore offer a new theoretical framework for conceptualizing the lower court confirmation process, the four tracks framework.[1] I propose conceptualizing the lower court confirmation process as a set of interconnected train tracks, and each lower court nomination as a train that follows these train tracks from nomination to confirmation. An actual train follows a particular track until it reaches a switch point. At these switch points, the train either continues on its original track or switches to a new track. A train may switch tracks for several reasons, and other trains and actors may influence whether the train switches tracks. On a long journey, a train may encounter numerous switch points, and thus multiple opportunities to switch tracks.

To fully understand the lower court confirmation process and why particular nominations may run into obstacles, it helps to use the train track simile, with the different tracks representing the different confirmation environments through which a nomination may pass. Each stage of the process presents a new switch point where the nomination may switch tracks. As a nomination proceeds through the different stages of the confirmation process, outside actors may take actions that push the nomination onto a different track and thus force it to confront a new confirmation environment. Because a nomination must successfully advance through all of the multiple stages of the confirmation process in order to be successfully confirmed, each nomination may actually follow a number of different tracks as it progresses through the complete confirmation process.

Nominations moving along their unique set of confirmation tracks may encounter both significant track changes and more minor detours. Although a significant track change can redirect a nomination permanently, a smaller detour may simply reroute the nomination temporarily; these minor detours may delay the nomination, but they also usually allow the nomination to return eventually to its default track. The four tracks framework thus captures the fluid nature of the Senate confirmation process and the fact that some obstacles are permanent, while others are only temporary. For example, private political disputes may momentarily delay nominations and send them on a detour, but these nominations may be allowed to return to the noncontroversial track as soon as the underlying issue is resolved. On the other hand, interest group objections permanently reroute nominations onto the public partisan track. The four tracks framework thus recognizes the multiple steps of the confirmation process as well as the fluctuating nature of the temporal political environment surrounding each nomination.

The four tracks framework builds on existing literature by offering a coherent framework for understanding the lower court confirmation process in its entirety. It continually recalls the multiple stages a nomination must successfully pass through, and so it allows us to delineate how nominations may be delayed or defeated at a particular stage, and which actors can influence confirmation outcomes at each of these stages. I show that senators and interest groups may each influence lower court confirmation outcomes in different ways at discrete points in the confirmation process. Furthermore, there are a myriad of different ways in which lower court nominations can be obstructed, and senators possess extremely powerful mechanisms through which they alone can influence confirmation outcomes. This framework thus gives equal weight to impediments that are usually overlooked, such as the use of senatorial courtesy and parliamentary procedures to delay—and sometimes defeat—judicial nominations.

Such a conceptualization is central to increasing our knowledge and understanding of the lower court confirmation process. Previous studies present the lower court confirmation process as a zero-sum game in which nominations are either confirmed or defeated by a vote on the Senate floor. Since most lower court nominations are eventually confirmed, recent studies focus on explaining confirmation durations rather than confirmation outcomes (Bell 2002b; Binder and Maltzman 2002; Martinek, Kemper, and Van Winkle 2002; Scherer, Bartels, and Steigerwalt 2008). These studies use duration (or hazard) models to determine what factors influence the length of time it takes for a particular nomination to move successfully through the confirmation process. They highlight which factors related to the nomination and the temporal political environment increase confirmation durations. However, these macro-level studies of confirmation timing do not aid us in understanding *where* in the process delay actually happens, *who* might be causing the delay, and, most important, *why* delay occurs.

To answer these questions, it is essential that we first understand the complete path nominations travel on the way to confirmation. By focusing on the inner workings of the lower court confirmation process, we can recognize the points at which key actors such as senators and interest groups may exert influence over judicial nominations and the different mechanisms by which nominations can be delayed or defeated. Only by appreciating the intricacies of the process itself can we begin to assess how and why trouble erupts over a particular nomination. The four tracks framework therefore provides a mechanism for uncovering precisely how and why nominations are delayed at different points in the confirmation process. I turn now to an overview of the history and construction of the lower court confirmation process.

Describing the Terrain: The Lower Court Confirmation Process

The judicial appointment process was designed to give control over the staffing of the federal bench to both the executive and legislative branches. Article II, Section 2, of the Constitution grants the president the power to nominate judges to the Supreme Court and the lower federal courts, and instructs the Senate to provide "advice and consent." From the beginning, the Senate interpreted this clause as granting it the right of refusal, and the Senate's confirmation process was designed accordingly. A key feature of the confirmation process is that nominations must advance successfully through numerous stages on their path to confirmation.

Although federal judges, along with executive branch nominees, are nominated by the president and confirmed by the Senate, and their nominations technically follow the same path to confirmation, similarities between judicial confirmations and other executive branch confirmations end there. As Gerhardt notes, the Constitution "establishes a presumption of confirmation that works to the advantage of the president and his nominees" by requiring only a simple majority to confirm nominees (2003, 41). Executive branch appointees "serve at the pleasure of the President," and only for as long as the appointing president holds office.[2] The president heads the executive branch, using cabinet secretaries and the agencies they run to carry out his orders, and there exists an understanding that the president may nominate whomever he pleases to these posts. Senators therefore rarely spend time on whether an executive branch nominee is fit for office.[3] Oppositely, federal judges are appointed for life terms, removable only by impeachment, and answer neither to the legislative branch nor to the executive branch once in office. Because of this independence, candidates for federal judgeships undergo a more rigorous confirmation process that truly focuses on vetting the nominee.[4]

As the analysis in this book depends on recognizing the different stages a judicial nomination must pass through, a description of the entire appointment process is needed. The modern-day judicial appointment process proceeds as follows:

1. The president (usually with input from the senators who represent the state where the vacancy occurred) nominates a person to the federal bench.
2. The nomination is forwarded to the Senate and referred to the Judiciary Committee.
3. The Judiciary Committee holds public hearings at which the nominee testifies; other persons (such as law professors or interest group representatives) might also be asked or permitted to testify.[5]
4. The Judiciary Committee votes on the nomination. If the committee votes in favor of the nomination by a simple majority, the nomination is forwarded to the Senate floor. If a majority of the committee votes against the nomination, the nomination fails.[6]
5. A floor vote is held in which the entire Senate votes on the nomination; a vote of a simple majority of senators is needed to confirm the nomination.
6. If the nomination fails to move through all of these stages by the end of the congressional term, the nomination automatically expires and is sent back to the president under Senate Rule XXXI.[7]

This capsule description of the judicial confirmation process delineates the multiple stages a nomination must pass through on the way to confirmation, as well as the numerous points at which the nomination may be defeated. Most notably, a nomination must pass successfully through each stage for the nominee to be confirmed. Thus, one crucial way of preventing the confirmation of lower court nominations is for key actors simply to refuse to schedule a hearing or a vote; these mechanisms of delay are more fully addressed in chapter 3.

This description also hints at the multitude of points at which senators alone may influence confirmation outcomes. While the role of interest groups garners considerable press and popular attention, the real power over lower court confirmation outcomes lies with senators. The four tracks framework thus highlights exactly how senators can influence lower court confirmations. The role of senators throughout the process varies depending on whether the appointing president and the Senate majority, as well as the home-state senators for each nominee, are from the same party. Unified government increases the propensity of senators to play a strong role in the presidential nominating process; divided government increases the likelihood that senators will wield more influence in the confirmation stage.

Explicating the different stages of the process also reveals where outside interest groups—key actors in the modern-day lower court confirmation process, but ones not mentioned anywhere in the U.S. Constitution—may attempt to exert influence over confirmation outcomes. Groups may participate formally by providing invited testimony at a nominee's confirmation hearing (Bell 2002a; Cohen 1998; Flemming, MacLeod, and Talbert 1998); however, such formal participation by interest groups has not been allowed since the 1980s (Bell 2002a, 108–11).[8] Blocked from testifying, interest groups have turned to informal lobbying techniques to influence judicial confirmation outcomes, such as lobbying senators, holding press conferences, and encouraging grassroots mobilization (Caldeira, Hojnacki, and Wright 2000). Interest groups use these tactics in an attempt to influence presidents in their selection of nominees and, once a nomination has been made, to influence senators' actions at the committee and floor stages.

Finally, the confirmation process as delineated above reveals that the president lacks a direct role in the confirmation phase of the judicial appointment process. The judicial appointment process consists of two distinct phases: the selection phase and the confirmation phase. Presidents possess the sole power to nominate people for vacancies on the federal court. Presidents therefore think strategically during the selection phase to try to anticipate potential confirmation battles (Goldman 1997; Goldman et al. 2005; Massie, Hansford, and Songer 2004; Nemacheck 2008a; Yalof 1999). Presidents consider how senators and other actors will respond to their choices, and then attempt to forestall or mitigate home-state objections or interest group opposition through strategic selection decisions. Massie, Hansford, and Songer (2004) find that presidential delay in filling lower court vacancies is "a function of politics," and that presidents take longer to select nominees when they face an unfriendly Senate and a more contentious political environment (153). Nemacheck (2008a) uses archival materials to illuminate how presidents strategically choose Supreme Court nominees in an attempt to decrease the uncertainty surrounding the nominee's future behavior on the Court as well as the nominee's fate during the Senate confirmation process.

Once a nomination is sent to the Senate, however, the president can influence the process only through indirect means. Presidents can take actions to try to resolve procedural blocks on their nominees (as discussed further in chapter 3). They can also lobby senators directly, or "go public" to press for their nominees to be moved through the process and confirmed.[9] For example, President George W. Bush used his bully pulpit to promote his judicial nominees; he held numerous press conferences and personally lobbied senators to try to force action on stalled nominations.

Holmes (2007, 2008a) systematically investigates when and why presidents go public to support circuit court nominees. She finds that presidents are most likely to utilize a public strategy when they want to appeal to certain key constituencies and when a nominee faces interest group opposition or an opposition Senate. Paradoxically, she also finds public presidential support for a circuit court nominee "troubled by partisan polarization and interest group opposition only causes increased difficulty for the nominee" (2007, 588).[10]

Presidents lack the constitutional authority to force the Senate to act, whether at the committee or the floor stage. And, since presidents always support their nominees, increased presidential activity does not fundamentally alter the landscape facing a nomination. In contrast, even though interest groups also act from outside the Senate, they can directly modify the confirmation environment by opposing a nomination and sending it down the public partisan track: as Scherer, Bartels, and Steigerwalt (2008) find, interest group opposition is the leading cause of both confirmation delay and defeat. The need to study group involvement in the lower court confirmation process also "becomes even more crucial . . . given that presidents are unable to overcome interest group opposition to nominees with the use of the bully pulpit" (Holmes 2007, 589). The four tracks framework thus focuses attention on those actors who can directly alter the confirmation environment a nomination faces.

Getting from Here to There: The Four Tracks to Confirmation

I have proposed that in order to understand the lower federal court confirmation process, we should conceive of judicial nominations as trains that follow different confirmation tracks en route to confirmation. At critical switch points, actors such as senators and interest groups can reroute the nomination onto a new confirmation track, forcing the nomination to confront a different—and potentially more perilous—political environment. By viewing the lower court confirmation process as a multistage process rather than a simple one-stage, zero-sum process, we are in a better position to understand whether and how senators and interest groups are able to make certain nominations contentious and thereby influence confirmation outcomes. Most important, this conceptualization recognizes that nominations may follow multiple tracks and confront various political environments and obstacles on the path to confirmation.

A judicial nomination may follow one of four tracks at any one time: the noncontroversial track, the senatorial courtesy track, the private political track, and the public partisan track. Nominations on the noncontroversial track proceed without any opposition or major delay. On the senatorial courtesy track, home-state senators object to a president's nominee and block the nomination from moving through the confirmation process. Individual senators or groups of senators may use what I term "private political" parliamentary tactics to stall a nomination indefinitely at the committee or floor stage. Finally, nominees on the public partisan track confront public opposition from senators and interest groups; these are the nominations commonly thought of as "controversial." Since there are multiple stages to the confirmation process, a nomination may be pushed from one track to another as it travels from stage to stage. Sometimes these track changes result in permanent diversions, while at other times nominations may be only temporarily diverted. Thus, while there are four primary tracks a nomination may follow, there are numerous possible permutations to the path a nomination may take over the span of the confirmation process. Figure 1.1 provides a flow chart of the possible complete tracks nominations may travel through the confirmation process.

The Four Tracks Examined

The following section isolates the four confirmation tracks and examines each one in detail. It also addresses the likelihood that a judicial nomination will face each of these four primary confirmation environments. I first present each track as an ideal type and characterize it according to its level of contentiousness, delay, and partisanship, as well as the amount of informal and formal interest group involvement. I then discuss the motivations that drive the key actors within each track. I end by systematically assessing how many circuit court nominations followed each track between 1985 and 2006, regardless of how many total tracks a nomination followed, and provide examples of prototypical nominations that followed each track.

NONCONTROVERSIAL TRACK

All judicial nominations begin their journey through the Senate confirmation process on the noncontroversial track. Senators' default position is to confirm lower court nominees, given both the traditional role home-state senators play in the selection process and the sheer number of lower court vacancies that must be filled every congressional term.

FIGURE 1.1 Flow chart of the four tracks to confirmation

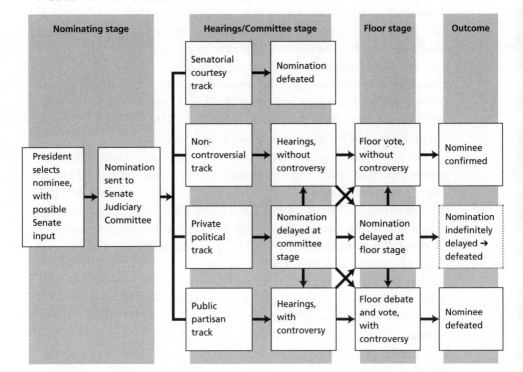

Nominations therefore follow the noncontroversial track unless and until they are diverted to a different confirmation track.

As the name implies, nominations on the noncontroversial track encounter no opposition. These nominations are confirmed routinely and easily, both by the Judiciary Committee and by the Senate as a whole. Noncontroversial confirmations involve short confirmation hearings, and few questions are asked of the nominee. Votes in committee and on the floor occur quickly and are usually unanimous; the nominees are highly likely to be confirmed by either voice vote or unanimous consent, rather than by a more procedurally cumbersome and time-consuming roll call vote. Finally, interest group participation is limited, if not completely absent. At the lower court level, interest groups become involved in support of a nomination only if it has drawn opposition. Thus, for noncontroversial nominations, the only interest group activity is usually the production of a positive report on the nominee's qualifications. Informal group lobbying is unnecessary, given the consensus in favor of the nomination.

The four tracks framework recognizes the fluidity of the judicial confirmation process and the reality that nominations can switch tracks multiple times as they progress from nomination to confirmation. Nominations may therefore be diverted from the noncontroversial track and, if
they are merely temporarily rerouted, may also return to this track. In
particular, a nomination may be temporarily rerouted onto the private
political track by virtue of a strategic hold and then return to the noncontroversial track once the dispute driving the hold is resolved. In such
situations the track diversion may last as little as a day.[11]

The overwhelming majority of lower court nominations follow the
noncontroversial track. Overall, there are 866 Article III federal judgeships: 9 Supreme Court justices, 179 circuit court judges, and 678 district court judges.[12] Between 1985 and 2006, a total of 272 nominations
were made to the circuit courts, and 208 were eventually confirmed.[13]
Of these 208 nominations, 161 (77.4 percent) confronted no interest
group objections and were confirmed unanimously by the full Senate;
another five nominations received one negative vote on the Senate floor
(table 1.1).[14] Four other nominations technically met the definition of
noncontroversial, those of Richard Clifton, Julia Smith Gibbons, Susan
Neilson, and John Rogers. However, these nominations were all blocked
for a period of time because of senatorial courtesy. Their stories are discussed in chapter 2.

Although the average time it takes for a nomination to move through
the confirmation process has grown in recent decades, almost all of these
161 noncontroversial nominations were confirmed quite quickly once

TABLE 1.1 Number of negative votes received by unopposed and opposed
circuit court nominations on the Senate floor, 1985–2006 (99th–109th
Congresses)

NEGATIVE FLOOR VOTES	UNOPPOSED NOMINATIONS	OPPOSED NOMINATIONS	TOTAL
0	165	10	175
1–10	6	0	6
11–20	1	2	3
21–30	3	5	8
31–40	0	7	7
41–50	0	9	9
Total	175	33	208

they began to move through the process (tables 1.2 and 1.3).[15] Specifically, 140 (87 percent) noncontroversial nominees received a Judiciary Committee vote within a month or less of their confirmation hearings; these calculations include both weekends and recesses during the congressional term. Of these 161 nominees, 106 (65.8 percent) were then confirmed by the full Senate within ten days of their committee vote, and 123 (76.4 percent) were confirmed within twenty days of their committee vote. Many of the noncontroversial nominees who waited more than twenty days to receive a floor vote after their nominations were sent to the floor were either confirmed directly after a congressional recess or saw their nominations diverted onto the private political track. Even with the increased contentiousness surrounding President George W. Bush's nominees, of the seven nominees who were first nominated during the 109th Congress and received unanimous committee and floor votes in that Congress, all seven received a committee vote within a month of their hearing, and five of the seven were confirmed within twelve days of their nominations being passed out of committee. Thus, as these numbers highlight, the vast majority of judicial nominees are confirmed quickly, easily, and without opposition, even with the increased scrutiny that has been given in recent years to circuit court nominations.

SENATORIAL COURTESY TRACK

A nominee's path to confirmation may not flow so smoothly, however. Lower court nominees may be stymied as soon as their nominations are sent to the Senate through the exercise of senatorial courtesy, sending their nominations onto the second possible confirmation track. Senatorial courtesy denotes the custom of senators calling on their fellow senators to grant them the "courtesy" of blocking the confirmation of a disliked nominee from their home state. Senators most typically invoke senatorial courtesy when the president declines to nominate the home-state senator's choice for a vacant seat or nominates someone to whom the senator objects (Denning 2001; Goldman 1997; Maltese 1995). The use of senatorial courtesy thus reflects the ongoing institutional struggle between the president and the Senate over judicial selection. When a home-state senator objects to a nominee, the nomination is diverted onto the senatorial courtesy track and, for all intents and purposes, is considered dead. Given its veto effect, the application of senatorial courtesy results in a significant track change, and only in rare instances do nominations rerouted onto the senatorial courtesy track later make the switch to another track that potentially allows for confirmation.

TABLE 1.2 Time to Judiciary Committee votes for noncontroversial nominations to the circuit courts, 1985–2006 (99th–109th Congresses)

NOMINATIONS	DAYS BETWEEN HEARING AND JUDICIARY COMMITTEE VOTE
74	0–10
39	11–20
27	21–30
11	31–40
3	41–50
2	51–60
1	61–70
0	71–80
0	81–90
0	91–100
1	101–200
0	201–300
3	301+

161 Total noncontroversial nominations

TABLE 1.3 Time to Senate floor votes for noncontroversial nominations to the circuit courts, 1985–2006 (99th–109th Congresses)

NOMINATIONS	DAYS BETWEEN COMMITTEE VOTE AND FLOOR VOTE
106	0–10
17	11–20
11	21–30
10	31–40
3	41–50
4	51–60
4	61–70
3	71–80
1	81–90
1	91–100
1	101–200
0	201–300
0	301+

161 Total noncontroversial nominations

From the early days of the Republic, the Senate has interpreted the advice and consent clause of the U.S. Constitution quite literally with respect to judicial appointments. The Senate created a confirmation process that allows its members to take an active role in vetting each and every judicial nominee—and in potentially rejecting them if found wanting. Furthermore, senators also argue for a strong role at the selection stage. Since district courts are located in particular states, and circuit court seats are generally "assigned" to particular states, senators advise the president as to suitable judicial nominees hailing from their states. Presidents rely on home-state senators since the senators are more likely to know who from the state might make a good candidate. Especially in relation to the district courts, senators have traditionally viewed the selection of nominees as a senatorial prerogative; this is especially true when the senator belongs to the same party as the president (Rowland and Carp 1996; Slotnick 1984). When presidents decline to follow a home-state senator's recommendation, the Senate as an institution usually reacts poorly.

Historically, a senator who objected to a nominee from his or her home state would make a speech on the Senate floor declaring the nomination "personally obnoxious," thereby signaling the other senators to support their colleague and vote against the president's choice for the vacancy (Goldman 1997, 43).[16] Senatorial courtesy reflects the well-known collegiality of the Senate and illuminates those instances when the Senate as an institution takes aim at the president. Senatorial courtesy traditionally concerned disputes between the president and a senator of his own party, since minority party members could not "expect to control the federal patronage in their states" (Harris 1952, 45–46). Senatorial courtesy is also a manifestation of the very real tensions between the executive and legislative branches as to their constitutional roles in the staffing of the federal bench. While the Senate interprets the advice and consent clause quite broadly, presidents argue both that the Constitution confers on the president the power to nominate and that senatorial courtesy results in the Senate delegating the power to confirm to an individual senator.[17]

Over time, Judiciary Committee chairs institutionalized the process of senatorial courtesy and extended this veto to all home-state senators, regardless of party (Binder 2007). The chair now sends out what are commonly called "blue slips" to the home-state senators for each nominee. Blue slips are literally blue slips of paper that ask each home-state senator whether he or she supports the nomination. If the blue slips for each nomination are not all returned, the chair generally refuses to schedule a confirmation hearing. Since nominations must receive a hear-

ing to be ultimately confirmed, a decision by the chair not to schedule a
hearing prevents the nomination from moving through the process and
effectively kills the nomination (Denning 2001; Goldman et al. 2001).

A clear and convincing mode of rejection, senatorial courtesy is powerful and effective owing to its low visibility and its occurrence very early
in the confirmation process. By preventing nominations from even receiving a hearing, the blue slip system provides home-state senators with
"an implicit 'silent veto'" (Goldman et al. 2001, 238). Historically done
behind closed doors, and calling on the well-known norm of collegiality of the Senate, rejections of nominations based on senatorial courtesy
receive little media coverage. Only since 2001 have Judiciary Committee
chairs publicized whether a home-state senator has failed to return a blue
slip for a nomination or has returned a negative blue slip. Before 2001,
senators were not obligated to make public their use of senatorial courtesy. While senatorial courtesy has become less and less of an automatic
rejection, the custom is still a powerful force in the Senate, and a nomination may be indefinitely delayed and killed because of the objections
of home-state senators.[18]

The number of nominations sent down the senatorial courtesy track
in recent years is rather small. Overall, twenty circuit court nominations
(7.4 percent of all nominations) between 1985 and 2006 were blocked
for any period of time due to home-state objections. In a typical instance of the use of senatorial courtesy, Senator Jesse Helms (R-NC)
blue-slipped Rich Leonard's nomination during the 104th Congress because he wanted President Clinton to nominate Terrence Boyle, a North
Carolina federal district court judge, instead. Helms's use of senatorial
courtesy effectively defeated Leonard's nomination; he never even received a committee hearing.

Chapter 2 systematically examines recent instances of nominations
being sent down the senatorial courtesy track. I find that most nominations were blocked through senatorial courtesy as a result of institutional
disputes, which illuminates the ongoing power struggle between the executive and the legislative branches over judicial selection. Additionally,
a number of nominations were blocked through senatorial courtesy in
retaliation for how nominations in a previous Congress had been treated,
providing our first glimpse of how judicial nominations serve as bargaining chips in unrelated disputes. Many of these nominations were
also eventually confirmed, again underscoring how nominations may be
delayed because of external disputes rather than because of objections to
the actual nominee.

PRIVATE POLITICAL TRACK

Third, some judicial nominations are delayed or impeded by private political fights. Nominations are turned down the private political track when individual senators use parliamentary procedures to delay or kill the nominations. These parliamentary procedures allow senators to obstruct nominations, sometimes anonymously, out of the public eye and without having to take a public position on the nominee, thus making them "private."[19] Additionally, these tools are used to advance political goals (as opposed to general policy), whether the goal is to exact leverage in an unrelated legislative dispute or to block an ideologically objectionable nominee from being seated on the federal bench.

Scrutiny of nominations sent down the private political track illuminates the extent to which judicial nominations are caught in the "normal" political disputes that characterize the modern-day legislative process. The most commonly used private political tactic is that of delay: nominations may be blocked from receiving hearings, committee votes, or floor votes until an agreement over those nominations has been reached, other issues are resolved, or, as was the case at the end of the Clinton administration, a new president takes office.[20]

Various ways to delay nominations are open to different senators. Senate and committee leaders can delay nominations by virtue of their power to set the committee and floor agendas. Judiciary Committee chairs can decide not to schedule hearings or votes on certain nominations (or even any nomination), while the Senate majority leader exercises almost complete control over which nominations will be brought to a vote on the floor. For example, in 2000, eight of Clinton's nine pending circuit court nominations were blocked, with only one nomination eventually being confirmed. Additionally, numerous nominees were denied even a hearing, including Helene White, who was nominated in January 1996 and renominated in 1998, and Enrique Moreno, Elena Kagan, and James Wynn, who were all nominated in 1999.[21] Control of Senate actions is one important reason why the two political parties strive to gain majority control of the Senate: an opposition majority party, which by definition controls both committee and floor actions, can make the path to confirmation especially rocky for the president's nominees.

It is difficult to pinpoint empirically the exact cause of delay, especially when the delay results from leadership actions. Clearly, not all delays can be attributed to private political fights. For example, delays in the advancement of judicial nominations during the 107th Congress might have been due to private political tactics being used to stymie President George W. Bush's nominees. However, then Judiciary Committee chair Patrick Leahy argued that the tragic events of September 11, 2001, as well as the anthrax attacks on Capitol Hill in October 2001, resulted in priorities being realigned, with judicial nominations sometimes being pushed aside so that the Senate could deal with more pressing matters, such as an anti-terrorism bill (Leahy 2001; Savage 2001). Additionally, President Bush's decision in March 2001 to forgo the traditional practice of having the American Bar Association (ABA) rate the professional qualifications of each of his nominees delayed Senate review of these nominees (Greenberger 2001); in response, the Judiciary Committee decided to submit the names of his nominees to the ABA once they were received in the Senate, and this practice was continued by all subsequent committee chairs during the Bush administration.[22]

Those senators serving on the Judiciary Committee can also delay confirmations, at least for a short period of time. Each senator on the committee is allowed to ask that a committee vote on a nomination be held over until the next committee meeting. While this tactic normally delays votes by only a week or two, it can result in substantial delays if the request is made immediately before a Congressional recess, or reiterated in subsequent weeks by other members of the committee to continue a block on a particular nomination.

Finally, all senators have available to them a range of weapons with which to stymie judicial nominations once the nominations reach the Senate floor (and so have passed successfully through the previous stages of the process). Specifically, senators may place a hold on a nomination or filibuster the nomination. Filibusters allow senators to prevent a nomination from being scheduled for a floor vote by forcing debate on the nomination to continue indefinitely. Alternatively, any senator may place a hold on a nomination by informing the Senate leadership that he or she will object if the leadership attempts to schedule a vote on the nomination. A hold thus also allows a senator to block a nomination from coming to a floor vote, but in a much lower-visibility manner than filibusters. Holds may be placed anonymously, such that even the Senate leadership might not know who is blocking the nomination; in these instances a senator privately notifies the party leadership of his or her intent to object, and the objection is not made public.[23] Senators may also ask colleagues to submit their request to the party leadership in order to delay identification. Unlike filibusters, holds receive little media coverage, if any, and they are usually not even noticed except by the nominee's home-state senators. And, with anonymous holds, attempts by a home-state senator to convince the blocking senator to release the hold are by definition doomed from the outset. Therefore, all of these procedural tactics may be used to delay, and possibly defeat, judicial nominations.

Studying private political fights is important, as these disputes involve the utilization of hidden tactics to stop an innately public process: a public hearing is conducted by the full Senate Judiciary Committee, the nominee testifies and answers questions, and the senators present all make public statements. A public vote is then taken by the committee. If the vote passes, the nomination is sent to the Senate floor, where a public vote is taken by the entire Senate, sometimes preceded by a public floor debate. Conversely, committee chairs, Senate leadership, and individual senators use the procedural tools at their disposal to prevent nominations from advancing along normal channels, and these actions are generally hidden from public view. Such actions are categorically different from public partisan nominations, in which senators and interest groups work publicly to defeat a nomination as it moves through the entire confirmation process. Once turned down the private political track, the nomination is not allowed to progress through the confirmation process, and the reasons for preventing confirmation are often completely unrelated to whether the nominee is viewed as suitable for a judgeship. An effective way to obstruct nominations, private political tactics receive little media coverage and waste very little political capital, two things publicly opposing a nominee inherently risks. As Renzin explains, "The confirmation fight is not being conducted in the public arena. Without a floor vote, or even public hearings, the Senate is waging its battle over appointments to the federal judiciary in almost complete anonymity" (1999, 168).

Because of the range of private political tactics and the varied motivations for their use, nominations may be permanently diverted onto the private political track or merely temporarily rerouted. Sometimes private political tactics are used to obstruct a nominee's path to confirmation. Alternatively, when senators utilize private political tactics for strategic purposes, nominations may visit the private partisan track only momentarily. For example, as the term implies, senators may place holds to restrain the targeted nominations, but then release the nominations once their goals are achieved. Nominations may even be diverted onto the private political track for as little as one day. Since nominations may be rerouted to the private political track as a result of strategic machinations, nominations often follow the noncontroversial or public partisan tracks while "visiting" the private political track in the interim.

The movement of a nomination on and off the private political track thus reflects the constantly fluctuating nature of the modern-day legislative process itself: while the overall temporal political environment remains relatively stable during any particular Congress, the day-to-day character of the Senate continually changes. On any given day numerous proposals are addressed, and each separate initiative provides the potential impetus for disputes to flare and bargaining to commence.[24] Nominations are neither immune to nor isolated from this reality, so nominations run the constant risk of being diverted onto the private political track as a result of one of these disputes. And because judicial nominations serve as highly convenient bargaining tools in these legislative disputes, individual nominations may be temporarily rerouted to the private political track more than once.

In this book I examine the use of a particularly potent private political tactic, the hold, focusing on those instances in which the use of private political tactics is clearly documented; it is possible that I have therefore underestimated the degree to which holds are used to obstruct the path of judicial nominees. Even though the holds examined in this study were confirmed publicly by the media, I contend they still represent "private" political tactics, because such maneuvers usually garner little media coverage or public attention. Even the most sophisticated of political observers—including those who work on the Hill[25]—are unlikely to know or follow which bills and nominations are subjected to holds at any given time. Additionally, even publicly announced holds are still a private and hidden mechanism in that they prevent the public action of a vote and possibly provide a shield for other senators who might also object but cannot take the political risk of publicly voting against the nomination in question. Finally, the use of these parliamentary tactics is less politically costly in the arena of staffing the federal bench than in other, more public domains, given the low level of media coverage judicial nominations receive overall.[26]

Between 1985 and 2006, 230 circuit court nominations were sent by the Judiciary Committee to the Senate floor. Once placed on the floor's Executive Calendar, these 230 nominations could be subjected to a hold. I identified ninety-six holds placed on sixty-six circuit court nominees during this time period.[27] Overall, 29.6 percent of the 230 nominations sent to the Senate floor were subjected to holds.[28] Many of these holds captured multiple nominations. For example, Senator John McCain placed a hold on five circuit court nominations during the summer of 2002 to force President George W. Bush to appoint McCain's choice to the Federal Election Commission; dozens of district court nominations were also caught in this hold. Some nominations were also subjected to more than one hold. For example, Susan Black's nomination was caught in a hold placed by Senator Larry Pressler in 1992 when Senator Richard Shelby placed another hold on Black's nomination for a completely different reason.

The most unanticipated finding is that the vast majority of these private political holds were strategic in nature rather than nominee-based. Senators place strategic holds in order to use the nomination as a bargaining chip in an unrelated dispute; the nomination provides the senator with strategic leverage in a fight over other nominations or legislation. Alternatively, senators place nominee-based holds when they object to the nominee him- or herself, usually for ideological reasons. While controversial nominees such as Marsha Berzon and Richard Paez, both nominated by Clinton to the Ninth Circuit Court, were subjected to nominee-based holds in 1999, such nominee-based holds occur rarely. Overall, nominee-based holds account for only 16.7 percent of all holds placed during this time frame. And surprisingly, almost every nominee blocked by such a hold was eventually confirmed. Conversely, strategic holds, in which nominations are used as bargaining tools, are quite common. For example, in December 1987, Senators Howard Metzenbaum and Ted Kennedy placed a hold on two Reagan circuit court nominations and four district court nominations to try to force the Department of Justice to release a report on the alleged financial improprieties of Faith Ryan Whittlesay, then ambassador to Switzerland. After the documents were released, all six nominees were easily confirmed.

Thus, senators use holds to delay lower court nominations quite often, but they do so because judicial nominations act as convenient leverage instruments in unrelated disputes. These findings are discussed in greater detail in chapter 3.

PUBLIC PARTISAN TRACK

The final possible track a nomination may follow is the public partisan track. Nominations are turned down the public partisan track when an interest group publicly expresses opposition to a nominee in the form of a press release, opinion piece in a newspaper, or public speech.[29] Publicly expressed opposition to a judicial nominee decisively results in a confirmation process marked by public contention and debate over whether the nominee will be confirmed; once redirected onto the public partisan track, nominations remain on this track unless temporarily diverted onto the private partisan track. The public partisan track is characterized by high levels of interest group participation and media attention. Senators both on and off the Judiciary Committee take public positions on the nomination. These nominations will likely receive negative votes in committee and on the floor, and they might even be defeated. The nominees generally confront long waits, the need for renominations in successive Congresses, and the possibility of multiple hearings or committee votes. Interestingly, and somewhat ironically, given the inherently public nature of these fights, these nominees are also more likely than many of their brethren to move through the entire confirmation process.

What increases the likelihood that a federal judicial nomination will be sent down the public partisan track? First, the type of nomination matters. All Supreme Court nominations are subjected to a very high level of scrutiny, opening the door for a more contested confirmation process (Maltese 1995; Silverstein 1994). Similarly, nominations to the circuit courts are increasingly scrutinized as the circuit courts have become the final arbiter on many important constitutional and statutory questions (Strauss 1987).[30] For example, the D.C. Circuit Court is many times referred to as the "second most influential court in the nation," and as such, nominations to this court receive especially intense examination (Berg 2003; Perine 2003). Second, nominations that may shift the balance of power on a particular court are also subjected to increased scrutiny. For example, many noted during President George W. Bush's first term that both the Sixth Circuit Court and the D.C. Circuit Court were rather precariously balanced ideologically, and that even one appointment could shift the ideological balance (and thus the future legal and policy outcomes) of these courts (Berg 2003; Horn 2003; Maltzman and Binder 2000).

Third, nominees viewed as ideologically extreme are more likely to see their nominations challenged. Charles Pickering's and Priscilla Owen's (perceived) extreme conservative ideologies caused the Democratic-led Senate Judiciary Committee to reject their confirmations in 2002, much like the reaction to Robert Bork's Supreme Court nomination in 1987. Therefore, the practice of nominating so-called stealth candidates has arisen, with presidents nominating persons with little or no public record in an attempt to see ideologically like-minded candidates confirmed.[31] Fourth, an opposition Senate greatly increases the chances that a president's nominees will be contested and defeated (Ruckman 1993; Segal 1987; Segal and Spaeth 1986). Finally, weaker presidents face more public opposition to their nominations (Watson and Stookey 1995).[32]

Whatever their particular features, public partisan nominations engender an enormous amount of scrutiny and opposition, and they require the president to expend a substantial amount of political capital to successfully confirm his nominees.

One of the most recent and well-known public partisan nominations was that of Priscilla Owen. Nominated by President George W. Bush to the Fifth Circuit Court, Owen's nomination was rejected on September 5, 2002, on a strict party-line vote in the Judiciary Committee. In a prototypical example of a public partisan nomination, numerous senators made public appeals for and against Owen's confirmation; interest group lobbying activity, both for and against, was varied and intense; and strongly partisan and ideologically based positions were taken by all. Showcasing a growing trend in lower court confirmation fights, the issue over Owen's nomination was not qualifications (as it would have been in earlier eras) but rather focused solely on how she was expected to rule on certain controversial issues once seated on the federal bench.[33] In particular, Democrats cited a June 2000 opinion in which then Texas Supreme Court justice Alberto Gonzales (who was White House counsel in 2002) called Owen's dissent in the case "an unconscionable act of judicial activism."[34]

However, contrary to conventional wisdom, such public partisan nominations are quite rare. Nominations are sent down the public partisan track as a result of the decision by key interest groups to publicly challenge these nominations. As discussed in chapters 4 and 5, interest groups provide senators with the information necessary to determine which nominees are ideologically extreme and vulnerable to defeat, information senators usually cannot acquire elsewhere. Of the 272 nominations made to the circuit courts between 1985 and 2006, only fifty-four (19.9 percent) were publicly objected to by interest groups and thus sent down the public partisan track.[35]

Interestingly, the majority of these opposed nominees were eventually confirmed. Of these fifty-four opposed nominations, forty-five (83.3 percent) received committee votes. Six opposed nominations were defeated in committee, but the committee then voted to forward two of these nominations (those of Daniel Manion and Susan Liebeler) to the Senate floor without a recommendation.[36] Thirty-eight of the forty-one nominations sent to the Senate floor received some type of floor action.[37] Thirty-three opposed nominations (61.1 percent) were eventually confirmed— almost all, however, after long and bruising confirmation fights.

In comparison to the 161 noncontroversial nominations (see tables

TABLE 1.4 Time to Judiciary Committee votes for public partisan nominations to the circuit courts, 1985–2006 (99th–109th Congresses)

NOMINATIONS	DAYS BETWEEN HEARING AND FIRST/ONLY JUDICIARY VOTE[a] COMMITTEE	NOMINATIONS	DAYS BETWEEN FIRST JUDICIARY COMMITTEE VOTE AND SECOND JUDICIARY COMMITTEE VOTE
2	0–10	0	0–10
5	11–20	0	11–20
10	21–30	0	21–30
5	31–40	0	31–40
3	41–50	0	41–50
5	51–60	0	51–60
0	61–70	0	61–70
0	71–80	0	71–80
1	81–90	0	81–90
0	91–100	0	91–100
8	101–200	0	101–200
2	201–300	0	201–300
4	301+	8	301+

[a] In total, forty-five public partisan nominees received committee votes, and eight of these nominees had committee votes in two successive Congresses. There were thus fifty-three committee votes conducted for public partisan circuit court nominations during this time period.

1.1, 1.2, and 1.3), nominations diverted onto the public partisan track faced considerable opposition in the Senate and extended waits. Of the forty-five nominations on the public partisan track that received Judiciary Committee votes, eight (17.8 percent) had two separate committee votes; in comparison, only four (2.5 percent) of the 161 noncontroversial nominations were subjected to two committee votes. Twenty-eight (62.2 percent) nominations on the public partisan track that received committee votes waited more than a month between the hearing and committee votes, and fourteen (31.1 percent) waited more than 100 days (table 1.4). All eight nominations on the public partisan track that were subjected to a second committee vote waited more than 300 days for the second vote to occur.

The thirty-three confirmed nominees who traveled the public partisan track also faced extensive waits between their final committee and floor votes (table 1.5): sixteen (48.5 percent) nominees waited more than fifty days, while seven nominees (21.2 percent) languished for more than 100 days on the Senate floor. If we include the time nominees subject to two separate committee votes spent languishing on the Senate floor in between their two committee votes, then twenty-one nominees (63.6 percent) waited more than fifty days, while twelve waited more than 100 days (36.4 percent). Finally, while all 161 noncontroversial nominations were unanimously confirmed by the full Senate, twenty-one of the thirty-three (63.6 percent) public partisan nominees received more than twenty no votes on the Senate floor (see table 1.1). Thus, while technically no nominations were rejected by the full Senate during the time period under analysis (but five nominees withdrew after failed cloture votes),[38] nominations sent down the public partisan track faced significantly more senatorial opposition than their noncontroversial counterparts.

One reason why nominees relatively infrequently find themselves on the public partisan track is that interest groups and senators must pick their battles carefully. Opposing a nomination takes considerable resources and political capital. Actors in the judicial confirmation process

TABLE 1.5 Time to Senate floor votes for public partisan nominations to the circuit courts, 1985–2006 (99th–109th Congresses)

NOMINATIONS	DAYS BETWEEN FINAL JUDICIARY COMMITTEE VOTE AND FLOOR VOTE	NOMINATIONS	DAYS BETWEEN FIRST JUDICIARY COMMITTEE VOTE AND FLOOR VOTE
4	0–10	4	0–10
6	11–20	4	11–20
3	21–30	2	21–30
3	31–40	2	31–40
1	41–50	0	41–50
2	51–60	2	51–60
5	61–70	5	61–70
2	71–80	2	71–80
0	81–90	0	81–90
0	91–100	0	91–100
5	101–200	4	101–200
1	201–300	0	201–300
1	301+	8	301+

33 Total public partisan nominations

acknowledge that opposing all disliked nominees is simply not possible, so decisions must be made as to which nominations are worth the fight.[39] Opposing nominations takes money and time, and opposing too many nominations strains the credibility of interest groups and senators alike (Abraham 1999; Bronner 1989a; Watson and Stookey 1995). Furthermore, senators are loath to vote against a president's nominations without ample ammunition and the supporting claim that "only these few nominees" are being challenged; it is still true that senators' default position is to vote to confirm a president's lower court nominations (Scherer, Bartels, and Steigerwalt 2008). For example, many argue that Anthony Kennedy's 1988 confirmation to the Supreme Court was relatively easy as a result of the political capital expended during the fight over Robert Bork's unsuccessful nomination in 1987 (Abraham 1999; Bronner 1989a). Similarly, Democratic senators used the slogan "168 to 4" in late 2003 to signal they were only opposing a few egregious George W. Bush nominations rather than the bulk of his nominations.[40]

However, a change from this usual pattern occurred during the 108th Congress (2003–2004). After President George W. Bush renominated a host of vigorously opposed nominees, including Priscilla Owen and Charles Pickering, who had both been defeated in committee during the previous Congress, the Senate Democrats proceeded to filibuster ten of their nominations, all of which were also opposed by interest groups. It was only after the so-called Gang of Fourteen stepped into the breach to broker a bipartisan agreement as to when filibusters against lower court nominations could occur that the stalemate ended. At the end of the day, five of the ten filibustered nominees were confirmed; the other five (Henry Saad, Carolyn Kuhl, William Myers, Charles Pickering, and Miguel Estrada) eventually withdrew.[41]

While interest groups are willing to publicly attack judicial nominations, they also choose their battles carefully. Senators pick their battles prudently as well, and are loathe to be portrayed as merely obstructionist. Presidents must also decide whether their judicial nominations are worth expending significant political capital to see them confirmed. However, once groups decide to oppose a nominee, this objection sends the nomination down the public partisan track where, even if confirmed, the nominee will face a long, hard road to confirmation. Public partisan nominations thus reflect the increased partisan tensions surrounding the staffing of the federal bench, as well as the heightened realization of the importance of lower federal court decisions on the major policy issues of the day.

Conclusion

Senators and interest groups can influence the outcomes of judicial nominations by causing these nominations to be diverted to different confirmation tracks for varying lengths of time. Since the vast majority of lower court nominees are eventually confirmed, the real question is what happens to them while they are en route to confirmation. The four tracks framework helps answer this question by illuminating how and when nominations may be delayed or defeated. By calling attention to the hidden ways in which nominations may be manipulated, the four tracks framework offers a comprehensive instrument for understanding the path nominees follow and the hurdles they may face.

This framework also reveals that much of the delay that characterizes the modern-day lower court confirmation process is not due to ideological objections to nominees but rather occurs because judicial nominations have become convenient bargaining chips in unrelated disputes. Rather than merely being a product of ideologically extreme nominees running into trouble, confirmation delays arise because senators use judicial nominations to gain leverage in unrelated disputes or to exact retribution for past infractions. The legislative process works through bargaining and compromise, and judicial nominations offer a convenient mechanism for senators to negotiate and resolve disputes. Each judicial nomination garners relatively little media or even senatorial attention, but each is also highly important to certain players in the legislative process. Senators thus strategically block nominations in order to attain their legislative goals, and this may occur even when the blocking senator strongly supports the blocked nominee. In other words, judicial nominations make convenient bargaining chips, and blocks on nominations—and the resulting delays—have become a routine cost of doing business in the modern Senate.

Two of the confirmation tracks illuminate how these weapons are used currently in the context of judicial nominations, and they also provide insight into how individual senators use these weapons more broadly to effectively negotiate and achieve their policy priorities. The four tracks framework thus also affords meaningful insight into the operation of the Senate. Both senatorial courtesy and holds are powerful informal customs that have become institutionalized over time. Senators, unlike their House counterparts, possess strong parliamentary weapons with which to impede nominations, legislation, and the operation of the Senate itself. The desire to make the Senate, in George Washington's phrase, the "saucer" to cool the passions of the House of Representatives "teacup" means individual senators wield enormous power. Studying judicial confirmations reveals the degree to which the normal politics of the Senate describes even the seemingly politically neutral job of confirming nominees to the federal bench.

The rest of this book offers an in-depth assessment of the senatorial courtesy, private political, and public partisan tracks. An empirical examination of all nominations to the circuit courts between 1985 and 2006 not only reveals how often nominations follow each of the confirmation tracks, it also casts a strong light on the political realities judicial nominees face today. In chapter 2 I examine the senatorial courtesy track and the ways in which senators can block the progress of nominees from their home states.

DEATH TO NOMINEES
Senatorial Courtesy and the Ability to "Kill" Judicial Confirmations

According to the four tracks framework explicated in chapter 1, each nominee should be viewed as a train that follows a unique set of train tracks from nomination to confirmation. By conceptualizing the lower court confirmation process as a set of interconnected train tracks, we can better understand the different confirmation environments nominees may face. The four tracks framework also reveals which actors can influence confirmation outcomes and at what points in the process they are able to do so. As discussed in chapter 1, most nominations follow the noncontroversial track. But a significant percentage of nominations will at some point be turned onto one (or more) of the other confirmation tracks. The rest of this book provides an in-depth assessment of these alternative tracks by empirically examining all nominees to the circuit courts between 1985 and 2006.

This chapter begins our empirical exploration of the four tracks framework by examining the first veto point in the Senate judicial confirmation process, and thus the first place where a nomination may veer off the noncontroversial track. Immediately after a nomination is sent to the Senate by the president, home-state senators may object to the nomination and propel it onto the senatorial courtesy track. A convincing mode of rejection, senatorial courtesy allows senators to kill a nomination, and to do so out of the public eye.

Senatorial Courtesy and Blue Slips: The Ongoing Institutional Struggle over the Power of Judicial Selection

Since the beginning of the Republic, senators and presidents have fought over the power to appoint federal judges. While Article II, Section 2, of the U.S. Constitution gives presidents the sole power to nominate federal judges, it also grants the Senate the authority to provide "advice and consent." The Senate takes seriously this advice and consent role and designed the federal judicial confirmation process accordingly. Most important, senators believe they should be allowed to recommend potential nominees for vacancies on the federal bench from their home states.

Within the federal judicial system, the lower courts are arranged geographically, so that seats on the federal bench at the district court and circuit court levels are "assigned" to particular states, with the exceptions of the Federal and D.C. Circuit Courts. District courts (the federal trial courts) are located within states, and, in much the same way that seats in the House of Representatives are allocated, some states are comprised of multiple districts, given their larger populations and correspondingly larger caseloads. A case involving federal law that arises in Oklahoma will be heard by a district court judge in Oklahoma.[1] The eleven numbered geographic circuit courts (the intermediate federal appeals courts) hear appeals from the multiple states that compose each federal circuit. For example, the Eleventh Circuit covers Georgia, Alabama, and Florida, and any federal case heard by a district court located in Georgia, Alabama, or Florida can be appealed to the Eleventh Circuit Court. For these circuit courts, each seat is considered to be assigned to one of the states covered by the circuit; thus, the Eleventh Circuit is composed of judges who hail from Georgia, Alabama, and Florida.

Presidents traditionally granted senators the courtesy of suggesting nominees to vacancies on federal courts located in their home state, on the assumption that local politicians know best. Senators are more likely to know the top lawyers from their states and to have connections with the local bar and local political parties. Not surprisingly, judicial appointments also provide ample opportunities for senators (and the president) to reward loyal supporters; in fact, until quite recently, most lower court appointments were based on patronage rather than policy considerations (Goldman 1997; Scherer 2005). As a result, senators from each state have the opportunity to play a role in both the selection and the confirmation phases of the lower court appointment process.[2] Since the mid-1970s, however, presidents have reasserted their control over the selection process, and senators have been relegated to a more consultative role.

Given the more direct connection between district courts and the states in which they are located, as well as their lesser policymaking role, presidents have generally granted senators much more of a role in the selection of district court nominees than in the selection of circuit court nominees (Goldman 1997; Harris 1953). Slotnick's (1980a) interviews with senators reveal their belief that district court appointments are primarily a senatorial prerogative, defined by bargaining with the president.

Goldman similarly explains that nominations to the district courts "typically are dominated by senators of the president's party," while circuit court vacancies "traditionally offer an administration more leeway in choosing nominees" (1997, 13). Finally, Rowland and Carp's (1996) in-depth examination of the district courts reveals that, especially in states with two home-state senators from the president's party, presidents have generally followed senators' recommendations.

As the Goldman quotation highlights, presidents historically turned to senators from their own party to suggest nominees (see also Binder 2007; Harris 1953; Rowland and Carp 1996; Slotnick 1980a, 1980b, 1984). When no home-state senator hails from the president's party, nominations generally reflect the president's preferences (Giles, Hettinger, and Peppers 2001; Songer 1982). However, out-party senators may be granted a role in the selection of judicial nominees. Binder and Maltzman (2004) find divided government and the institutionalization of the blue slip procedure mean recent presidents must consult more with opposition party senators during the selection stage. For example, explicit arrangements have been made between home-state senators or between senators and the current administration to provide out-party senators with a role in the nominating process.[3]

Presidents may, of course, choose to reject or ignore the stated preferences of the relevant home-state senators. Presidents do so at their peril, however, for senators may in return call upon their fellow senators to grant them "senatorial courtesy." Senatorial courtesy is invoked when a senator asks his or her colleagues to support the senator against the president and allow the senator to kill the nomination. In its modern incarnation, senators retaliate by blocking the offending nominations as soon as they are formally sent to the Senate. It is important to note that senatorial courtesy can occur between senators and a president of the same party, since the objection is not to the nominee but rather to the process used to select the nominee; in fact, senatorial courtesy traditionally emerges from an intraparty dispute. The custom of senatorial courtesy highlights both the power of institutionalized Senate norms and the ongoing struggle between the president and the Senate over what the Senate's advice and consent role entails.

THE DEVELOPMENT OF THE MODERN-DAY PRACTICE OF SENATORIAL COURTESY

Senatorial courtesy gained its name from the original manner in which a home-state senator objected to and thereby killed a nomination.

Drawing on the Senate norms of collegiality and deference, a senator would declare the nominee "personally obnoxious" in order to signal his colleagues to support the senator over the president (Harris 1952, 39; Goldman 1997, 43). The other senators would then vote against the nominee on the Senate floor. Senatorial courtesy thus reflects the strong institutional ties senators feel to their chamber and fellow colleagues, as well as the belief that senators should have a say in choosing judicial nominees from their home states.

The earliest instances of senatorial courtesy occurred barely three months into the Senate's first session in 1789. The Senate rejected George Washington's nomination of Benjamin Fishbourn to be the naval officer for the Port of Savannah because Georgia's two senators supported another candidate. Two weeks later, the two Georgia senators again objected to one of Washington's nominees, this time one of his candidates for commissioner responsible for negotiating with Indians in Georgia (Gerhardt 2003; Harris 1953; McDonald 1994). In both instances the home-state senators supported another candidate, and their fellow senators responded by backing their colleagues. Similarly, in the early 1950s, four district court nominees nominated by President Truman were rejected by the full Senate because of opposition from their home-state senators; all of the objecting senators were fellow Democrats.

Presidents and their staff recognize the possible ramifications of not consulting home-state senators when nominating candidates for the lower federal courts. William D. Mitchell, attorney general under President Hoover, said in a 1929 radio address, "It would be futile, of course, for the President to nominate a United States District Court Judge who could not be confirmed because of the determined opposition of the Senators in his home state."[4]

Over time, the custom of allowing home-state senators a veto over judicial nominees from their state developed into a formalized practice known as the blue slip process. Blue slips are literally blue slips of paper that ask senators for their "opinion and information" concerning home-state nominees (Binder 2007, 8; see also Slotnick 1980a). Beginning in 1913, Judiciary Committee Executive Docket books reflected the routinization of the blue slip procedure and contained information not only on the status of each nomination but also on the views of each home-state senator and when they were solicited (Binder 2007, 7). Until 1955, a negative blue slip meant the Judiciary Committee would forward the nomination to the floor with a negative recommendation; the home-state senator could then state his or her objections before the final floor vote. However, beginning in 1956, under Chairman James Eastland, a negative blue slip signaled certain death for the nominee: a negative blue slip would now allow home-state senators to stop all Judiciary Committee action, thereby killing the nomination (Binder 2007; Denning 2002; Gerhardt 2003; Goldman et al. 2001).[5]

Ironically, the development of the blue slip process increased the power of opposition party senators in the selection phase by granting a veto to all home-state senators, regardless of their party affiliation. Originally there existed an "uneven extension" of the power to block home-state nominees to members of the opposition party (Harris 1953, 224). As Binder (2007) documents, the blue slip process was designed in 1913 to help the then majority party reduce uncertainty as to a nomination's fate on the floor, since the norm of senatorial courtesy dictated that one's colleagues reject a disliked nomination on the floor, even if the nomination successfully made it out of the Judiciary Committee. Out-party senators' views were solicited to help decrease uncertainty and improve the management of the floor proceedings. By the mid-twentieth century, however, the use of blue slips had been transformed from an advisory practice to "a potential veto tool for home state senators regardless of whether or not they hailed from the president's party" (Binder 2007, 2).[6] More recently, on March 2, 2009, Republican senators sent a letter to newly inaugurated President Obama stating that if Republican senators "are not consulted on, and approve of, a nominee from our states, the Republican Conference will be unable to support moving forward on that nominee . . . we, as a Conference, expect [senatorial courtesy] to be observed, even-handedly and regardless of party affiliation. And we will act to preserve this principle and rights of our colleagues if it is not."[7]

Much like other informal Senate customs, a negative blue slip is only as powerful as the Senate leadership, in this case the Judiciary Committee chair, allows it to be. While senatorial courtesy has been formalized over time, it is still an informal custom and not part of the codified Senate rules. As a result, different committee chairs have granted negative blue slips various amounts of veto power. Usually a positive recommendation is needed from both home-state senators for a nomination to move forward, but chairs have sometimes decided to honor negative blue slips only from senators in their own party or to block nominations only when both home-state senators object. Especially in situations in which a senator not in the president's party objects to a nominee and is also in the

Senate minority, the chair may decide to move the nominee over the objections of the home-state senator and risk the possibility that the senator will block or impede the nominee in other ways.

For example, when Edward Kennedy became chair of the Judiciary Committee in 1979, he declared that the full committee would decide whether a blue-slipped nominee would receive a hearing; his decision was seen as an attempt to forestall objections to Carter's attempts to appoint more minorities and women to the federal bench (Epstein and Segal 2005, 89; Sollenberger 2003). His successor, Strom Thurmond, also allowed some blue-slipped nominations to progress. Patrick Leahy, upon gaining the chairmanship in 2001, determined that two positive blue slips were necessary for a nominee to receive a hearing. Conversely, after the Republicans regained control of the Senate in 2002, Chair Orrin Hatch decided in May 2003 to schedule Carolyn Kuhl, a nominee from California for the Ninth Circuit, for a hearing and committee vote over the objections of both Democratic home-state senators, Barbara Boxer and Dianne Feinstein. In response, the Democrats filibustered Kuhl's nomination on the Senate floor.[8] Chairs may also decide to extend the reach of senatorial courtesy: during the 107th Congress, Leahy allowed Michigan Democratic senators Carl Levin and Debbie Stabenow to exercise a veto over all Sixth Circuit nominees in order to protest Senate Republicans' treatment of two Clinton nominees from Michigan.[9]

Currently, we know relatively little about the modern use of senatorial courtesy as a mode of rejection. Most studies of senatorial courtesy focus on senators' "advice" role in helping select nominees for lower court vacancies in their home states (Carp and Stidham 1993; Gerhardt 2003; Goldman 1997). Binder and Maltzman (2004) analyze the degree to which senators act as a constraint on presidents' decisions about whom to nominate and find that the senators' advice role in the nominating phase influences how swiftly presidents move to fill lower court vacancies. Similarly, Hendershot (2008) explores changes in the relationship between the president and Senate over time with respect to senators' advice role; he finds that some periods reflect true "advice and consent" paradigms, while in other periods senators are restricted to merely assessing nominees at the confirmation stage. However, these studies do not focus on senators' power to reject a nomination through senatorial courtesy once the nomination is formally sent to the Senate.

Those studies that do examine senatorial courtesy as a mechanism of rejection generally focus on describing how this informal veto practice works in theory, as well as its ramifications, as opposed to systematically assessing its actual usage (Chase 1972; Denning 2002; Gerhardt 2003; Goldman et al. 2001, 2003; Harris 1953; Jacobi 2005; Scherer 2005). Slotnick (1980a) provides one of the few empirical analyses of senatorial courtesy by surveying senators as to their use of senatorial courtesy as well as their feelings on the process. Interestingly, he concludes that "[senatorial courtesy's] major function seems to be to delay, not defeat, a nomination" (Slotnick 1980a, 73). Denning (2002) offers a more recent if mostly anecdotal analysis of the blue slip process. He argues that in the two decades since Slotnick's study, senatorial courtesy has transformed once again into a powerful mechanism of defeat. Thus, while the practice of senatorial courtesy is extremely powerful and widely acknowledged, its actual usage is still somewhat of a mystery. We do not know precisely how often negative blue slips are returned, and it is not clear whether a negative blue slip merely delays a nominee's progress or signals certain death for the nominee.

This chapter seeks to fill this gap by investigating the use of senatorial courtesy by home-state senators against circuit court nominations made between 1985 and 2006. By assessing how often senatorial courtesy is used and why, we can begin to understand the different political environments judicial nominees may confront. I first outline the possible motivations behind the use of senatorial courtesy and then determine how often each has been active. I find institutional battles over the power of lower court selection continue to be fought today, and judicial nominees many times serve as innocent pawns in these long-simmering disputes. Furthermore, the heightened use of institutional senatorial courtesy means blue slips once again act more as a delaying mechanism than as an absolute roadblock to confirmation.

SENATORIAL COURTESY AND ITS MOTIVATIONS

At its core, the use of senatorial courtesy reflects the tug-of-war between the president and the Senate over who should have the final say in naming lower court nominees. Since the lower federal courts are arranged geographically, nominees traditionally hail from the state or region in which the court is located. Senators maintain they are better suited to identify qualified candidates to represent their state on the federal bench than the president. The location of district courts within states provides senators with a strong argument for why they should be allowed input as to the people who will resolve legal conflicts affecting their constituents. At the circuit court level, each seat on each circuit is assigned to a particular state in order to alleviate potential state-bias problems. Not surprisingly, the home-state senators connected to these seats want to be included in the selection process.[10] As Harris noted in 1952, "An objection to a nomination does not mean that the nominee is actually 'personally obnoxious' to the objecting senator; it frequently involves no animus whatever, but merely indicates that the senator has another candidate" (39).

In recent years presidents have reasserted their power over judicial selection, and institutional fights between presidents and senators have inevitably resulted. For example, Republican senators blocked President George H. W. Bush's judicial nominees when he attempted to reassert control over the selection phase. In particular, the blue slip process has become "the formal vehicle for sanctioning a president's failure to abide by senators' expectations of consultation prior to making judicial nominations from their states" (Denning 2002, 224). Thus, the predominant reason for the invocation of senatorial courtesy is institutional. Institutional senatorial courtesy reflects the ongoing struggle between the legislative branch and the executive branch over the power to select judges and over what the Senate's constitutional advice and consent role truly encompasses. Institutional senatorial courtesy arises when senators believe they have not been adequately consulted about nominations to vacancies in their state, and so senators call on their colleagues to support their institutional claim to the power to select judicial nominees. Institutional senatorial courtesy often includes objections by senators of the same party as the president.

Invocations of senatorial courtesy may also have a retaliatory basis. Senators invoke retaliatory senatorial courtesy when they feel a previous president's nominees were treated unfairly during prior Congresses. If the current administration refuses to renominate them, senators may decide to block the new nominees in retaliation, and to gain leverage in convincing the current president to nominate the original candidate. Retaliatory senatorial courtesy most commonly occurs between presidents and senators of opposite parties; it also reflects the broader institutional dispute over the Senate's advice and consent role, as the retaliation is partly a response to a lack of consultation with the new administration.

Finally, senators may use senatorial courtesy to block nominees they dislike for ideological reasons. Ideological senatorial courtesy occurs when the objecting senator views a particular nominee as "personally obnoxious" along ideological lines. Ideological senatorial courtesy usually occurs in disputes between presidents and senators of different parties. Much like the other motivations for senatorial courtesy in relation to judicial nominees, ideological senatorial courtesy disputes also reflect at their core a dispute over senators' role in the selection phase, as these candidates would not have been nominated if the senators had been adequately consulted.

Overall, senators use senatorial courtesy to block lower court nominees for three main reasons: institutional, retaliatory, and ideological. All three motivations reflect to varying degrees the struggle between presidents and senators as to what the Senate's advice and consent role truly encompasses. The question now becomes, how often do senators use senatorial courtesy for each of these reasons? The following section provides an in-depth assessment of when and why senatorial courtesy was used by home-state senators to block circuit court nominees between 1985 and 2006.[11]

The Use of Senatorial Courtesy in the Modern Era

Between 1985 and 2006, of the 272 nominations made to the circuit courts, twenty (7.4 percent) were blocked through senatorial courtesy. This number includes eight nominations that were initially blocked by senatorial courtesy but were eventually allowed to move through the entire confirmation process. Only twelve (4.4 percent) nominations overall were killed by senatorial courtesy during this time period, but for 60 percent of the blue-slipped nominations, the negative blue slip proved to be determinative.[12] These results reflect the ever-evolving nature of the Senate's blue slip process and the continuing question of whether a negative blue slip represents—or should represent—a decisive veto. As outlined above, the power of blue slips alters depending on who holds the chair of the Judiciary Committee and which party controls the presidency and the Senate. As a result, during the past two decades, nominations diverted onto the senatorial courtesy track have at times been allowed to progress through the entire confirmation process.

Table 2.1 reports the number of nominees who were blue-slipped during each Congress in relation to the number of new nominations made to the circuit courts during that Congress.[13] Presidents Reagan and Bush (41) had no nominees blocked by senatorial courtesy, while Clinton had eight nominees stopped by senatorial courtesy and Bush (43) had twelve. These findings are interesting on two levels. First, unified government occurred during the 103rd, 108th, and 109th Congresses, so the lack of home-state objections to nominees during the Reagan and Bush (41) administrations cannot be explained merely by the presence of unified government. Second, these findings illustrate the increasing ten-

TABLE 2.1 Number of circuit court nominations blocked by senatorial courtesy in comparison to total number of new nominations, 1985–2006 (99th–109th Congresses)

	NOMINEES RECEIVING NEGATIVE BLUE SLIPS	NOMINESS RECEIVING POSITIVE BLUE SLIPS	TOTAL
99th	0	33	33
100th	0	26	26
101st	0	23	23
102nd	0	30	30
103rd	0	22	22
104th	2	15	17
105th	2	20	22
106th	4	25	29
107th	11	21	32
108th	0	22	22
109th	1	15	16
Total	20	252	272

Note: A negative blue slip means that a senator either returned the blue slip without approving the nominee or declined to return the blue slip. A positive blue slip means that a senator returned the blue slip and approved of the nominee.

sion over recent presidential prerogatives to select lower court nominees without Senate input.[14] However, the numbers for the 107th Congress are somewhat inflated: as mentioned earlier, then Judiciary Committee chair Leahy allowed Michigan senators Levin and Stabenow to block, at least for a while, all nominees to the Sixth Circuit, regardless of their state of origin, in retaliation for the treatment of two Michigan nominees during the Clinton administration.[15] Additionally, Richard Clifton was blue-slipped by both Hawaii senators, but eventually his nomination was allowed to move forward after negotiations commenced between the senators and the White House.[16] Finally, the historical treatment of nominees from certain circuits has led to the court of appointment being extremely important: as table 2.2 shows, nominees to only five circuit courts were blue-slipped during the period under examination.[17] In fact, fourteen of the twenty blue-slipped nominees were nominated to either the Fourth Circuit or the Sixth Circuit.

Table 2.3 provides some basic demographic information about these twenty blue-slipped nominees in relation to the party of the appointing president. Five of the eight Clinton nominees blocked by senatorial courtesy were minorities. Of these nominees, two were nominated to the Fourth Circuit, two to the Fifth Circuit, and one to the Sixth Circuit. As discussed below, Senator Jesse Helms refused to allow any North Carolinian to be confirmed to the Fourth Circuit in retaliation for the treatment of Terrence Boyle during the first Bush administration, and his actions twice prevented the confirmation of the first black judge to the Fourth Circuit. Similarly, the Texas senators blocked two of President Clinton's nominees to the Fifth Circuit, and both were Hispanic. Four of the six female nominees were blocked during the 107th Congress, and, ironically, three were blocked in retaliation for the treatment of two women nominated to the Sixth Circuit during the Clinton administration. Fi-

TABLE 2.2 Number of nominations blocked by senatorial courtesy, by court of appointment, 1985–2006 (99th–109th Congresses)

	BLUE-SLIPPED NOMINEES
1st Circuit Court	0
2nd Circuit Court	0
3rd Circuit Court	0
4th Circuit Court	4
5th Circuit Court	2
6th Circuit Court	10
7th Circuit Court	0
8th Circuit Court	0
9th Circuit Court	3
10th Circuit Court	1
11th Circuit Court	0
Total	20

Note: The D.C. and Federal Circuit Courts are not included in this table because nominees to these courts do not have home-state senators.

TABLE 2.3 Demographic information on circuit court nominees blocked by senatorial courtesy, 1985–2006 (99th–109th Congresses)

	MINORITIES	WOMEN	WHITE MEN
Republicans	0	4	8
Democrats	5	2	2

Note: The numbers on this table reflect the fact that one nominee, Kathleen McCree Lewis, is both female and a member of a minority group.

nally, senatorial courtesy was not applied to any nominations made by a president from the home-state senator's party during this period, though such actions have occurred frequently in the past. For example, Goldman (1997) relates the many skirmishes between Franklin D. Roosevelt and Democratic home-state senators.

Intraparty fights over senators' judicial selection power did arise during the time period under analysis, but they manifested in ways other than senatorial courtesy. The most striking example occurred when Republican James Jeffords placed a hold on all judicial nominations currently on the Senate floor in November 1989 to protest President George H. W. Bush's new policy concerning lower court selection. President Bush determined that senators should provide him with at least three names for each lower court vacancy in their state. He then intimated he would generally pick a nominee from this list, but that he would not be bound by the list. Republican senators rebelled, arguing that the norm of providing a single name should prevail. This fight continued for months, and one result was Jeffords' hold. Republican senators did not—or rather could not—use senatorial courtesy in this instance because the nominating process itself was indefinitely stalled. Thus, the intraparty disputes over senators' selection power that occurred during this time period are captured by the examination of holds on the Senate floor in chapter 3.

Why These Nominees? The Motivations behind Senatorial Courtesy in Recent Decades

Overall, the use of senatorial courtesy in recent years has been limited. While forty-one circuit court nominees between 1985 and 2006 failed to receive even a hearing, the blue slip process frustrated only twenty of these nominees. Why were these particular nominees blocked? Given the small number of nominees subjected to senatorial courtesy during the time period under analysis, an in-depth examination of the motivations behind each use of senatorial courtesy is possible. The analysis reveals that all of these instances of senatorial courtesy reflected some form of an institutional clash between the Senate and the then current administration.

Table 2.4 lists the reason each nominee was blocked by senatorial courtesy, arranged by appointing president. Of the twenty instances of negative blue slips, six (30 percent) reflected the objecting senator's ire that she or he was not adequately consulted in the decision-making process—that is, the institutional form of senatorial courtesy. Twelve nominees (60 percent) were blue-slipped in retaliation for the treatment of a

TABLE 2.4 Motivation for use of senatorial courtesy to block circuit court nominations, by appointing president, 1985–2006 (99th–109th Congresses)

MOTIVATION FOR OBJECTION	REAGAN NOMINATIONS	BUSH (41) NOMINATIONS	CLINTON NOMINATIONS	BUSH (43) NOMINATIONS	TOTAL
Institutional	0	0	4	2	6
Retaliatory	0	0	3	9	12
Ideological	0	0	1	1	2
Total	0	0	8	12	20

previously favored nominee. The remaining two nominees (10 percent) were blue-slipped because of overt ideological objections.

Conventional wisdom holds that most nominees run into trouble in the Senate because of ideological objections from opposition senators. This belief carries over to the use of senatorial courtesy as well as the other mechanisms of delay individual senators may utilize. Studies of confirmation durations do reveal strong relations between the temporal political environment (such as whether there is divided government) and the length of a nominee's wait (Binder and Maltzman 2002; Martinek, Kemper, and Van Winkle 2002). However, as the findings herein reveal, between 1985 and 2006, only two nominees were blocked because of explicit objections to the nominee's perceived positions—that is, through the application of ideological senatorial courtesy. Rather, recent uses of senatorial courtesy primarily reflect institutional disputes between the blocking senators and the current administration.

First, Carolyn Kuhl, nominated to the Ninth Circuit Court in 2001, was blue-slipped by California senator Barbara Boxer because of her history of opposition to reproductive rights.[18] The second instance of ideological senatorial courtesy reflects more of a traditional partisan dispute. Colorado senator Wayne Allard blue-slipped, with the support of numerous other Republican senators such as James Inhofe and Pat Roberts, the nomination of James Lyons to the Tenth Circuit Court in 1999. Bill and Hillary Clinton had asked Lyons to investigate their role in the White-water land deals during the 1992 presidential campaign, and his investigation exonerated the Clintons of any wrongdoing. Allard contended Lyons's report concealed Bill Clinton's true involvement in these land deals. The opposing senators likened Lyons's nomination to President Nixon appointing one of his Watergate attorneys to the federal bench

(*Wall Street Journal* 1999). Thus, in these two cases, the primary objection voiced was ideological.

Strikingly, however, such ideologically based uses of senatorial courtesy explain only a bare minimum (10 percent, to be exact) of all of the instances of senatorial courtesy used against circuit court nominations between 1985 and 2006. Rather, the overwhelming majority of nominations blocked due to senatorial courtesy reflect either institutional disputes or retaliation.

Six of the twenty blue-slipped nominations were blocked due to clear institutional disputes: Clinton nominees Helen White, Kathleen McCree Lewis, Jorge Rangel, and Enrique Moreno, and George W. Bush nominees Richard Clifton and Randy Norman Smith. Newspaper accounts concerning each of these nominations indicated that the objecting home-state senator was primarily upset that he or she was not adequately consulted as to the initial nomination. Clinton nominees Helene White and Kathleen McCree Lewis were blue-slipped by Michigan Republican senator Spencer Abraham because Clinton nominated McCree Lewis and White instead of Abraham's favored candidate, district court judge Jerry Rosen.

Similarly, Texas Republican senators Phil Gramm and Kay Bailey Hutchinson blocked the nominations of Jorge Rangel and Enrique Moreno to the Fifth Circuit. In particular, they were upset that Rangel and Moreno were both nominated based on the recommendations of the Texas Democratic House delegation. They also opposed Moreno on the basis of his qualifications. Moreno was rated "well qualified" by the American Bar Association, but he received a rating of "not qualified" from the Texas Judicial Advisory Group, a nonpartisan committee of Texas attorneys formed in 1986 by Senator Gramm to review nominees to the lower federal courts in Texas (Koppel 2000; Zuniga 2000). Gramm and Hutchinson argued that by not consulting them about the most qualified Texans, Clinton nominated an inferior candidate.[19]

During the George W. Bush administration, Richard Clifton was blue-slipped for a number of months by the two Democratic senators from Hawaii, Daniel Akaka and Daniel Inouye, as a result of their belief that Bush did not adequately consult them. The senators allowed Clifton's nomination to move forward after Bush agreed to confer with them on the next Hawaii vacancy. Clifton was then easily confirmed with these two senators' support. Finally, Diane Feinstein of California was permitted by then Judiciary Committee chair Patrick Leahy to blue-slip Randy Norman Smith's nomination to the Ninth Circuit Court; Feinstein argued the seat "belonged" to California rather than to Smith's home state of Idaho. Smith eventually joined the Ninth Circuit during the 110th Congress, but only after an Idaho vacancy on the court appeared and he was renominated for that position.

In each of these six cases, institutional disputes over the power of nominee selection frustrated the nominations. The senators' main complaints concerned a lack of presidential consultation as to vacancies in their home states. While some blocking senators may disapprove of any nomination made by an opposition president, it is notable that these same senators did vote for other nominees proposed by the same president when consultation did occur. For example, Senator Abraham voted for Michigan Sixth Circuit nominee Eric Clay. And Senator Feinstein supported Smith's nomination once he was nominated for an Idaho Ninth Circuit vacancy rather than the California vacancy.

Notably, the majority of nominees blocked by senatorial courtesy (twelve out of twenty, or 60 percent) were blue-slipped in retaliation for past political grievances (see table 2.4). Strikingly, all of these retaliatory senatorial courtesy disputes concerned nominations to a particular seat on two different circuit courts. The first use of retaliatory senatorial courtesy concerns the North Carolina seat on the Fourth Circuit Court. In October 1991, President George H. W. Bush nominated Terrence Boyle, a former aide to Senator Jesse Helms and a sitting district court judge, to this position. Boyle never even received a hearing; many argued this was primarily due to the expected slowdown in confirmations as the presidential election approached. As the newly enshrined President Clinton soon discovered to his dismay, Helms was extremely upset and desired retribution. When Clinton refused to renominate Boyle, Helms proceeded to block the three Fourth Circuit nominees Clinton proposed from North Carolina (Richard Leonard, James Beatty, and James Wynn) for the entirety of Clinton's presidency. After the Republicans regained the presidency in 2000, Bush (43) again nominated Boyle in May 2001. However, as soon as the Democrats regained control of the Senate after James Jeffords defected in June 2001, the junior senator from North Carolina, Democrat John Edwards, blue-slipped Boyle's nomination to protest Helms's treatment of Clinton's North Carolina nominees. Boyle finally received a Judiciary Committee hearing and vote in 2005, after Edwards left the Senate, but he never received a floor vote; on January 9, 2007, the White House (over Boyle's objections) announced it would not renominate Boyle again (Barrett 2007).[20] Another North Carolinian, Allyson Duncan, was confirmed to the Fourth Circuit in 2003 after Edwards reached an agreement with the newly elected Republican senator (and Helms's replacement), Elizabeth Dole.

The second retaliatory use of senatorial courtesy concerns seats allocated to Michigan on the Sixth Circuit Court. President Clinton nominated Helene White and Kathleen McCree Lewis to two vacancies on the Sixth Circuit in 1997 and 1999, respectively. As discussed above, both were blue-slipped by Senator Abraham. After the Democrats regained control of the Senate in 2001, Michigan Democratic senators Debbie Stabenow and Carl Levin followed the precedent set by Senator Helms during the Clinton years and proceeded to block all of George W. Bush's nominees to the Michigan seats on the Sixth Circuit.[21] Additionally, then Judiciary chair Patrick Leahy also allowed them to block *every* current nominee to the Sixth Circuit. Eventually the non-Michigan nominees, Julia Smith Gibbons of Tennessee and John Rogers of Kentucky, were allowed to proceed, and both were confirmed easily. When the Republicans regained control of the Senate in 2003, they held committee hearings on the four Michigan nominees over the Democrats' objections. The nominations of Henry Saad, Richard Griffin, and David McKeague were then filibustered on the Senate floor. As part of the Gang of Fourteen deal, discussed more fully in chapter 6, the nominations of Griffin, McKeague, and Susan Neilson were eventually confirmed; Henry Saad withdrew in 2006. Stephen Murphy and Raymond Kethledge were then nominated to the Sixth Circuit in late 2006.[22] Their nominations again faced opposition from the two Michigan Democratic senators during the 110th Congress. This impasse was finally resolved after seven years, when President Bush and the Michigan senators reached an agreement in April 2008 (Thomas 2008). Under the agreement, Kethledge's nomination was allowed to move forward. Murphy's nomination to the Sixth Circuit was withdrawn, and he was renominated for a district court seat. In his place, Helene White, who had waited four years without even a hearing under President Clinton, was again nominated for the Sixth Circuit, this time by President Bush (43). She was successfully confirmed in June 2008. These senators invoked senatorial courtesy to force the current administration to renominate previously scorned nominees. In this case, the use of retaliatory senatorial courtesy worked: Levin and Stabenow were ultimately successful in seeing at least one of their favored nominees confirmed to the Sixth Circuit.

These retaliatory senatorial courtesy disputes highlight the breakdown of bipartisanship on both sides of the aisle and the desire by home-state senators to be consulted during the selection phase by the president, regardless of party. In each case, senators exacted retribution for the treatment of past nominees. While the existence of retaliatory senatorial courtesy is not surprising, what is unexpected is the extent to which senators have used this weapon against the president—and the unlucky nominees—since 1993. Retaliatory senatorial courtesy thus also reveals how judicial nominations have become favored bargaining chips in larger political disputes.

Conclusion

Although conventional accounts suggest most nominations are killed by senatorial courtesy arising out of ideological objections to the nominee, the reality is quite different. The twenty uses of senatorial courtesy against circuit court nominations since 1985 principally reflect ongoing institutional disputes between senators and presidents over who should hold the power to select lower court nominees. Senators maintain they should have a strong role at both the advice and consent stages of the appointment process. These recent disputes reveal senators' displeasure at the reduction of their traditional selection role. Presidents have gradually sought to reassert their power to nominate lower court judges. In response, senators have resisted this power shift and tried to kill the nominations of those selected unilaterally by the president. Each use of senatorial courtesy thus inherently reflects the belief that the home-state senator was not adequately consulted. It is still the case, however, that presidents and home-state senators generally agree on candidates for judgeships: while twenty nominees were blue-slipped, 252 nominees enjoyed home-state support.

A number of instances of senatorial courtesy applied against circuit court nominations also show senators seeking retribution for the treatment of past nominees. Current presidents may be punished for how previous Senates treated favored nominees, and contemporary nominees are held hostage in these disputes. Strikingly, in only one case was the actual nominee objected to. In all other cases the implication was that the nomination would be allowed to move forward if future nominations reflected more collaboration between the president and home-state senators. Both Hawaii senators supported Clifton's eventual confirmation, while the two Michigan senators eventually voted in support of the nominations of Griffin, McKeague, Neilson, Kethledge, and Murphy. Similarly, Edwards voted for Duncan's compromise nomination. Much as Slotnick found in 1980, many of these blue-slipped nominees were delayed rather than defeated.

Senatorial courtesy is thus being used as a weapon in institutional (and partisan) fights that look more and more like the normal politicking that characterizes the contemporary legislative process. Nominations provide useful negotiation instruments, especially in Senate–presidential disputes. Senators wish to retain their control over the staffing of the lower federal courts and to influence the development of legal policy. Senators may therefore invoke senatorial courtesy as a way of ensuring their voices are heard at the advice stage of the judicial appointment process. As this chapter and the next show, senators are not reluctant to use the parliamentary tools available to them to try to win these battles. The concern is that judicial nominees are stuck in the middle.

Chapter 3 examines another parliamentary procedure senators may use to delay—and possibly defeat—nominees, the hold. Continuing the argument begun in this chapter, an in-depth analysis reveals that holds are routinely used to block judicial nominations. Even more striking, many of these holds are utilized to resolve legislative disputes, and these holds commonly capture nominations completely unrelated to the dispute at hand; rather, nominees have become convenient bargaining chips in the tit-for-tat game that characterizes the modern-day U.S. Congress.

3

"HERDING CATS"
Holds and Private Political Fights

Chapter 2 outlined the use of senatorial courtesy, an informal custom that allows home-state senators to block an objectionable judicial nominee from progressing past the nomination stage. This chapter begins our examination of what can happen to nominations once they receive home-state senator approval and begin to move through the confirmation process. It first explores the myriad of ways in which particular senators can delay judicial nominations at different stages throughout the confirmation process. These mechanisms make up the private political arsenal that senators may employ to influence confirmation outcomes. It then investigates the use of a parliamentary procedure by which senators can exert enormous influence over judicial nominations, the hold. An informal custom that has become institutionalized over time, holds allow senators to impede a nomination once it reaches the Senate floor. By placing a hold on a nomination, senators send nominees down the private political track while utilizing a powerful private political tactic.

The use of holds in relation to judicial nominations is almost entirely overlooked. In fact, we know very little about the use of holds at all. This chapter therefore undertakes an extensive examination of the use of holds in order to shed much-needed light on this powerful yet hidden parliamentary tool.

Conventional wisdom assumes that senators obstruct and delay nominations they find ideologically objectionable, using whatever means available. As discussed in the previous chapter, however, while senators sometimes invoke senatorial courtesy to defeat ideologically objectionable nominees, they more commonly use negative blue slips to express a disagreement with the president over the nominating process itself. This chapter assesses when and why holds are used to determine if factors or disputes other than ideological objections motivate senators to impede judicial nominations. By looking closely at each hold applied to a circuit

court nomination between 1985 and 2006 and categorizing the motivation behind each hold, we can construct a more accurate picture of the
lower court confirmation process and the different confirmation environments nominees may face. A central finding is that much of the delay and
obstruction that mark the modern-day lower court confirmation process
is a function of nominations being used as convenient bargaining chips
in unrelated disputes

The Increasing Delay of Judicial Nominations

As presidents, senators, interest groups, and the public have increasingly recognized the importance of the makeup of the federal bench,
attention has shifted to the lower federal court confirmation process.
More nominations are contentious, and nominees (including unopposed
nominees) are taking longer to move through the confirmation process.
In addition, the lower court confirmation process has become a central
battleground for public policy disputes. Not surprisingly, many therefore
assume that ideology and partisanship account for much of the delay
in the current confirmation process. However, such a belief prompts a
straightforward empirical question: What causes nominations to be delayed, sometimes for months or years, or to be derailed completely?

Recent studies find that contemporary judicial nominees have taken
longer and longer to be confirmed at all levels of the federal judiciary (Bell
2002b; Binder 2001; Binder and Maltzman 2002; Goldman et al. 2003;
Hartley and Holmes 1997, 2002; Martinek, Kemper, and Van Winkle
2002; Shipan and Shannon 2003). Hartley and Holmes (1997) report
that the time between referral to the Senate Judiciary Committee and
confirmation on the Senate floor for all lower court nominees rose from
an average of 25.4 days during the Nixon administration to an average
of 56 days during the Clinton administration. Martinek, Kemper, and
Van Winkle (2002) find that this delay is relatively new: Carter circuit
court nominees took an average of 50.9 days to move from nomination
to confirmation, while Clinton circuit court nominees took an average
of 100.3 days. Cohen (1998) reports that between 1995 and 1997, the
average length of time it took between nomination and confirmation for
Clinton nominees rose from 79 days to 212 days. Delays only increased
during the George W. Bush administration: Rutkus and Bearden (2009)
find Bush's confirmed circuit court nominees averaged 350 days from
nomination to confirmation, a 47 percent increase over Clinton's circuit
court nominees and a 407 percent increase over the average wait time
experienced by Carter's circuit court nominees.

Some studies also attempt to discern *why* some lower court nominations move faster than others. Because almost all lower court nominees are eventually confirmed, studying Senate floor votes reveals little. Scholars have therefore used duration (or hazard) models to determine which factors affect how long it takes lower court nominees to be confirmed.[1] These studies reveal a number of personal and political factors influence confirmation durations, such as the nominee's American Bar Association (ABA) rating, which evaluates a nominee's professional competence, integrity, and judicial temperament, and how late the nomination came in the appointing president's term (Bell 2002b; Binder and Maltzman 2002; Martinek, Kemper, and Van Winkle 2002). These studies do not address, however, how these nominations are delayed, at what point in the process they are delayed, or why they are delayed; such macro-level analyses cannot answer these important questions. The one exception is a recent study by Scherer, Bartels, and Steigerwalt (2008) that partly addresses the "why" by showing how interest group objections significantly increase confirmation durations for opposed nominations.

To answer these questions of how, when, and why delay occurs, we must engage in a micro-level analysis of the judicial confirmation process and the ways senators can impede the progress of nominations. Senators have available to them several mechanisms of delay, many of which can be utilized free from public scrutiny.

Mechanisms of Delay

Overall, there are two sets of actions open to senators to possibly delay judicial nominations once they reach the Senate: (1) scheduling decisions by the Judiciary Committee chair and Senate leadership and (2) parliamentary tactics used by individual senators to block specific nominees.[2]

SCHEDULING DECISIONS

First and foremost, the chair of the Judiciary Committee and the Senate majority leader exercise control over committee and floor actions, respectively. The Judiciary Committee chair can refuse or delay scheduling a committee hearing or a vote on a nominee, and the majority leader can refuse or delay scheduling a floor vote on a nominee once the nominee is favorably voted out of committee and placed on the Executive Calendar. Such refusals and delays occur frequently and for a variety of reasons. The chair or majority leader may decide to act on noncontroversial nominees first; as then chairman Patrick Leahy explained in 2001, "I'm trying to get the ones who are non-controversial [first]. We're trying to get through as many as we can" (Holland 2001b). Similarly, then chairman Orrin Hatch stated on February 11, 1998, on *The NewsHour with Jim Lehrer,* "I think the President, if he sends up qualified, noncontroversial nominees, they go through very quickly. If they have problems and they're not qualified, then it's a problem."

Similarly, presidents often send groups of nominations to the Senate at one time. Obviously, nominees cannot all have hearings at once, and this is especially true for circuit court nominees, as senators need time to vet and closely question these important nominees. An informal practice has been followed for almost two decades that only one circuit court nominee will be scheduled to testify at each committee hearing.[3] Because committee hearings need to be scheduled with enough time between meetings that senators and their staffs can be prepared (with usually no more than two confirmation hearings scheduled per month), nominees may find themselves waiting (im)patiently for their hearing to be scheduled. Thus, for example, if eight circuit court nominees are nominated on the same day, some nominees may wait three months or more for a Judiciary Committee hearing without anyone necessarily wanting to delay their progress.

The Judiciary Committee also attends to a multitude of other legislative issues. Not surprisingly, the pace of nominations slowed in the aftermath of September 11, 2001; the Judiciary Committee was particularly swamped, as most bills proposed in relation to the terrorist attacks, such as the USA Patriot Act, fell under its jurisdiction. Finally, Senate recesses, such as the annual monthlong August recess, may also substantially delay a nominee's progress.

Delays have also resulted from institutional squabbles between senators and the administration over the investigations conducted by the FBI and the ABA. Judiciary Committee chairs have declined to schedule hearings and committee votes—usually with the vocal support of the other committee members—because of delays in receiving these reports. The FBI and the ABA both conduct investigations on every judicial nominee. The FBI's investigation thoroughly scrutinizes the nominee's background and takes place before the nomination is formally made by the White House, while the ABA rates nominees as to their professional qualifications.[4] The FBI generally takes at least two months to investigate a potential nominee; the ABA attempts to finish its investigation of circuit court nominees in approximately six weeks.[5]

During the George H. W. Bush administration, a dispute arose over who on the Judiciary Committee—if anyone at all—should be allowed to view the FBI's reports. President Bush, upset about leaks concerning Anita Hill's allegations of sexual harassment against Clarence Thomas, declared in October 1991 that the Judiciary Committee would not receive the FBI's entire report but rather only a summary prepared by the White House. In response, the Judiciary Committee's members unanimously argued that they needed to be able to review the full FBI file so that the committee did not have to conduct its own investigations into nominees' backgrounds. The issue was finally resolved in February 1992, but during the five-month stand-off, thirty-six judicial nominations were delayed.

Similarly, numerous debates (and thus delays) have taken place over the years regarding the ABA's evaluations of judicial nominees' professional qualifications. The ABA rates nominees based on their professional competence, integrity, and judicial temperament. These debates center on concerns that the ABA's ratings at times reflect the political and ideological judgments of the members of the ABA's Standing Committee on the Federal Judiciary and not merely neutral evaluations of the nominee's professional qualifications (Grassley 1990; Greenberger and Cloud 2001; LaMarche 2001; Lindgren 2001). A recent study finds that, all else being equal, liberal nominees are more likely to receive a unanimous "well qualified" rating from the ABA than their more conservative counterparts (Vining, Steigerwalt, and Smelcer 2009). Many argue that evaluations of a nominee's judicial temperament can veer from assessing whether a nominee is unbiased and open-minded and instead hone in on whether a nominee holds certain policy positions (see, e.g., Grassley 1990). This debate came to a head in March 2001, when President George W. Bush decided that the White House would no longer send the names of potential judicial nominees to the ABA to be rated.[6] The Bush administration defended this decision as necessary given even the possibility of bias against more conservative-leaning nominees (see Howlett 2001, quoting then Attorney General John Ashcroft). The Senate Judiciary Committee decided in return to send the names of all of those formally nominated to the ABA itself, and it further refused to hold hearings on these nominees until the ABA's ratings were received. Thus, while the first nominations were submitted to the Senate on May 9, 2001, the nominees' committee hearings were delayed until the ABA's evaluations were received by the committee.[7] Each of the subsequent Judiciary Committee chairs during the Bush (43) administration continued this practice, thus subtly delaying the time to confirmation for each nominee.

Finally, the Judiciary Committee chair controls the scheduling and fate of judicial nominations while they are still in committee. From time to time, chairs have abused this power, for personal and partisan reasons. The most vivid example occurred in 1999 when then chairman Hatch shut down the entire confirmation process not once but twice in order to force the nomination and then the confirmation of his choice, Ted Stewart, for a district court seat in Utah. When a district court vacancy opened in late 1998, Hatch recommended that President Clinton appoint Stewart. When Clinton refused, Hatch brought the confirmation process to a standstill in January 1999, and he refused to hold any committee hearings or votes. His actions delayed forty-two nominees for almost six months.[8] Hatch allowed these nominations to move forward only after Clinton agreed in June 1999 to appoint Stewart. Not surprisingly, Stewart's nomination moved very quickly through the Judiciary Committee. However, when Democrats protested that nominees who had been waiting much longer than Stewart should be confirmed first, Hatch again shut down the process, canceling all committee hearings and votes as well as putting holds on all nominations that were on the Senate floor, in order to force a floor vote on Stewart. Two weeks later, Stewart was confirmed.

Once nominees make it out of committee, the Senate majority leader controls floor activities, including the scheduling of nominee confirmation votes. All nominations, judicial or otherwise, are placed on the Senate's Executive Calendar, and the majority leader must schedule time for the Senate to consider measures on the Executive Calendar, as opposed to the general Legislative Calendar. In recent years, majority leaders have waited to confirm groups of nominees all at once. Some majority leaders have, informally, only brought nominations up for a vote once a month or even once every other month, depending on the number of nominations, as a way to speed floor business. For example, majority leaders may group nominations together in one unanimous consent agreement at the end of a week, such that a vote for the unanimous consent agreement constitutes a vote in favor of every nomination included in that agreement. The increased contentiousness of the process in recent years has also increased the amount of time it takes for nominations to be dealt with on the floor and the chance that certain nominees will face a delay in receiving a floor vote.

Finally, other legislative issues may push aside judicial nominations. For example, the tragedy of September 11, 2001, the simultaneous anthrax scare, and the glut of legislation surrounding homeland security issues (including the creation of the Department of Homeland Security)

caused numerous measures, including judicial nominations, to be post-
poned for months. President Bill Clinton's impeachment trial ground
the Senate to a halt in 1998. Numerous lower court nominations were
delayed by Clarence Thomas's Supreme Court confirmation in 1991 and,
more recently, the confirmations of John Roberts and Samuel Alito in
late 2005 and early 2006, vacancies that, quite obviously, took precedence over all others. In sum, the judicial confirmation process does not
operate in a vacuum. Pressing legislative issues, more important nominations, and institutional disputes between the Senate and the president
can lead to long delays in the processing of even routine nominations. As
a result, a clear understanding of confirmation delay must also account
for scheduling delays unrelated to particular nominees.

PROCEDURAL OR PARLIAMENTARY TACTICS

There are also three key procedural tools senators may use to block a
judicial nomination, sometimes indefinitely. In contrast to the previously
discussed reasons why nominations may be delayed, these procedural
actions allow individual senators to impede the progress of a particular
nominee. More important, these mechanisms may be used by any senator, including those who do not hold leadership positions.

In stark contrast to the House of Representatives, which operates under strict majority rule and a rigid power hierarchy, the Senate's rules and
informal customs grant each individual senator a large degree of power
over Senate operations, including the progress of judicial nominations.
First, any senator on the Judiciary Committee may ask that a vote on a
nominee be held over until the committee's next meeting. If a committee vote is held over until the next meeting, a vote must be held at that
meeting unless a different senator asks that the vote again be held over.
Such a tactic is commonly used when senators would like additional
time to review a nominee's record and does not necessarily signal that
the senator has an objection to the nominee; for example, Orrin Hatch
requested that Charles Pickering's committee vote be held over for a week
to provide his Republican supporters more time to lobby committee
Democrats (Sammon 2002). Committee members may also utilize this
procedure for other reasons. For example, in August 1991 Arlen Specter,
upset that Edward Kennedy had placed a hold on one of his home-state
nominees, blocked committee votes on sixteen nominees in retaliation, a
move that caused each nominee to wait an additional month for a committee vote, as the original vote had been scheduled for the day before
the August recess.

Second, once nominations are sent to the Senate floor for a vote by the full Senate, senators may place a hold on the nomination, thus signaling their intention to object to the nomination if it is brought up for a floor vote. A hold can be placed on a nomination as soon as it is passed out of committee and reaches the Senate floor, and holds can last indefinitely. The hold is an extremely powerful device, as majority leaders are loathe to bring up nominations that might be filibustered and waste valuable floor time. Additionally, holds may be placed anonymously such that senators are stymied from determining who has placed the hold and, more important, why.

Third, if a nomination is brought up for a floor vote and a senator objects, he or she may exercise the right to filibuster the nomination, thereby preventing the nomination from coming to a vote until a three-fifths majority of senators votes to end debate (a process known as gaining cloture).[9]

Relatively few examinations of these procedural mechanisms exist. A small number of scholarly works discuss filibusters (Alter and McGranahan 2000; Binder and Mann 1995; Binder and Smith 1996; Burdette 1940; DeNardis 1989; Fisk and Chemerinsky 1997).[10] Other than the filibuster against Abe Fortas's elevation to chief justice of the United States in 1968 (Abraham 1999; Murphy 1988; Shogan 1972), the use of the filibuster in relation to judicial nominations is rarely examined (Beth 2002). In fact, filibusters over lower court nominations were basically unheard of until the recent filibuster of ten George W. Bush nominees to the circuit courts during the 108th and 109th Congresses.[11]

Similarly, while some newspapers may record the use of holds on particular nominations and bills, scholarly accounts of their existence and use are sketchy at best. Holds receive only passing mention in most works on congressional procedure and actions (see, e.g., Beth and Bach 2003; Carr and Bach 2002; Oleszek 1996; Saturno 2003; Sinclair 1989). To date, only one study has looked extensively at the use of holds. DeNardis's 1989 dissertation provides an overview of the development of holds as well as three case studies of instances in which holds were used to delay and derail certain bills in the mid-1980s; however, he does not systematically analyze their usage.[12] Finally, the use of holds is unstudied—and usually overlooked—in the realm of judicial appointments.[13] Therefore, this chapter is dedicated to systematically analyzing the use of this potent parliamentary tool as applied to judicial nominations and uncovering when and why senators decide to send nominees down the private political track.

The History of Holds

Current Senate rules and customs reflect an institutional reliance on the norm of individual power and influence. Unlike the House of Representatives, which is driven by the power of the majority, the Senate was created to ensure that the passions of the majority could be checked and that the important issues of the day would be fully debated and discussed. Famously, George Washington compared the Senate to a saucer, arguing that the Senate would act to cool House legislation just as a saucer cools hot tea. To ensure deliberation is the order of the day, Senate rules and customs encourage extended debate, and they bestow upon each senator the power to bring the Senate to a halt and make certain that his or her concerns are heard. Parliamentary procedures such as filibusters were crafted to give power to the one—or at least to the minority—rather than to the whole.[14] Individual senators therefore have the power to severely curtail Senate operations. Former majority leader Trent Lott likened trying to maintain control over other senators to "herding cats."[15]

Similarly, internal Senate customs developed that were designed to elevate the concerns of the one over the concerns of the many (DeNardis 1989, 30).[16] One such custom is the hold. The hold is not found in the rules of the Senate but rather is an informal practice that gained power and prominence in the 1970s, though historians cannot pinpoint its exact origin (DeNardis 1989, 235). Early use of the hold concerned senators asking the Senate leadership to "hold off" on moving a particular piece of legislation as a personal courtesy in order to grant the senator time to learn more about the subject or avoid scheduling conflicts. Tradition limited such holds to two weeks, and after such time the legislation again moved forward (DeNardis 1989; Ornstein 1999). Over time, however, the hold morphed from an instrument of courtesy and reciprocity into a device of obstruction and delay.

Ornstein argues that, by the 1970s, the hold had become "a weapon of partisan and ideological welfare, one reinforced in a body that relies for its scheduling on unanimous consent agreements" (1999, 6). Holds were used with increasing frequency to block bills and nominations for more political reasons. Sinclair argued in 1989 that "the new Senate style" reflected a change from a norm of reciprocity to a "norm of individualism" in which "senators are . . . much more likely to make expansive use of the powers the Senate rules confer upon the individual," and the use of holds on both legislation and nominations by this new breed of senator flourished in the 1980s (96; see also DeNardis 1989; Ornstein 1999).

However, even these new "political" holds usually lasted no more than a month. But senators who wished to permanently obstruct legislation rather than merely delay it could do so: these senators would ask colleagues to place a hold on the legislation in question after each two-week period expired. This practice, which became known as a "revolving hold," could potentially delay a piece of legislation or a nomination indefinitely (Ornstein 1999). Finally, by the 1990s, senators fully recognized the usefulness of holds in extracting concessions and engaging in behind-the-scenes negotiations with nominees and bills as the central bargaining chips (Ornstein 1999). The two-week time limit has since been abandoned (though it is unclear when this change occurred), and the current practice is that one person may place a hold and thereby block a bill or nomination indefinitely.

By placing a hold, a senator informs his or her floor leader that he or she will object to a particular bill or nomination or to any unanimous consent agreement covering that bill or nomination, and the senator implicitly asks that the measure not be called up for consideration without giving the senator advance notice.[17] Thus, each hold is dependent on the majority leader being willing to recognize and support the hold.

Majority leaders can override holds merely by scheduling a vote on the offending measure; if the majority leader decides to bring up the measure and the senator still objects, the senator can then decide to exercise his or her right to filibuster. However, "recent majority leaders have accordingly tended to honor holds, both as a courtesy to their colleagues, and in recognition that if they choose not to do so, they may well confront filibusters that they prefer to avoid" (Beth and Bach 2003, 20). Filibusters are costly since they prolong debate and eat up precious floor time. This potential cost leads majority leaders to generally support other members' holds, especially in relation to lower court nominations, which concern few senators and, in general, draw little media attention. In turn, holds allow senators to indefinitely block nominations without having to publicly fight the nomination on the Senate floor and potentially shut down the Senate through a filibuster. Obviously, a senator who releases a hold and decides not to filibuster the measure can still vote against the measure on the floor, but that is a very different and much less powerful strategy than staging a filibuster.

The hold is an extremely powerful practice given its private nature. Rather than publicly voting against a bill or nomination, a hold allows a senator to block the measure, and to do so almost completely out of the public eye. Senators are not required to announce their holds, the Senate leadership is not required to acknowledge holds, and media coverage of such arcane parliamentary procedures is understandably low. Additionally, a hold can be placed anonymously, and anonymous holds can be extremely frustrating to the senator sponsoring the bill or nominee. Senator J. James Exon declared, "There is a hold on S. 1407 and this Senator cannot even find out which Senator or the staff of which Senator has placed a hold on that bill."[18] Numerous attempts have been made over the years to eliminate the use of such holds, though none has been successful as of yet.[19] Even public holds are unlikely to garner substantial media attention, and holds grow even more powerful when applied to judicial nominations. Because judicial nominations garner little media attention[20] and because very few senators care about each individual nominee,[21] holds placed on judicial nominations are extremely effective. Due to the low visibility of judicial nominations, holds allow senators and the administration to bargain over issues out of the public eye.

Different Types of Holds

Holds garner little popular or scholarly attention but are a potent mechanism of private political delay a single senator can utilize. Why are holds used, and what is the driving motivation behind the use of each hold? I argue that all holds can be understood as falling into one of two broad categories: (1) holds based on opposition to a particular bill or nomination and (2) holds placed for strategic reasons. First, senators can place a hold on a bill or nomination to signal their opposition to the bill or nomination in question. In these instances the bill or nomination itself is the subject of the dispute. The objecting senator may dislike the nominee's personal views or the content of the bill. Given my focus on judicial nominations, I will refer to these holds as "nominee-based holds."

Second, senators can utilize holds for strategic reasons. When disputes among senators or between senators and the president arise, senators may use holds to try to resolve these disputes. The bill or nomination trapped in the hold is chosen not because the senator objects to the bill or nomination but because of the bill's or nomination's importance to her foe. The nomination or bill thus becomes a strategic weapon in the dispute. I term these holds "strategic holds."

NOMINEE-BASED HOLDS

Conventional wisdom maintains that most holds are placed when a senator dislikes the views of a particular nominee. Similarly, reports abound of nominees being delayed because of partisan desires to block the judicial appointments of an opposition president. We can thus identify two distinct types of nominee-based holds, ideological holds and partisan holds.

Ideological holds are based solely on an objection to the views held by the nominee. A senator may block the nominee because of positions the nominee holds on specific issues or because of the nominee's overall judicial philosophy. Senators Howard Metzenbaum, Alan Cranston, and others placed holds on the nomination of Edward Carnes to the Eleventh Circuit Court in 1992. Carnes served as an assistant attorney general for the state of Alabama, and his main duty was to prosecute defendants in capital cases. Death penalty opponents and civil rights leaders loudly protested his nomination, arguing both that the death penalty was applied disproportionately to blacks in Alabama and that Carnes had defended a biased system that unfairly kept blacks off death penalty juries.

Similarly, Senator Robert Smith placed holds in 1999 on Ninth Circuit Court nominees Marsha Berzon and Richard Paez. Both Berzon and Paez drew heavy fire from conservative senators and interest groups due to their positions on a myriad of issues. A *Washington Post* editorial stated that "Smith's spokeswoman says he has slapped a hold on them because their answers to questions on abortion, the death penalty and guns do not meet with the senator's approval and that he believes there should be a litmus test for federal judges on abortion" (*Washington Post* 1999). Smith later added, "They are activist judges. They are out of the mainstream of American thought, and I don't think either one should be on the court" (quoted in Abrams 2000). These two examples highlight how senators may decide to utilize ideological holds to block nominees whose record and personal ideology they oppose, especially when they fear the nominees may be confirmed otherwise. This fear is not unjustified, as the overwhelming majority of lower court nominees are eventually confirmed; in fact, all three of the nominees discussed above were ultimately confirmed.

Partisan holds, the second type of nominee-based holds, are used by senators to further their party's political agenda. Senators generally utilize partisan holds as a mechanism to prevent the further confirmation of nominations made by an opposition president. In these instances holds are placed not because a specific nominee's ideology is problematic (as is the case with ideological holds) but rather because the out-party hopes to regain the presidency and appoint its own nominees. Thus, an entire group is seen as problematic owing to its partisan allegiances and likely judicial philosophy, even if individual nominees—or even every nominee—might actually be acceptable to the senator placing the hold. The likelihood of such holds increases substantially as presidential elections draw near. After such a hold is placed, it is doubtful that any of the blocked nominations will move forward, though specific deals might be brokered.

Before Robert Dole resigned as Senate majority leader in the summer of 1996 to concentrate on his presidential election campaign, he stated publicly that he would not allow any more judicial nominations to move forward until after the election. He himself placed a partisan hold on all pending judicial nominations, a hold made even more powerful in that no other member of the Senate besides the majority leader can override a hold. In this case, while Dole admitted he had no real objection to the nominees, he based his hold on the premise that nominees from a Republican president (i.e., himself) would be more desirable.[22] The situation was resolved after Dole resigned his post and Trent Lott became Senate majority leader. Lott believed it was unfair to systematically block Clinton's nominees, and he brought a sizable number of nominations to a vote before the session ended (Roger 1996). Partisan holds thus reflect the growing partisan tensions surrounding judicial appointments, in part due to the move from patronage-based appointments to policy-based appointments (Scherer 2005). Partisan holds also illuminate how the nature of the Senate itself is subtly changing as the majority party's authority has increased in recent years and collegial relations among senators have begun to fracture along partisan lines (see, e.g., Campbell, Cox, and McCubbins 2002; Den Hartog and Monroe 2008; Gailmard and Jenkins 2007; Lazarus and Steigerwalt 2009).

STRATEGIC HOLDS

Senators block nominees (or bills) with nominee-based (or legislation-based) holds because they dislike the nominees (or bills) themselves. However, a senator does not necessarily have to object to a nominee to place a hold on the nomination; in fact, senators many times place holds on nominees they otherwise support. Instead, senators may trap nominations because of their strategic value. Ornstein explains that holds are increasingly used "not to hold up a nominee who was personally or ideologically opposed by one or more Senators but to hold any available or vulnerable nominee hostage to some other wholly extraneous objective of a Senator" (1999, 7). Making legislation and confirming nominees are not always pretty processes, and strategic holds present a valuable mechanism by which back-room negotiations may take place. Given the motivations behind strategic holds, senators place these holds even against nominations made by a president of their own party. Three main types of strategic holds can be identified.

First, a senator may place a hold on a judicial nomination or bill in order to gain leverage in a dispute. These "leverage holds" provide the objecting senators with a mechanism by which to force the hand of whomever they are feuding with. With leverage holds, senators choose which nomination(s) or bill(s) to block by determining which one is most important to their foe. By blocking the nomination or bill, the senators hope to force their opponent to the bargaining table. The most distinctive feature of these holds is that the blocked nomination or bill usually has little connection to the dispute at hand and is instead merely a tool of convenience. In fact, the blocking senator might vigorously support the nomination or bill in question while also recognizing its usefulness as a bargaining device.[23] For example, if Senator X objects to a bill Senator Y has sponsored, Senator Y may place a hold on a nominee from Senator X's home state to force Senator X to bargain with Senator Y over the aforementioned bill. Similarly, leverage holds may be directed at the current administration or at an executive agency. In these situations, judicial nominations and other executive branch nominations make extremely good bargaining devices because the nominations are important to the administration but are not usually important to the broader Senate or public. Examples of disputes with the executive branch might include issues surrounding other executive appointments, reports senators would like certain agencies to release, or concerns with agency regulations.[24]

The two best examples of leverage holds on judicial nominations both concern disputes between senators and the then current administration. Both holds also showcase how the blocked nominees may be independent of the issue at hand. In December 1987, Senators Howard Metzenbaum and Edward Kennedy placed a hold on two circuit court nominees and four district court nominees to try to compel the Department of Justice (DOJ) to release documents about the actions of Faith Ryan Whittlesay during her term as ambassador to Switzerland. Whittlesay was accused of improperly soliciting private contributions to pay for embassy entertainment. The DOJ conducted an inquiry and recommended the appointment of a special prosecutor to investigate Whittlesay's actions. However, the final decision in such matters resides with the attorney general, and Attorney General Edward Meese decided against appointing a special prosecutor. Senators Metzenbaum and Kennedy wanted the DOJ to release its internal report and other documents pertaining to Whittlesay's actions and the surrounding investigation.[25] The DOJ refused, and the senators promptly placed a hold on six judicial nominations.[26] Eventually the DOJ released the documents, and the holds were promptly lifted.

Even more striking is the leverage hold placed by Senator John McCain during the summer of 2002 on all nominations pending on the floor of the Senate to force President George W. Bush—a fellow Republican—to nominate McCain's choice for the Federal Election Commission (FEC). McCain, a strong supporter of campaign finance reform, wanted Bush to replace Karl Sandstrom, whose term on the FEC had expired sixteen months earlier. McCain was especially motivated to remove Sandstrom after Sandstrom voted—long after his term had expired—to implement a series of regulations interpreting the new McCain-Feingold campaign finance reform law that, in McCain's words, "emasculated" the new law (Holland 2002). Angry at Bush's refusal to appoint a replacement, McCain put a hold on all sixty-two presidential nominees awaiting Senate confirmation, including eighteen judicial nominees.[27] None of the blocked nominees had any connection to either McCain or the FEC; rather, blocking these nominations presented a convenient way for McCain to force Bush's hand. Eventually Bush agreed to appoint McCain's choice, Ellen Weintraub, to the FEC. Dozens of nominees were then quickly confirmed.[28] In this case, not only did McCain block a large number of nominees, he also intentionally blocked nominations made by a president of his own party. Strategic holds thus allow senators to gain leverage in intraparty as well as interparty disputes.

Second, holds may be used in retaliation. For example, if Senator X places a hold on a bill sponsored by Senator Y, Senator Y might then place a hold on a nominee from the home state of Senator X in retaliation. Such "retaliatory holds" generally do not reflect objections to the blocked nominee but rather act as a mechanism of reprisal directed against the offending senator. While retaliatory holds are similar to holds used primarily to gain leverage (as we can assume Senator Y wants Senator X to release her original hold), these holds belie the normally collegial nature of the Senate. Rather than working out the problem that prompted the original hold, a senator in this situation reacts angrily by attacking a bill or nomination important to the offending senator. The primary motivation behind retaliatory holds is therefore punishment rather than bargaining. Retaliatory holds may also be placed later in time to avenge a past offense. While retaliatory holds are primarily about retribution, many times there are ways for the issues to be resolved and the holds to be lifted.

The ideological hold placed on Edward Carnes in 1992 led to a retaliatory hold on Susan Black. Senator Richard Shelby, upset that his nominee was being blocked, placed a retaliatory hold on Black, who was also nominated to the Eleventh Circuit. Shelby argued that Carnes, nominated and sent to the Senate floor before Black, should be confirmed first, out of "a sense of fairness," so he put a hold on Black's nomination to try to force Carnes's nomination forward (Wagner 1992).[29] Shelby's staff was quick to acknowledge that the senator fully supported Black's nomination, stating that he had "no problem with Ms. Black" but rather was focused on gaining confirmation for his home-state nominee (Wagner 1992).[30]

The hold placed on David Sentelle in 1987 presents an even clearer case of retaliation. Senator Edward Kennedy put a retaliatory hold on Sentelle's nomination after Jesse Helms placed a hold on Melissa Wells, the ambassador designate to Mozambique.[31] Kennedy chose to block Sentelle because of his long-standing ties to the North Carolina senator: Sentelle was active in North Carolina GOP politics and had served on Helms's Senate campaign committees. Sentelle was also chosen because he was already serving as a district court judge, so Kennedy felt the repercussions of his hold were limited. Kennedy did not oppose Sentelle's nomination; the hold was placed solely to convince Helms to remove his hold on Wells. The stand-off ended after Wells was confirmed over Helms's vocal objections; Sentelle was then easily confirmed.

In 2006, Senator Sam Brownback's opposition to a district court nominee led to a slew of retaliatory holds. Brownback, a staunch gay marriage opponent, placed a hold on Janet Neff, a Michigan district court nominee, after reports emerged that she had attended a commitment ceremony for a lesbian couple (Lewis 2006). In response to Brownback's hold, Michigan senators Carl Levin and Debbie Stabenow retaliated by placing holds on two other Michigan district court nominees. When this tactic failed, Patrick Leahy placed a hold on all judicial nominations currently on the Senate floor, many of which Brownback strongly supported. Senator Jim Inhofe then became involved in the negotiations because Leahy's hold—which Inhofe blamed Brownback for—impeded the progress of an Oklahoma district court nominee. Eventually Brownback lifted his hold, the other senators lifted theirs in return, and the nominees were all confirmed.

Finally, strategic holds may be used in institutional disputes between the White House and senators over how judicial appointments should be determined and allocated. Institutional holds are used in response to two primary disputes: first, the nomination went to a nominee from another state and the senator feels that, based on established custom or principle, a nominee from his or her state should have received the nomination; or second, the senator believes another seat on a particular circuit court is unneeded.[32] Such disputes especially arise in relation to circuit court vacancies: each circuit serves several states, and each seat on the court is usually considered assigned to a particular state within that circuit. While again similar to leverage holds, institutional holds are easily differentiated as the nomination blocked is usually the direct source of the dispute, though the nominee herself might be perfectly acceptable.

Jerry Smith of Texas was nominated to the Fifth Circuit Court in 1987. Louisiana senator Bennett Johnston placed an institutional hold on Smith's confirmation once it reached the Senate floor and threatened a filibuster because Johnston felt the vacancy should go to a nominee from Louisiana instead of Texas. Johnston argued that the seats on the Fifth Circuit should be allocated based on caseload (which would increase the number of seats from Louisiana) rather than population (which benefited Texas). Johnston did not have any problems per se with Smith himself; rather, he blocked the nomination to force the administration and the Senate leadership to redistribute the seat assignments on the Fifth Circuit. In this case, Johnston objected to the nomination (as it went to a Texan) but not the nominee (whom he eventually voted for), and the dispute was resolved when the Reagan administration agreed that the next Fifth Circuit vacancy would go to a non-Texan.

Similarly, a number of senators, led by Charles Grassley, objected to Merrick Garland's nomination to the D.C. Circuit Court beginning in 1995 on the grounds that the circuit's workload did not support a twelfth seat.[33] Garland's nomination was not opposed for any other reason, and, after another D.C. Circuit Court vacancy eventually occurred, he was confirmed in 1997.[34] The story of his nomination is explained well by Senator Arlen Specter: "A great deal has been said today on this floor which is of great importance but not really tremendously related to Merrick Garland's nomination."[35]

The above discussion illuminates five distinct reasons why senators place holds on judicial nominations or bills: ideological disagreements, partisan animosity, bargaining leverage, retaliation, and interbranch disputes. Of the five motivating reasons for holds, three are unrelated to the nominee or bill being blocked. Leverage holds, retaliatory holds, and institutional holds are all by-products of some sort of external dispute, and in these instances senators block nominations or bills because of their perceived usefulness in helping to resolve the existing dispute. Conversely, ideological holds and partisan holds indicate clear objections to a bill or a nominee's issue positions or overall judicial philosophy. These holds cannot be resolved; they can only be overcome or capitulated to.

How often do senators use these different holds in relation to judicial nominations? The preceding stories demonstrate that we can find examples of every type of hold, but how often does each type of hold occur? Conventional wisdom, as well as analyses of confirmation delay, maintains that nominees are usually blocked due to ideological objections or partisan attempts by the out-party to prevent a president's nominees from being confirmed (Binder and Maltzman 2002; Martinek, Kemper, and Van Winkle 2002). On the other hand, a 2003 hearing by the Senate Rules Committee revealed a Senate wherein holds are routinely used as a mechanism of back-door negotiations over bills and nominations alike. As Trent Lott stated at the June 17, 2003, hearing, "It has become increasingly common for holds to be placed on nominees and bills for reasons that have nothing to do with the nominee or the bill. Instead, bills and nominations are held hostage because a Senator is trying to leverage something from the Administration or from another Senator. These so-called 'leverage holds' are routinely used by members from both parties."[36]

Given the above elaboration of the five reasons why nominations may subject to holds and turned down the private political track, it is quite probable that many holds on judicial nominations have been used to gain leverage or exact retribution rather than to block objectionable nominees. Thus, the rest of this chapter investigates why nominees to the circuit courts have been subjected to holds on the floor of the Senate. The main thrust of this analysis is to determine the reasons and motivations for the numerous holds that have affected nominations made between 1985 and 2006.[37]

The Modern-Day Practice of Holds

I conducted a series of comprehensive, multilevel searches of newspaper archives for all articles mentioning some type of hold or block placed on judicial nominations between 1985 and 2006 (the search methodology is explained in appendix A). Once I determined that a hold had been placed on a judicial nomination awaiting Senate floor action,

TABLE 3.1 Number of holds and number of circuit court nominations affected by these holds, 1985–2006 (99th–109th Congresses)

	HOLDS PLACED	NOMINATIONS AFFECTED
99th	16	12
100th	6	6
101st	0	0
102nd	6	4
103rd	0	0
104th	10	7
105th	11	8
106th	16	10
107th	5	5
108th	20	13
109th	6	4
Total	96	69

Note: In total, sixty-six nominees were blocked by holds. The table gives a figure of sixty-nine, reflecting the fact that three nominees had separate holds applied to their nominations in two different Congresses. Each distinct hold was counted separately.

I identified which circuit court nominees were subjected to each hold. Finally, I examined the written record detailing each hold in order to categorize the motivation behind each hold based on the five categories elucidated above.

Between 1985 and 2006, a total of 272 nominations were made to the circuit courts.[38] Two hundred thirty nominations were passed out of committee and sent to the Senate floor; consequently, these nominations could be subjected to a hold.[39]

I identified a total of ninety-six holds placed on sixty-six circuit court nominees during this time period.[40] Table 3.1 reports how many holds were placed during each Congress. No holds were placed on circuit court nominees during the 101st or 103rd Congresses, though during both Congresses, district court nominees were subjected to holds. In some instances particular nominees were subjected to multiple holds during a particular Congress, and each hold that was placed against a nominee was counted separately in this study. Three nominees were trapped by discrete holds in two successive Congresses; again, each distinct hold is counted separately in this study.[41]

Table 3.2 continues this analysis by reporting how many holds each nominee received. Of the sixty-six nominees blocked by holds, 27.3 per-

TABLE 3.2 Number of holds placed on each nomination to the circuit courts, 1985–2006 (99th–109th Congresses)

HOLDS PLACED ON NOMINATION	NOMINATIONS RECEIVING THAT MANY HOLDS	%
0	206	75.7
1	48	17.6
2	11	4.0
3	4	1.5
4	1	0.4
5	2	0.7
	272 Total nominations	

cent were subjected to two or more holds, with two nominees, William Fletcher and Richard Paez, each caught by five different holds.

What types of holds were utilized against these nominations? All of the newspaper articles identifying a hold against a judicial nomination also explained the motivations behind the hold (see appendix A). As many accounts as possible were read in order to determine the correct categorization for the hold. Table 3.3 reports the number of each type of hold placed on circuit court nominations during each Congress. Each of the five types of holds was used during this time period. Strikingly, nominee-based holds occurred relatively infrequently. Instead, the vast majority of nominations were caught in strategic holds used to gain leverage or to retaliate for past offenses.

Some descriptive statistics highlight these findings. Eleven ideological holds were placed against circuit court nominations,[42] a little less than 12 percent of all holds, and partisan holds were directed at five nominations (5.2 percent).[43] Two nominees had ideological holds placed against their nominations in two different Congresses; both were eventually confirmed.[44] Therefore, in total, nominee-based holds accounted for only 16.7 percent of all holds placed during this period.

In comparison, the remaining 83.3 percent of holds can clearly be characterized as strategic holds. Specifically, twenty-nine nominations (30.2 percent) were caught in institutional holds, thirty nominations (31.3 percent) were caught in leverage holds, and twenty-one nominations (21.9 percent) were trapped by retaliatory holds. The vast majority of holds placed between 1985 and 2006 thus reflect strategic maneuvering by senators rather than objections to ideologically extreme nominees.

Judicial nominations have become a key bargaining tool in the modern Senate, and strategic holds allow senators to negotiate out of the public eye and with few repercussions.

Strategic holds many times capture judicial nominations by coincidence: in a number of instances, the strategic hold was applied to whoever happened to be on the floor at the moment, rather than nominations chosen specifically for their strategic value. In such instances, the senators viewed stopping all nominations from proceeding as the most advantageous mechanism for achieving their goals. Slowing down the entire confirmation process provides a brutally effective stick during negotiations, especially when the carrot is allowing all nominations to be confirmed easily upon release.

When particular nominees were trapped by strategic holds because of their perceived value to the overarching dispute, the blocking senator almost always supported the chosen nominees. However, one might argue that a strategic hold placed on multiple nominations may act as a cover for a nominee-based hold against a specific nominee. A senator might place a leverage hold, and provide a reasonable explanation of a dispute that might prompt such a leverage hold, while in reality using the hold to block particular, ideologically objectionable nominees. While it is difficult to know if senators and their staffs are expressing the true

TABLE 3.3 Types of holds applied to circuit court nominations, 1985–2006 (99th–109th Congresses)

	IDEOLOGICAL	PARTISAN	LEVERAGE	RETALIATORY	INSTITUTIONAL	TOTAL
99th	3	0	8	0	5	16
100th	0	1	2	2	1	6
101st	0	0	0	0	0	0
102nd	1	0	0	1	4	6
103rd	0	0	0	0	0	0
104th	2	4	3	0	1	10
105th	3	0	3	5	0	11
106th	2	0	4	10	0	16
107th	0	0	5	0	0	5
108th	0	0	5	0	15	20
109th	0	0	0	3	3	6
Total	11	5	30	21	29	96
(%)	(11.5%)	(5.2%)	(31.3%)	(21.9%)	(30.2%)	

reasons for their holds, there are five discrete measures we can use to try and discern the objecting senator's true intent.

First, many of these holds applied not just to the circuit court nominations counted in this study but also to numerous district court nominations and other executive nominations. For example, John McCain's leverage hold in 2002 over an FEC nomination captured five circuit court nominations and eleven district court nominations, as well as dozens of other executive nominations. Similarly, Larry Pressler's institutional hold in 1992, which affected only two circuit court nominations, blocked twenty-nine district court nominations. Finally, the starkest example is Robert Byrd's 1985 institutional hold, which blocked seventy judicial, ambassadorial, and high-level cabinet nominations, along with more than 5,000 military promotions. While not impossible, it seems improbable that a senator would block dozens, if not thousands, of nominations just to prevent the confirmation of one.

Second, does evidence exist as to the supposed issue, unrelated to the captured nominations, the blocking senator would like resolved? With each of the strategic holds counted here, clear evidence of the alleged dispute can be found. For example, while James Inhofe obviously disliked all of Clinton's nominees, he made his intentions clear weeks before each retaliatory hold was placed that he would use such retaliatory holds to protest Clinton's future use of recess appointments for contested nominees. Similarly, then minority leader Tom Daschle placed a hold on all pending judicial nominations in March 2004 in order to protest George W. Bush's use of recess appointments for divisive nominees. Once Bush agreed to stop using such recess appointments, Daschle agreed to immediately confirm twenty-five judicial nominations, including five circuit court nominations. While such evidence of the alleged disputes is not entirely conclusive, it at least demonstrates that senators are not blocking judicial nominations based on false allegations, and that they many times resort to strategic holds on judicial nominations only after other avenues of resolution have failed.

Third, if senators are placing widespread holds with the goal of blocking particular nominees, do holds ever remain on particular nominees after a hold is lifted on some? The answer is a resounding no. In no instance did a strategic hold that affected multiple nominations evolve into a hold affecting only one nomination indefinitely.[45] In fact, all of the ideological holds observed herein were eventually lifted, and all of the blocked nominees were confirmed. The only instance of a hold being removed slowly occurred with Howard Metzenbaum's leverage hold in 1988 on six judicial nominations to force the DOJ to release certain documents. Metzenbaum released all the nominations except that of Stephen Trott, owing to Trott's position as associate attorney general. However, as soon as some of the papers were released, the hold on Trott was immediately lifted, and he was easily confirmed, with Metzenbaum voting in favor of his nomination.

Fourth, if the senator used the supposed dispute as a cover for an ideological hold, another indication of such an action might be how long after the dispute was resolved the strategic hold was finally lifted. The evidence against suggests that senators place strategic holds on nominations in order to resolve the publicly announced disputes rather than for other, hidden purposes. With every strategic hold observed in this study except two, as soon as some sort of agreement was reached, the strategic holds were immediately lifted and the nominees allowed to progress through the process; these previously blocked nominees were usually confirmed in a matter of days, unless they were also simultaneously caught in another hold.[46] This finding holds true even in those instances in which the agreement related to actions to be taken in the future, such as President George W. Bush's agreement in 2002 that he would nominate Ellen Weintraub for the FEC by the end of the congressional session. The first exception concerns the retaliatory hold placed by James Inhofe in late 1999 over Clinton's use of recess appointments, which was broken in February 2000 when then majority leader Trent Lott decided to override Inhofe's hold and push through a cloture vote.[47] The second exception was Alfonse D'Amato's 1992 retaliatory hold on Stuart Summit (a George H. W. Bush nominee); D'Amato removed his hold, but Summit was not confirmed for other reasons.[48]

Finally, we can assess the blocking senator's possible motives in one last, decisive way: once the strategic hold was lifted, did the senator vote against any of the previously blocked nominees on the Senate floor? If the senator voted against certain nominees on the floor, we might then have some indication that the senator was placing the strategic hold as a cover for ideologically based objections. Here again, the findings suggest senators are not placing strategic holds as a mechanism to surreptitiously block objectionable nominees. Eighty strategic holds were placed on sixty-two different nominees. Forty-nine (79 percent) of these nominees eventually received Senate floor votes. Of these nominees, fifteen were voted against by senators who had placed strategic holds on them. However, thirteen of these nominees had been objected to previously for ideological reasons, and the senator placing the strategic hold in each case had also publicly stated his or her ideological objection to the nominee. In fact, six of these nominees were filibustered during the 108th Congress; in all of these cases the senator who placed the strategic hold also voted in favor of the filibuster. In contrast to a simple floor vote, these filibusters received a considerable amount of press coverage, and each of the blocking senators was on record as opposing the nominees. Once again, it seems doubtful that a senator willing to support a public filibuster against a nominee would also find it necessary to obscure his or her true motives for placing a hold on the same nominee. In the other two instances the holds were not removed; rather, the nominations were brought to a vote over the objections of the blocking senators.[49] Overall, 69.4 percent of nominees who had been subjected to strategic holds received "yea" confirmation votes from those senators who had blocked their confirmations, and the remaining fifteen nominees were publicly objected to by the blocking senators. In sum, these five measures all provide clear evidence that senators utilize strategic holds to resolve unrelated disputes rather than as a cover for ideological objections.

A final question remains: how often did senators place holds against nominations made by a president of their own party? During the time frame under study, nineteen holds, or almost 20 percent of all holds, were placed by senators from the same party as the president. Unsurprisingly, all of these nineteen holds were strategic holds, and these same-party holds accounted for 24 percent of all strategic holds. The stories of these five sets of holds highlight their strategic rather than objecting nature. In 1998, Senator Patrick Leahy blocked three Clinton nominations to try to force Republicans to vote on other long stalled judicial nominations. Senator Alfonse D'Amato blocked five Reagan nominations in 1988 to protest the treatment of two New York District Court nominations. Senator Larry Pressler blocked thirty-one judicial nominations, two of them to circuit court vacancies, over a dispute with the George H. W. Bush administration over federal judgeships in South Dakota. A group of Democratic senators blocked a number of Clinton nominations in 1999 to force Republicans to finally bring Marsha Berzon's and Richard Paez's nominations to a vote (and this maneuver did result in an agreement that their floor votes would take place). In each of these instances, senators used nominees from their own party to fight for other, more battle-weary nominees. Last, Senator John McCain, as discussed earlier, blocked five of George W. Bush's circuit court nominations during the summer of 2002 to compel Bush to nominate his choice for the FEC. McCain's strategic hold accounted for all holds placed on circuit court nominations during the 107th Congress. In each of these cases, senators used judicial nominations they supported (and that had been nominated by their own president) to try to force some other party to act, highlighting how holds on judicial nominations are many times applied to nominees outside the scope of the dispute.

These findings lead to three important conclusions. First, nominee-based holds are utilized much less frequently than commonly assumed. While nominations may be delayed or defeated because of ideological and partisan-based objections, the use of holds for such reasons is rare. In comparison, strategic holds are used frequently, and these holds account for a sizable amount of the confirmation delay captured by earlier studies.

Second, strategic holds are usually placed on judicial nominations to help senators try to resolve disputes totally unrelated to the particular nominees trapped by the hold. Many times the objecting senator supports the blocked nominee, and the nomination might have even been made by the senator's own party leader. Strategic holds aid senators in negotiations and are placed as a matter of convenience rather than as a reflection of an actual objection to the trapped nominee. Simply put, judicial nominations offer opportune bargaining chips. As a Republican Senate Judiciary Committee staffer explained in a 2002 interview, "A lot of times a hold has nothing to do with the nominee. . . . Politicians want to get their bills passed, and many times they have ten different people against, so everything gets traded. . . . If the senator has a nominee in his pocket, the other senators are more likely to be amenable to negotiations. Everything is a chess board, and judges are pawns for where they can get on the board. And this is true for both sides."

Third, the routine use of strategic holds on judicial nominations speaks more broadly to the power of individual senators—including those who are not party or floor leaders—to influence the Senate's basic operation and its ultimate policy outputs. The ability of individual senators to place holds on bills and nominations allows them to, in effect, direct both how and when the Senate considers those measures. The strategic use of holds can therefore yield substantial benefits, as well as cause considerable delay. By placing a hold, the objecting senator forces his or her adversaries to (and many times back to) the bargaining table. The senator also creates a Catch-22 for the Senate majority leader: the majority leader must now either honor the hold, and implicitly aid the blocking senator, or take steps to end the hold, thereby consuming precious floor time and risking a full-fledged filibuster. Thus, from a leadership perspective, encouraging expedited negotiations may be the best strategy. As a result, the pace of deliberations on a measure may be directly related to these behind-the-scenes negotiations.

Furthermore, strategic holds can lead to significant policy victories. Since overriding holds is costly in terms of Senate floor time, supporters cannot simply ask the majority leader to attempt cloture every time a hold is placed on a bill or nomination. The supporters must instead determine what price they are willing to pay to try to appease their opponent. The end result is that placing a hold can lead to meaningful changes with important public policy consequences. Consequently, placing a strategic hold is in many ways a win-win situation for the blocking senators. The senators are likely to achieve some, if not all, of their goals, and do so with very little cost to themselves. On the other hand, strategic holds present a lose-lose situation for the measure's supporters and the Senate itself. Strategic holds tip the balance of power toward the minority, or even to a single individual. The passage of important legislation may be delayed, or even derailed. And the arcane and hidden nature of holds makes it difficult for supporters to garner public pressure against the blocking senators. Thus, the use of holds is a low-cost, high-reward strategy that serves its proponents well.

Conclusion

A main cause of judicial confirmation delay is holds placed on nominations. Holds allow senators to block nominations out of the public eye. Furthermore, holds are used far more often to gain a position of leverage in an unrelated matter than to block an ideologically objectionable nominee. Earlier macro-level analyses highlighted factors that increase the likelihood of confirmation delay, but these studies were unable to determine exactly how judicial nominations were being delayed, by whom, and for what reasons. By focusing on a parliamentary mechanism senators can use to obstruct nominations, many times indefinitely, we can begin to uncover how nominations are delayed and, more important, why.

While the use of holds (and senatorial courtesy) does not explain all the delay in the lower court confirmation process, it does explain a sizable amount. Even more important, an examination of each hold reveals precisely why these nominations were delayed. Senators commonly place holds on judicial nominations to gain leverage in wholly unconnected disputes. Because judicial nominations receive little public and media attention, and because each nomination is important to only a few players in the legislative process, judicial nominations have become an important vehicle for playing the tit-for-tat game of bargaining and compromise that characterizes the modern political process. This finding illuminates the crucial role bargaining plays more generally in Senate decision making and how senators utilize holds on nominations and bills to gain the upper hand in these negotiations. While holds were historically used to buy senators more preparation time before the final vote on the bill or nomination, currently they offer senators a hidden yet extremely powerful mechanism with which to strategically obtain (or force) their policy goals.

Chapters 2 and 3 have investigated how and why judicial nominations are delayed and sometimes defeated. The use of senatorial courtesy and holds underscores the power individual senators can exert over judicial nominations at certain points in the confirmation process. Home-state senators may single-handedly defeat nominations soon after they are sent to the Senate, and any senator may place a hold on a nomination. Most striking is the finding that these two parliamentary mechanisms are generally not utilized because of ideological objections to the nominees themselves. Rather, the use of senatorial courtesy reflects institutional disagreements over the power of selection, while nominations are caught in strategic holds as senators attempt to gain leverage in exogenous disputes. The lesson learned here is twofold: senators can exert enormous influence over confirmation outcomes, and judicial nominations have become a favored tool to resolve legislative disputes. Nominations may be diverted onto the private political track while internal political deliberations commence. Such diversions can be relatively brief, and unlucky nominees may watch their nominations rerouted numerous times. Judicial nominations have thus become a central part of the game of politics, and the nominees are the ones paying the price.

However, the exercise of senatorial courtesy and holds does not capture all of the possible confirmation environments judicial nominations may face. Nominations may also follow the public partisan track. Examining the public partisan track reveals the role of the final important player in judicial confirmation politics: outside interest groups. When nominees confront public objections to their nominations by interest groups, they are turned down the public partisan track.

The rest of this book offers an in-depth examination of the role of interest groups in the judicial confirmation process. While there has been considerable popular and media attention given to interest groups in the judicial confirmation process, we know relatively little about the different roles interest groups play, how the other players in the system view them, how interest groups operate when making key decisions, and the degree to which interest group participation influences confirmation outcomes. The following chapters thus focus on exploring different dimensions of interest group activity in the lower court confirmation process. Chapter 4 begins this analysis by reporting the results of interviews with Senate staffers. These staffers were asked what functions they believed outside interest groups actually perform and the impacts these activities have. Chapter 5 uses interviews with interest group leaders to discuss how groups decide to become involved in a lower court confirmation fight, and chapter 6 concludes the analysis by exploring the impact of interest group objections on whether a circuit court nominee will be successfully confirmed.

4

INTEREST GROUPS AND JUDICIAL CONFIRMATIONS
A View from the Senate

While considerable media and popular attention has been concentrated on the role outside interest groups play in the modern-day federal judicial confirmation process, in reality, we know relatively little about the activities of these groups. Conventional wisdom suggests that outside groups drive the process itself, setting the terms of the debate and dictating the activities of like-minded senators. For example, the cover of the April 8, 2002, edition of the *National Review* featured a picture of then Judiciary Committee chair Patrick Leahy attached to marionette strings with the headline, "Strings Attached: How Liberal Interest Groups Control Senate Democrats." Similarly, Judge Charles Pickering stated, in response to a question about why he was filibustered in 2005 but unanimously confirmed to a district court seat in 1990, "During this period of time these far-left special interest groups gained power and they had control of Democrats on the Judiciary Committee, and through the Senators on the Committee they gained control of the entire Democratic apparatus" (Giachino 2006).

The previous chapters showed, however, that other factors might be at work in explaining why some nominees face long delays: nominees may be blocked by their home-state senators through the exercise of senatorial courtesy or their nominations may be turned down the private political track through the use of holds. Most important, the analysis in chapters 2 and 3 revealed that the capture of nominations by private political tactics is usually incidental to the actual disputes: nominations are captured by these parliamentary procedures out of convenience or because of their bargaining significance. Thus, senators do not merely trap nominees to appease like-minded interest groups.

Nonetheless, we do know interest groups play an influential role in the lower court confirmation process. Since the start of the second Reagan administration, interest groups have been major players in the process as they, along with presidents and senators, have increasingly recognized the far-reaching and long-term consequences of who sits on the federal bench. While groups have historically recognized the importance of Supreme Court vacancies (see, e.g., Abraham 1999; Frank 1991; Maltese 1995; Silverstein 1994), only recently have they turned their attention to lower court selection. In the mid-1980s and early 1990s, judicial watchdog groups formed on the left and the right, and other groups began monitoring lower court nominations as well. For groups concerned with policy issues in which court decisions play a prominent role—issues such as gay marriage, abortion rights, discrimination, and the death penalty—the Senate confirmation process affords one more arena in which to pursue their goals.

The remaining chapters of this book explore what roles interest groups play in the lower court confirmation process and the impact of these activities. I begin by examining the different functions interest groups perform. Interest groups historically participated formally in the judicial confirmation process by testifying at confirmation hearings. Previous studies focus on assessing when groups testified and whether, through testifying, these groups influenced a lower court nominee's likelihood of confirmation (Bell 2002a; Cohen 1998; Flemming, MacLeod, and Talbert 1998). Since the early 1990s, however, Judiciary Committee chairs have restricted the formal involvement of groups, so groups have turned to more informal mechanisms of participation.

We know relatively little about groups' informal activities. Seminal studies examine informal interest group activity in the context of particular, highly contested nominations (Bell 2002a; Caldeira, Hojnacki, and Wright 2000; Caldeira and Wright 1995, 1998), but no study to date has examined the full extent of the functions groups perform in the lower court confirmation process, including whether groups play any role in uncontested nominations.

This chapter adds a different perspective to the debate over interest group activity by asking those who are most likely to be affected—senators and their staffs—what functions they believe interest groups perform. Senators and Senate staffers recognize that outside groups are a formidable force in the modern legislative arena. But are groups essential players in the lower court confirmation process, or are they a necessary evil that must be dealt with? Are groups the puppet masters of like-minded senators, or do they fill roles senators and their staffs cannot? This chapter aims to answer these questions by examining the results of interviews with thirty-two Senate staffers and one former senator.

Before I turn to the interview results, I will briefly lay out what we do know. Studies find that interest groups play an important role in influencing members of Congress generally (see, e.g., Austen-Smith 1993; Cigler and Loomis 1998; Denzau and Munger 1986; Hojnacki and Kimball 1999; Schlozman and Tierney 1986; Wright 1996). In the judicial confirmation process, groups perform a crucial information-transmission role (Caldeira, Hojnacki, and Wright 2000; Caldeira and Wright 1995, 1998; Scherer 2003; Scherer, Bartels, and Steigerwalt 2008). Groups used to fulfill this role by testifying at confirmation hearings about the nominee's background and perceived views, and by providing reports from group members who resided in the nominee's home state. When formal participation was curtailed, groups turned to informal information-transmission mechanisms, such as written reports and lobbying (Bell 2002a). The question, however, is why such a task for outside groups is even necessary. The next two sections explain why information on judicial nominations is both essential and lacking, and provide an overview of what formal and informal sources of information are available to senators and their staffs.

The Need for Information on Judicial Nominations

Collecting and analyzing information on nominees is a crucial component of the judicial confirmation process. During every presidential term, hundreds of lower court vacancies need to be filled. Presidents need information about potential nominees for each vacancy, and senators and their staffs need information about each nominee once the nominations are formally sent to the Senate.

Members of the Judiciary Committee require considerable amounts of information, as they must determine whether every nominee is suitable for the federal bench. The Senate's committee structure requires committees to do the brunt of the work on bills and nominations related to their specific areas; as a result of this specialization, other senators depend on the committees to provide them with detailed information once a bill or nomination makes it to the Senate floor (Gilligan and Krehbiel 1989, 1990; Krehbiel 1991). With dozens of nominees awaiting Judiciary Committee attention at any one time, committee members and their staffs must try to determine which nominees require a more thorough investigation and which nominees can be quickly vetted. The quandary is that information gathered about one nominee does not help senators assess other nominees. As Caldeira, Hojnacki, and Wright (2000) explain, "Nominations strain the resources of Senators, for no two nominations are alike. Whatever information or expertise senators acquire about one nominee is not transferable to the next. On each nomination, senators must learn about a nominee's policy views and any controversial decision made by the nominee" (67).

As the nation has expanded in population and in size, the number of federal judgeships has multiplied, and the need for information about potential nominees has grown accordingly. In addition, as lower court confirmations have become the new battleground, the Senate's need for information has grown as well. Finally, "the demand for information on controversial nominees is high *and* constant" (Caldeira, Hojnacki, and Wright 2000, 54). Senators must therefore rely on both formal and informal sources of information to effectively vet judicial nominees.

FORMAL SOURCES OF INFORMATION

Senators rely on four main sources of formal information on lower court nominees. First, every nominee completes a Judiciary Committee questionnaire. Nominees provide information about their background, education, financial interests, and work experiences, including information about any significant cases they have litigated. Nominees who have previously served as judges, whether at the local, state, or federal level, are asked to supply copies of their ten most significant decisions, as well as data on the number of times their decisions have been reversed by a higher court. Nominees are also asked to make available copies of all other published materials, such as books or articles, and any public speeches. The Judiciary Committee may also make other requests, such as asking for copies of a judge's unpublished opinions.[1] This information is available to every senator who serves on the committee.

The committee's investigatory staffers then vet each nominee by reviewing this information. The week prior to a nominee's confirmation hearing, the nominations counsel prepares a report that is sent to the members of the committee and any other senator who requests it.[2] This memo provides information about the nominee, with the aim of highlighting facts or cases of interest. As the chief nominations counsel explained in 2002, "It's usually just very straight information with an eye to what I know they will be concerned about. They're going to be concerned about the death penalty, abortion rights, civil liberties, and labor because these are Democrats. That's what they are very concerned about, so I let them know that. But it's not an opinion piece."

Second, the Federal Bureau of Investigation (FBI) conducts a background check on each nominee. This investigation takes place at the request of the White House prior to the formal nomination, and the report is initially sent only to the White House. The FBI's investigation consists of interviews with friends, family, co-workers, and employers, as well as inquiries into employment and arrest records. The FBI's investigation focuses on ensuring that the prospective nominee does not have any personal issues that may disqualify him or her from holding a lifetime appointment, such as substance abuse, serious financial problems, or potentially illegal or unethical activities. Once a person is formally nominated, a copy of the report is forwarded to the Judiciary Committee. Because of the confidential nature of the information collected by the FBI, only senators serving on the committee plus one staff member in each of the chair's and ranking minority member's offices are authorized to view this file. It is understood that information contained in a nominee's FBI file will not be discussed publicly, even if a senator objects to a nominee based on something discovered during the FBI's investigation.[3]

Third, the American Bar Association (ABA) conducts an in-depth investigation of each nominee. Lower court nominees are asked to fill out a lengthy questionnaire and to provide the ABA with copies of all previous writings or speeches. Confidential interviews are then conducted with at least forty individuals who have knowledge of the nominee's professional experiences and behavior. The ABA's investigation focuses on assessing nominees' professional competence and qualifications, as well as their integrity and judicial temperament (American Bar Association 2007; Grossman 1965). The ABA then rates each nominee as either "well qualified," "qualified," or "not qualified" for the position to which the candidate is nominated. The ABA publicly announces the rating given to each lower court nominee, as well as whether the rating was unanimous. The ABA does not, however, release any other information or a summary of these investigations to the White House, Senate, or public. If a nominee receives a "not qualified" or a split "not qualified/qualified" rating, the ABA may be asked to testify at the nominee's committee hearing and explain the reason for the "not qualified" rating.[4]

From the mid-1940s until March 2001, the ABA's investigation took place during the presidential selection phase, at the request of the White House. The ABA's rating would then be forwarded to the Senate post-nomination. In March 2001, President George W. Bush decided to discontinue the ABA's role at the presidential selection phase in response to growing complaints that the ABA's ratings were biased against conservative-leaning nominees.[5] Then Judiciary Committee chair Patrick Leahy determined that the committee would send the names of nominees to the ABA for evaluation, and wait to proceed on each nomination until a rating was received (Hudson 2001). While Republican senators did not necessarily agree with the initial decision, Orrin Hatch continued the practice once he regained the chairmanship in 2003 (Davidson 2003). Then, on March 17, 2009, newly inaugurated President Barack Obama announced the restoration of the ABA to its traditional pre-presidential-selection role.

The ongoing dispute over whether the ABA's ratings are biased against conservatives (see, e.g., Vining, Steigerwalt, and Smelcer 2009) only serves to illuminate the considerable impact these ratings have on judicial confirmations. Regardless of political affiliation, ABA ratings are the benchmark by which actors in the judicial selection process determine whether a particular nominee can be considered qualified to serve on the federal bench. Presidents use the ABA's ratings to determine which proposed candidate should receive a nomination; a low rating prior to presidential selection may prevent candidates from being formally nominated (Goldman 1997; Hall 1979). Once a nomination is sent to the Senate, senators look to ABA ratings to provide a clear signal as to the nominee's level of professional qualifications and fitness to be confirmed to the federal bench. Although a high ABA rating does not ensure a successful confirmation, it does generally shield nominees from facing an overly contentious path to confirmation (see, e.g., Martinek, Kemper, and Van Winkle 2002).

Finally, the nominees themselves provide further information in two ways. First, each nominee testifies at a Judiciary Committee hearing and answers oral questions from committee members.[6] Hearings may last a few hours or may continue for days—Robert Bork testified for five days—and the committee may ask a nominee to return for a second hearing, as they did in the summer of 2002 with Fifth Circuit Court nominee Charles Pickering. Nominees renominated in successive Congresses by the same president may also be subjected to additional committee hearings in the later Congresses, though this is not a hard-and-fast rule. These hearings are open to the public, and hearing transcripts are published by the Senate. Supporters and opponents of the nominee may be invited to testify as to the nominee's fitness for the bench. However, Judiciary Committee chairs have generally not allowed such outside testimony since the late 1980s (Bell 2002a, 87). Second, the nominee may be asked by senators to answer a series of written follow-up questions.[7]

There are thus four sources of formal information that the Senate Judiciary Committee receives. Committee members use these formal information sources to assess each nominee and determine whether the nominee should be confirmed. Most of this formal information is also available to the other senators and their staffs.

INFORMAL SOURCES OF INFORMATION

The conundrum is that these formal sources of information do not alleviate the enormous resource constraints confronting senators. Given the sheer number of nominations made each congressional term, senators and their staffs lack the time and resources to cull the mountain of information produced on every nominee; this is especially true if a nominee has a substantial written record from previous experience as a judge or law professor. When Senator Edward Kennedy became chair in 1979, he began the practice of hiring investigatory staffers to allow the committee to independently vet judicial nominees. However, as of 2002, as noted by the then current nominations counsel, the majority staff had only two staffers whose full-time job was to vet nominees.

Senators also require more than just raw information about the nominee and his or her background; they need information that can help them distinguish between the dozens of nominations pending at any one time and determine which nominees are acceptable and which require additional scrutiny. Senators additionally seek information about what Caldeira and Wright term "the 'politics' of nominations" (1995, 45). Senators must ascertain not only whether a nominee may hold troubling views but also how mobilized groups and voters in their home states view the nominee: since senators cannot fight every nomination, they need to determine which fights their constituents will support. As a result, senators and their staff rely heavily on a more informal source of information, interest groups.

Interest groups help senators identify which nominees require additional attention. Leading judicial watchdog groups provide senators and their staffs with information on nominees. Many times groups send detailed reports on a nominee's background and views, with special attention to potentially problematic judicial decisions or writings; the report may also highlight important political information about the nomination and home-state support. In this way, groups fill the gap left by the formal information sources by providing information designed specifically to help senators differentiate among the multitude of nominations pending each congressional term.

Currently we lack empirical, systematic evidence about the extent of groups' information-transmission role. I therefore interviewed Senate

TABLE 4.1 Descriptive statistics on Senate staff members interviewed

	TOTAL INTERVIEWED	TOTAL CURRENT STAFF	TOTAL FORMER STAFF	TOTAL SENATE JUDICIARY COMMITTEE STAFF
Democrats	18	14	4	12
Republicans	14	9	5	9
Total	32	23	9	21

staff to determine how often groups send information, to whom they send it, and how this information is used by its recipients. The results of these interviews are detailed below.

The Interviews

During the summer of 2002, I interviewed thirty-two current and former Senate staff members (table 4.1).[8] I also interviewed former senator Howard Metzenbaum (D-OH), who served on the Judiciary Committee between 1977 and 1994. I interviewed current and former staffers for the Judiciary Committee as well as current staffers who handled judicial confirmations for senators not on the committee. At the time of the interviews, twelve of the individuals interviewed worked for the Judiciary Committee and another nine interviewees were former committee staffers. The remaining eleven interviewees worked at the time as staff for senators who served on other committees. Eighteen individuals interviewed worked for Democrats and fourteen worked for Republicans. Many of the current staffers held the same position during the Clinton administration and thus could provide observations about the role of interest groups during both the Clinton and George W. Bush administrations. The nine former committee staffers provided an institutional memory dating back to the Reagan administration.

The interviews probed each interviewee's view of the role of interest groups in the judicial confirmation process. The interviewees were asked specifically about the types of information they received from interest groups and how often they received such information, their relationships with different interest groups, and the role they believed interest groups played in making particular confirmations contested. Finally, staffers who worked in the Senate during multiple presidential administrations were asked about any variations they observed in the functions played by outside groups during the different administrations. Most of these interviewees asked not to be directly quoted; these staffers are identified in the text by their political party and whether they worked for a senator on or off the Judiciary Committee.

I used a combination of structured and semistructured interview techniques. First, to provide a more systematic examination of how those in the Senate view outside interest groups, I posed the same series of questions to the interviewees. I then examined their answers much as John Kingdon did in his seminal study, *Congressmen's Voting Decisions* (1989). Kingdon asked a set series of questions of all his interview subjects. He then quantified their answers by counting how many interviewees gave similar answers to the same question. This approach allowed him to uncover systematic answer patterns across subjects and within discrete groups. I used this method for questions about the overall role of interest groups, as well as their information-transmission role. As a result, I was able to draw conclusions about the views held by my interview subjects, as well as to discover important differences between subgroups of interviewees. Second, I utilized semistructured interview questions to probe more broadly into the interviewees' view of interest groups and the confirmation process overall. I then analyzed these answers looking for broad, consistent themes. Three primary questions drove these interviews: (1) How important is interest groups' information-transmission role in the lower court confirmation process? (2) What other functions do interest groups perform in the lower court confirmation process? (3) Are there noticeable differences in the roles liberal and conservative groups play in the lower court confirmation process?

Interest Groups and Information

Thirty interviewees were asked, "What do you see as the role of interest groups in the judicial confirmation process?" If a staffer described multiple roles for interest groups, each of the roles was recorded as a separate response. Therefore, the total number of responses in table 4.2 is more than the total number of staffers who were asked the question. In response to this question, 83 percent of those interviewed (twenty-four staffers and Senator Metzenbaum) answered that the main function interest groups performed was providing research and information about the nominees (table 4.2). Staffers described the reports they received from interest groups as "invaluable" and an "easy" and "huge" source of information.

All of the staffers seconded the arguments advanced in previous stud-

TABLE 4.2 Senate staff responses concerning the roles of interest groups in lower court confirmations

	RESEARCH AND INFORMATION (%)	SET AGENDA (%)	MEDIA AND PUBLIC RELATIONS (%)	GRASS-ROOTS MOBILIZA-TION (%)	SUPPORT SENATORS IF IS A BATTLE (%)	INFLUENCE SENATORS' VOTING DECISIONS (%)	NOT MUCH AT ALL (%)
Democrats	19	5	2	2	1	0	0
	(63)	(17)	(7)	(7)	(3)		
Current staff	13	4	2	2	1	0	0
	(43)	(13)	(7)	(7)	(3)		
Former staff	5	0	0	0	0	0	0
	(17)						
Committee staff	14	2	2	2	1	0	0
	(47)	(7)	(7)	(7)	(3)		
Republicans	6	1	4	2	1	1	2
	(20)	(3)	(13)	(7)	(3)	(3)	(7)
Current staff	3	1	2	1	0	1	1
	(10)	(3)	(7)	(3)		(3)	(3)
Former staff	3	0	2	1	1	0	1
	(10)		(7)	(3)	(3)		(3)
Committee staff	3	0	3	1	1	0	2
	(10)		(10)	(3)	(3)		(7)
Total	25	6	6	4	2	1	2
	(83)	(20)	(20)	(14)	(7)	(3)	(7)

Note: The numbers reported for "Democrats total" also include responses given by former senator Howard Metzenbaum.

ies that information is a vital commodity lacking in the judicial confirmation process overall and that the Judiciary Committee is not equipped to acquire or provide the information senators and staff both on and off the committee require. All of the participants voiced a desire for complete information on each nominee's background and views. A common complaint expressed during the interviews was the dearth of available information; information on nominees frequently was described as not forthcoming or readily available.

Even staffers serving on the Judiciary Committee felt they often lacked necessary information on each nominee. The week of a confirmation hearing, all committee members receive the memo composed by the

chief nominations counsel and a copy of the nominee's completed questionnaire.[9] For nominees viewed as noncontroversial, this information
is generally sufficient. However, when questions arise as to a nominee's
fitness for the federal bench, staffers reported that these items lacked
the substance needed to help them make an informed decision about
the nominee. Staffers also noted their inability to conduct their own
investigations. Each staffer must therefore find ways to augment his or
her knowledge. Not surprisingly, many turn to interest groups to fill
this gap.

Judiciary Committee staffers also frequently mentioned that they were
responsible for numerous other issues beyond judicial confirmations, and
so the research provided by interest groups freed them to focus on other
priorities. As a Democratic committee staffer explained, "It's knowing
that the groups are doing [research] that we are able to focus our ener-
gies on other things. If they didn't, we probably would make an effort,
but we have to focus on all the other things the Committee does. . . . I
can devote less of my staff time to reading every case, if we're going to be
getting very detailed reports from interest groups. Obviously, you have
to take them with a grain of salt, and review what they've done, but it's a
very good starting point."

The workload and the importance of judicial nominations also vary
by office. A staffer working for a more junior member of the Judiciary
Committee explained that information received from the committee and
from interest groups the week of the hearing is invaluable, especially as
she is the only staffer in her office working on judicial nominations. She
further noted her approach to using the various sources of information. If
the nomination is somewhat contentious, she relies mostly on the committee's memo; however, if the nomination is contested, she looks more
closely at the interest groups' evaluations. Overall, she relies more on the
interest groups' research, since interest groups generally can devote more
resources to vetting each nominee than the committee can.

In comparison, many of the committee Republicans said conservative
interest groups were not a significant source of information for them (see
table 4.2). These staffers explained they received little to no information from interest groups (though many of them wished they did), and
many further commented that any information they did receive from
groups was usually information they already possessed, whether it came
from then chairman Leahy's office, the Department of Justice, or their
own research. As noted throughout this chapter, the more conservative a
senator, the less likely he or she was to receive information from interest

groups, and especially from groups on the left, who primarily fulfilled the information-transmission role during the 107th Congress.

Thus, overall, groups transmit needed information to committee members and their staff. Partisan differences emerge when this information-transmission function is examined more closely, as conservative offices rarely receive information from interest groups (and this was true even during the Clinton administration), while more liberal offices receive such information frequently and rely on it a great deal.

For those not serving on the Judiciary Committee, the formal information available through the committee was also viewed as inadequate for assessing nominees. There are a number of reasons why this might be so. The Judiciary Committee does not customarily send information about every nominee to every senator; rather, it does so only when asked. The vast majority of staff members I spoke with said that the amount of material they received from the committee was usually insufficient for their needs. As one moderate Republican explained, often he receives "only superficial or no information" on a nominee from the committee. Consequently for non-committee members, the information provided by interest groups fills this crucial gap. A Democratic staffer observed, "Especially with controversial nominees, [interest groups] provide information on that nominee that you may not get from the White House or the Judiciary Committee which is considered 'official information,' so the interest groups rely a lot on 'unofficial information.'" A moderate Republican staffer noted that "there are so many nominations that there is not the time or the resources to check out each and every one, [and] you don't have all the information you need, so interest groups play a crucial role in providing background information, and pointing out who are the potential controversies." Interestingly, this same staffer also maintained that one must look to information from interest groups because information from the majority and minority offices of the committee is "inherently unreliable to rely on because it has a biased view." As judicial nominees are not usually on a non-committee staffer's radar before they hit the Senate floor, interest groups play a large role in bringing attention to worrisome nominees (see Table 4.2). Thus, many staffers reported relying heavily on interest groups both to provide them with basic information and to alert them to problematic nominees (see also Scherer, Bartels, and Steigerwalt 2008).

Information from the Judiciary Committee was also found to be lacking in "insider information." Staffers expressed frustration at not knowing the status of nominees from their states and commonly said they did not know what was blocking their nominees' progress. When asked about her biggest frustrations, one staffer replied, "Information. I wish it could get to us faster. . . . I just want to know, so I can pass it on or know what's going on and know what to do. . . . You know those email alerts you get from CNN? I'd like to get one of those from the committee. 'Alert: there's a hold,' or 'Alert: your nominee is coming up.' . . . But they have so many. . . . When you call [the committee staff is] really friendly. . . . But I have to call them." Interest groups thus appreciably augment formal information sources for non-Judiciary Committee members.

WHERE YOU SIT DETERMINES WHAT YOU READ

Beyond providing information about a nominee's background and views, interest groups also supply necessary information about the politics of particular nominations. However, one of the most interesting interview findings that emerged is that constituency concerns do matter, but only for certain senators. Overall, key differences in the types of information senators find useful exist between senators serving on the Judiciary Committee and those not currently serving on the committee.

For those serving on the committee, constituent concerns matter little. Committee staffers all dismissed the impact of constituent concerns on their bosses' decision-making calculi when determining whether to vote for a particular judicial nominee. A former Republican committee staffer explained, "We don't pay attention to any letters, as [Senator X] has such a safe seat. A lot of times the mail criticizes him for not being conservative enough, and that just doesn't matter on nominations."[10] Similarly, a current Republican committee staffer, when asked whether constituency concerns influenced his boss's vote, said, "Probably not. It's useful for us to see how many resources we need to dedicate to defending a nominee or explain [Senator X's] position on a nominee." While home-state nominees invoke constituent considerations, for the vast majority of nominees, committee senators focus on the nominee's background and views rather than on home-state political calculations.

Therefore, the groups with the greatest access to committee members and their staff are the leading judicial watchdog groups. As of 2002, these were the Alliance for Justice and People for the American Way on the left, and the Judicial Selection Monitoring Project on the right. These three groups monitor federal judicial selection on behalf of hundreds of smaller groups. They focus mainly on providing analyses of the nominees and their views rather than on offering more strategic or constituency-based information.

Many of the committee staffers I spoke with also specifically noted that they relied more heavily on information from national groups than on information from local groups. As one current committee staffer explained, he believes the national groups are more "plugged in," and he knows the "groups do a lot of legwork to check how local people feel." Moreover, since he "know[s] those at the national interest groups personally," he trusts them when they report local reactions. Other staffers reported similar views. Thus, for those senators on the Judiciary Committee, reelection concerns are not the primary impetus for granting an interest group access and influence. The question then arises, what is the primary concern of senators on the Judiciary Committee?

Simply put, many committee staffers felt that the decision of whether to support a judicial nominee was one "removed from politics." Staffers on both sides of the aisle argued that their senators were concerned with the role of the federal courts and the individual impact each nominee might make, rather than how each vote might affect their reelection chances. As one committee staffer explained, in a statement echoed by many, "The Judiciary Committee members . . . have a role to play in reviewing nominations that is completely separate from their constituents, and they take that role seriously, and they want to know what those who have concerns on substance think, whereas a Senator who's not on the Committee and not involved in the state or Circuit, when they cast their vote they're more concerned about how it's going to play at home. . . . [The committee members] make their decisions on their own judgment. They've taken on this responsibility, and they want to carry it out seriously."

Much like Fenno's (1973) conclusions in his seminal study, *Congressmen in Committee,* about why senators choose to serve on the Senate Foreign Relations Committee, the Judiciary Committee staff all agreed that senators join the committee out of a concern for the creation of public policy through the courts. Consequently, the policies (expected) to be created by those serving on the federal courts take center stage in these senators' deliberations. As a result, those groups that focus on providing such information—the primary actions of the leading judicial watchdog groups—play a central role in aiding committee members in making their decisions. Conversely, membership groups that primarily transmit information about constituency concerns and potential electoral ramifications play a much lesser role in influencing the views of committee members. Some staffers on the committee expressed skepticism about constituent contacts and views: "I think that there is a real sense that a lot of people who call are activated by these networks and in the end they won't actually know what the result is anyway. . . . I don't think that we have a huge concern about how [Senator X] votes on a particular nominee is going to get those folks upset with him because they probably won't know" (Republican committee staffer).

On the other hand, for those senators not serving on the committee, constituent concerns take priority. One staffer commented, "It's the constituents who drive the decision making, and how the Senator is going to respond to the nominee." A Republican staffer explained that for his office, an interest group's biggest influence was the likelihood that it could affect who was voting for his boss: "If [the interest group] got a lot of responses from [our] constituents, then we watch that very closely." Senators not on the committee therefore listen more closely to the objections of membership groups tied to their states and issues of importance to them. For example, for senators active on women's issues and abortion, the objections of membership-based groups such as the National Organization for Women and NARAL on the left and Concerned Women for America on the right—and the mobilized constituents they bring with them—are extremely important. These findings, at least for non-committee members, bolster the arguments made by Scherer (2003, 2005) that groups are able to exert influence because of senators' fears of electoral retribution.

Non-committee senators and their staffers are much more worried about constituent interests and less trusting of national groups than their counterparts on the Judiciary Committee. What the national interest groups can do is round up local constituents for senators and staff to talk with: "We use them [the national groups] as a source to get to our local constituents. We don't just take their word for anything, because sometimes the local constituents differ." This Democratic staffer continued, "You always want to quote the local office. . . . You always want to be able to say I talked to Mrs. Jane Smith and this is what she thinks." Similarly, a Republican staffer suggested that national groups should always bring local constituents with them. He related that the meeting he had immediately following our interview was with the president of the League of Women Voters. While he was personally excited (and flattered) to meet with her, he explained that her visit would be much more powerful politically if she brought along local members from the state, as "the message is clearer if the group is from [our state]," especially as that transmits unmistakable constituency (and, consequently, electoral) cues.

Thus, constituency and reelection concerns predominate on both sides of the aisle for senators not serving on the Judiciary Committee.

These staffers are less interested in the reports coming from national groups and more interested in letters and phone calls from their constituents. That said, not all constituent responses are valued equally: "The ways in which people contact are varied, and they are not equal in their effectiveness" (Verba 1993, 678). Many staffers explained that much of the correspondence they receive on judicial nominations is generated through interest groups. Groups send out "alerts" or bulletins that encourage their members to call or write their senators. To aid these efforts, interest groups have created mechanisms that allow interested members to send emails and faxes to senators directly from their Web sites.

Referred to as "Astroturf lobbying," this mechanism of manufactured grassroots activity can generate considerable action, but it can also be a deterrent to true debate, as offices are forced to determine where the calls are coming from and how much they actually reflect home-state concerns.[11] Thus, while senators and their staffs are highly responsive to constituent concerns, they also make clear distinctions between different types of constituent contacts, such as weighing 100 handwritten letters more highly than the same form letter with 100 different signatures. One staffer said he would speak to anyone who calls, but he also recognized the difference between the people who read an editorial on a situation affecting nominations to their circuit court and have "honest questions" versus the people who call to say "vote for candidate X" and know only the talking points generated by a particular interest group. He further explained, "On lots of controversial issues we get millions of calls because someone is spending money, and they just don't matter that much as they are not a good reflection of the state's views." He added that if a local mayor or community leader or worker in the state or local chapter of an interest group calls, those are the contacts that he relates to the senator, but 100 phone calls from "John Smiths" that were generated by a group's phone tree do not carry nearly the same weight: "They may not be totally ignored, but it's just different." Thus, while non-committee senators assess constituency concerns when making their decisions on judicial nominees, they have also learned to distinguish between the types of constituency contacts and their corresponding import.

Finally, a former Judiciary Committee staffer highlighted how committee members do rely on local chapters of national organizations. Mark Gittenstein, chief counsel under Senator Biden when he was chair, explained that interest groups could help committee senators lobby non-committee senators. He commented, "The [groups] in Washington were not nearly as effective as the ones in the field talking to members . . .

Because they knew the members. The local NAACP or something like that more likely than not knows the members" (2002).[12] Thus, committee staffers find local organizations useful as a means of shoring up support from other senators once a nominee moves to the Senate floor, but not as an instrument to help their senators determine how to vote for a nominee in committee.

In sum, whom a senator listens to is highly dependent on where the senator sits. For senators not on the Judiciary Committee, electoral concerns dominate, and local membership groups exert enormous influence. These staffers want to hear from those in their home state. Oppositely, committee senators take their role of staffing the federal bench seriously. For these senators, the desire to make good public policy, much like the senators Fenno interviewed thirty years ago, dominates their decision-making processes, rather than the need to appease constituents at home. National groups provide these senators with important substantive information they can use to determine how to vote on a nomination, but grassroots lobbying efforts serve only to alert committee senators to how much time they need to devote to defending their positions.

Other Interest Group Roles

Interviewees noted two other key functions interest groups perform, with an interesting split along party lines (see table 4.2). Twenty percent of respondents—four Democratic staffers, Senator Metzenbaum, and one moderate Republican staffer—stated that groups help set the agenda by identifying which nominees should be targeted for defeat, while another 20 percent of respondents—four Republicans and two Democrats—maintained that interest groups mainly played a public relations role.

Staff members I spoke with, especially those not on the committee, noted their reliance on interest groups to help determine which nominees were most vulnerable: "The role of interest groups is pretty huge, especially for a non-Senate Judiciary Committee member, because we pay attention when groups bring us information, because unless the nomination is pretty egregious, it is not even on our radar screen until it hits the floor. Thus, the role of the interest groups is to bring attention to a nomination before it hits the floor, to call and tell us which ones to be concerned about" (Democratic staffer not on the committee). The role of interest groups as strategists can go even farther. As one Democratic staffer explained, "interest groups are good about picking [senators] to lead the fights," as they are knowledgeable about who might be willing to be a lead spokesperson or put a hold on a nominee. Alternatively, numerous Republicans pointed to the important task they believe interest groups fulfill in terms of media and public relations.

This party division with respect to the secondary role of interest groups is not entirely surprising. First, because the interviews were done during a period of Democratic control of the Senate and Republican control of the presidency, liberal groups were the ones determining which of George W. Bush's nominations were viable targets for defeat. Conservative groups in turn had their greatest impact on the presidential selection process rather than the Senate confirmation process.[13] Similarly, since Republicans were focused on supporting President Bush's nominations to the federal bench, their view of interest groups as useful conduits for media relations is also not unexpected. However, the interviews also revealed that conservative interest groups play much less of a public and organized role than liberal interest groups, and this was true even during the Clinton administration. In fact, two of the Republican committee interviewees (7 percent) said they did not believe groups played much of a role at all in the judicial confirmation process.

Interviewees who highlighted the information-transmission role of interest groups were asked how often they received such information from groups. Interesting partisan distinctions again appeared, as well as differences based on whether the staffer served on the Judiciary Committee (table 4.3). Of the twenty-one staffers asked how often they received information from groups, 57 percent answered that they received information only on contentious nominees, though many of these staffers further commented that they received information "all the time" about these contested nominees. This dual response was usually given by those working on the Judiciary Committee. Eight staffers (38 percent) replied that they received information "rarely" or "never." Strikingly, seven of these eight staffers were Republican. The three Republican staffers who "never" received information from groups all served on the committee and worked for rather conservative senators. Thus, while Democratic staffers receive a considerable amount of information from interest groups, the groups do not seem to send Republicans similar levels of information, and this was especially true of Republican committee staffers. The Republican staffers who did report receiving a decent amount of information from groups all worked for senators not on the committee. The lone Republican who "almost always" received information from outside groups worked for a moderate non-committee senator known to reach across the aisle on a number of issues.

TABLE 4.3 Senate staff responses concerning how often they received information from interest groups

	ALMOST ALWAYS (%)	ONLY ON CONTROVERSIAL NOMINATIONS (%)	RARELY (%)	NEVER (%)
Democrats	7	8	1	0
	(33)	(38)	(5)	
Current staff	6	6	1	0
	(29)	(29)	(5)	
Former staff	1	2	0	0
	(5)	(10)		
Committee staff	6	5	0	0
	(29)	(24)		
Republicans	1	4	4	3
	(5)	(19)	(19)	(14)
Current staff	1	3	4	3
	(5)	(14)	(19)	(14)
Former staff	0	1	0	0
		(5)		
Committee staff	0	1	2	3
		(5)	(10)	(14)
Total	8	12	5	3
	(38)	(57)	(24)	(14)

Finally, with regard to groups' information-providing role, eighteen interviewees were asked, "Do you ever receive information from interest groups on the opposite side of the aisle?"[14] This question was asked of eleven Democrats and seven Republicans, all of whom had stated earlier that they at least sometimes received information from outside groups (table 4.4). Overall, 67 percent of respondents stated they received information from groups across the aisle. However, when we look at these results by party, we discover that all eleven Democrats received at least some information from conservative groups, while only four of the seven Republicans received information from liberal groups.

The results in table 4.4, combined with those shown in table 4.3, indicate that groups are cognizant of the need to use different strategies when targeting committee senators versus non-committee senators.

Groups also seem to recognize the utility of targeting various senators. Those who did not receive any information from groups and those who had never been targeted by groups across the aisle were all staffers who worked for conservative committee members who were highly supportive of all of President George W. Bush's nominees. On the other hand, those who received information constantly and from groups on both sides of the aisles were all either Democratic committee staffers or staffers working for moderate, swing-vote senators.

These findings afford an important glimpse into one of the unique features of lower court confirmation politics vis-à-vis the role of interest groups: groups must lobby their friends. In a significant study of the effect of interest group lobbying on the outcome of Robert Bork's nomination to the Supreme Court in 1987, Austen-Smith and Wright (1994, 1996; but see Baumgartner and Leech 1996) find that groups engage in

TABLE 4.4 Senate staff responses concerning whether they received information from interest groups traditionally aligned with the other party

	YES (%)	FEW TIMES/ONCE (%)	NEVER (%)
Democrats	8	3	0
	(44)	(17)	
Current staff	8	2	0
	(44)	(11)	
Former staff	0	1	0
		(6)	
Committee staff	5	3	0
	(28)	(17)	
Republicans	4	0	3
	(22)		(17)
Current staff	3	0	2
	(17)		(11)
Former staff	1	0	1
	(6)		(6)
Committee staff	1	0	3
	(6)		(17)
Total	12	3	3
	(67)	(17)	(17)

"counter-active" lobbying of their friends on Supreme Court nominations only to offset the effects of lobbying by opposition groups. However, the above results illuminate the fact that, with regard to lower court nominations, groups spend quite a lot of time lobbying their friends. The question is, why?

Simply put, the historical deference given to presidents and home-state senators to select lower court judges deters senators from voting against nominees without ample cause. Groups must assume that each senator will vote yes on a given nominee unless sufficient evidence becomes available to provide the senator with an acceptable reason to vote no (see also Scherer, Bartels, and Steigerwalt 2008). Interest groups therefore must devote much of their resources to convincing even their friends to vote no. Consequently, liberal groups routinely targeted liberal senators such as Charles Schumer and Barbara Boxer in order to galvanize opposition to particular Bush (43) nominees. Given this reality, groups opposed to a nominee recognize that spending time lobbying one's opposition (i.e., a member of the president's party) diverts precious resources, as the chance that these senators will vote against one of the president's nominees is extremely small; only in situations where groups lobby a member of the president's party who is known to be receptive to the views held by the group might such a strategy work (and only once opposition party senators have joined the fight). Thus, Lincoln Chaffee, a moderate Republican, was lobbied heavily by liberal interest groups during the 107th Congress, while conservative senators Jon Kyl and Jeff Sessions received no contact from any liberal groups.

PARTISAN DIFFERENCES AMONG GROUP ACTIVITIES

The final notable finding from the staff interviews was the emergence of clear partisan differences regarding the amount and character of interest group lobbying. As of 2002, there existed a widespread belief that few conservative groups were consistently involved in the lower court confirmation process. A Republican staffer with leadership ties expressed a need to "create the groups" on the right. He felt conservatives such as Ralph Reed and Pat Robertson concentrated on nominations during the Reagan and Bush (41) administrations, but not more recently. He continued, "You would think the corporations would pay attention, but generally they are too busy doing business. We have to ask for help, the other side gets volunteers, and so we fight an uphill stream."

More important, all of the Republican interviewees claimed there was a "dearth" of interest groups on the right that provided information on nominees; instead, conservative groups were seen as playing mainly a media and public relations role (see table 4.2). For example, one Republican staff member commented that he could not think of a single group on the right from which he received information, while another stated that conservative groups had "never" provided any type of legal analysis or background information that his office did not already have. Several staffers noted that one group, Judicial Watch, sent numerous blast faxes, but the staffers then all reiterated that they could not think of any group that sent information, and especially not consistently. As one current Republican committee staffer commented, "[I] get nothing" on the nominees from conservative groups, and it is "frustrating." What he really wished for was an extra hand: "If there are a hundred cases and someone can say, 'Really look at these five especially,' that would be a lot of help. We're not getting it, and I really wish we did! It's just not there . . . or not being done." One moderate non-committee Republican commented, "It's not a matter of wishing for groups on the right but a matter of getting information on all sides. I get more from the left, perfected, they know how to do it, are just more effective. I think the right feels an inherently liberal bias in the media and so would not listen to them, and [do] not feel they get a fair hearing, so that may be partly why I appreciate information from all sides because the groups can slant information in any way." Similarly, another non-committee Republican stated, "I wish there were more sources of information to look through. I can't think of a single group on the right that I get information from. There are splinter groups who care only about one single issue, but there is not any one general group that sends information."

Instead, many staffers argued that the main function of conservative groups was media and public relations, another crucial lobbying tactic. Former Republican staffers indicated that conservative groups in earlier periods also concentrated more on media-related strategies. One former Republican committee staffer who had served during the Reagan administration described how conservative groups took the lead in convincing the public that Reagan's nominees were really no different from Carter's, Ford's, or Nixon's. Conservative groups did not provide information or lobby members; instead, he described how these groups worked to target the media and project the message of the Reagan administration. Similarly, another former Republican committee staffer said conservative groups did not conduct independent research but rather provided grassroots support once committee senators had made their decisions. He believed conservative groups had "zero influence" on the choices senators made and instead were used after the decision was made to mobilize elite and grassroots support for the senators' positions. Many times these groups actually received their information from the committee staff.[15] However, one Republican committee staffer expressed his wish for more help from conservative groups in "projecting their message."[16]

The activities of conservative groups and Republican offices are often highly coordinated. A former committee staffer explained how his office would work with the head of the Project for the Judiciary, a conservative think tank, on op-ed pieces about the Republican position on judges. If their office had certain positions they wanted broadcast, they would feed arguments to the columnist, which he would then write up in opinion pieces published in key newspapers. Likewise, a senior administration official in the George W. Bush White House spoke in a 2002 interview about weekly strategy meetings attended by administration officials, Senate and committee leadership, and the leaders of key conservative groups. Thus, conservative groups do perform an important function in the judicial confirmation process, but it is a very different one from the role played by liberal groups.

Conclusion

Interviews with Senate staff revealed that interest groups play different roles in the judicial confirmation process. Because Senate staff and senators are those most likely to interact with groups and be affected by their actions (as they are the main targets of group lobbying activities), I asked these key players where they felt groups fit into the process. I then compared their answers with some of the main theories offered by other scholars vis-à-vis the role of outside groups in politics in general and in the judicial confirmation process in particular.

These interviews with current and former Senate staff produced four main findings. First, the overall role interest groups, especially liberal groups, play in the judicial confirmation process is to provide information. Although this function has been noted previously, the interviews uncovered the degree to which groups provide information because the committee cannot meet the information needs of those serving on and off the committee, whether the senator desires nominee-based information or more process-oriented information.

Second, senators who serve on the committee have very different information needs than non-committee senators. Committee senators desire objective, substantive information about the nominee, while non-committee senators crave strategic information about constituent views.

And while committee members focus on the public policy aspects of staffing the federal bench, non-committee senators primarily pay attention to how their votes on nominees may affect their reelection chances.

Third, the lobbying strategies interest groups utilize differ in the context of judicial confirmations as opposed to other policy arenas. Because senators are predisposed to vote for a president's nominees, groups must lobby everyone, including their friends, to ensure an outcome in their favor. More lobbying must be done, and it must be directed at more friends than usually occurs in other policy arenas.

Finally, from the point of view of those in the Senate, the interviews illuminated significant partisan differences as to the role interest groups play in the confirmation process. Liberal groups primarily provide information, while conservative groups principally perform a media and public relations function. Democrats thus rely on liberal groups to identify the most problematic nominees, while Republicans rely on conservative groups to wage the necessary public relations campaigns.

This chapter focused predominantly on groups' information-transmission role, which takes place early in the process as groups provide senators and their staffs with information on nominees to help them cull the large number of judicial nominations pending at any given time. This information helps senators and their staffs identify which nominees need to be scrutinized more carefully.

However, groups also perform another important task, that of publicly objecting to nominees they believe will be harmful to their goals if seated on the federal bench. Once a particular nominee begins to move through the confirmation process, groups must decide whether they will publicly object to the nominee and wage a campaign to defeat him or her. Because of limited resources, groups cannot oppose every nominee, and so they strategically and sparingly oppose objectionable nominees. These objections raise a "fire alarm" and send valuable ideological and institutional cues to senators about the nomination (Scherer, Bartels, and Steigerwalt 2008). Chapter 5 addresses how groups decide which nominees they will oppose and which they will allow to move through the process unimpeded.

INTEREST GROUPS AND THE DECISION TO OBJECT
Sending Confirmations down the Public Partisan Track

Senators and their staffs require in-depth information on every single judicial nominee. Interest groups help fill this information gap by serving as an important informal source of information. When a nominee begins to move through the confirmation process, groups may decide to adopt a more active lobbying strategy and publicly object to the nominee. By publicly opposing a nominee, groups decisively turn the nomination onto the public partisan track.[1] Opposed nominees then face a concerted campaign to defeat their nomination and a long and rocky path to confirmation. Through interviews with the leaders of key judicial watchdog groups, this chapter reveals how groups decide which nominees to oppose.

The decision by an interest group to publicly object to a nominee has powerful consequences for the tone (and often the outcome) of the nomination. Once an interest group attack is launched, the president (and supporting senators) must spend precious political capital and resources in support of the nominee. But presidents can fight only so many battles. Presidents must work with Congress to see their nominees confirmed, their legislative priorities enacted, and their executive goals realized, and each of these activities requires the expenditure of resources and political capital. When a judicial nominee is opposed, the president must determine whether fighting for the nominee is worth the potential costs in political capital and the possible need to defer or forgo other high-priority goals.

While presidents almost always work to ensure their Supreme Court nominees are successfully confirmed, the large number of lower court nominations made every term means presidents must carefully calculate which nominations are worth the fight. Eleanor Acheson, who was assistant attorney general for the Office of Policy Development and handled judicial nominations under President Clinton, said in an interview that while Clinton cared deeply about seeing his nominees confirmed, at times other priorities took precedence, such as Clinton's impeachment trial (Acheson 2002). These calculations may also change over time. For example, President George W. Bush nominated Terrence Boyle in May 2001 to the Fourth Circuit, and pushed for Boyle's confirmation during the next five years. However, the Democrats regained control of the Senate in the 2006 midterm elections. Now facing an opposition Senate, Bush made the decision to end this battle and declined to renominate Boyle; Boyle made it clear he did not voluntarily withdraw his nomination (Barrett 2007). As this story shows, group objections require presidents to devote resources that could be directed toward other goals to see their nominees confirmed. In some cases presidents may decide that the battle is not worth the effort. Thus, once nominations are turned down the public partisan track, the cost of a successful confirmation rises considerably.

An example concerning Supreme Court nominations highlights how the presence or absence of an interest group objection can directly influence a nominee's path to confirmation. In 1986, two vacancies on the Supreme Court occurred simultaneously as a result of Chief Justice William Burger's retirement. President Reagan nominated then associate justice William Rehnquist to be elevated to the position of chief justice. The proposed elevation of Rehnquist created an open associate justice seat, and Antonin Scalia was subsequently nominated for this position. Liberal interest groups had to decide whether they would oppose either nomination, given President Reagan's stated goal of appointing "strict constitutional constructionist" justices (Abraham 1999, 291). The leading groups, along with Democratic senators, decided only one of the nominees could be challenged.[2] They then determined that the best strategy was to challenge Rehnquist's elevation to the chief justice post, as the seat for Scalia would vanish if Rehnquist's promotion was denied.[3] As Jeffrey Robinson, chief counsel for then Judiciary Committee chair Joseph Biden, explained in a 2002 interview:

> They [Rehnquist and Scalia] both came at the same time, and it was explicitly a trade-off. I believe that a decision was reached that it was not practical to say you were going to fight against two people, and therefore the focus was on Rehnquist. . . . I think [senators and interest groups] recognized that there's only so much that you can do. And the other practicality is that if the Rehnquist nomination had been defeated . . . then the slot for Scalia [would go] away. . . . And [the decision to target Rehnquist

made sense] in terms of what was available in the record and in terms of who was more likely to be defeated.

Liberal groups and Democratic senators expended large amounts of energy and resources trying to defeat Rehnquist's elevation, and Rehnquist received the largest number of no votes for a confirmed justice up to that point, thirty-three. However, the major players felt they lacked the resources to launch a concurrent fight against Scalia, and so did not expend any resources to fight his nomination. Scalia was confirmed unanimously by the Senate a mere half-hour after the contentious Rehnquist confirmation vote took place. "The protracted Rehnquist battle may well have drawn some fire away from Scalia, leaving the Senate too fatigued to take up another political crusade against him" (Abraham 1999, 294). The decision by interest groups to oppose a nominee turns the nomination decisively down the public partisan track. However, when groups decline to oppose a nominee—even a nominee with a possibly "extreme" record—the nominee will most likely be confirmed swiftly and easily. The story of the simultaneous Rehnquist and Scalia nominations highlights both the importance of the decision to object to a judicial nominee and how these decisions directly affect whether nominations are turned onto the public partisan track.

Surprisingly little is known about how interest groups make the decision whether to publicly oppose a particular nominee. A number of studies assess the role of groups in Supreme Court confirmations, but these studies usually focus on group activity during particular controversial confirmations (Bork 1990; Bronner 1989a; Frank 1991; Goings 1990; Lichtman 1990; Myers 1990; Pertschuk and Schaetzel 1989; Vieira and Gross 1998; Watson 1963) or assess the impact of group activity on confirmation outcomes (Caldeira 1989; Caldeira and Wright 1988; Overby et al. 1992; Segal, Cameron, and Cover 1992). The studies listed all examine group activity once groups have begun a confirmation fight. They do not investigate how groups decide to become involved in the first place.

A few studies examine the role of interest groups in lower court confirmations. Flemming, MacLeod, and Talbert (1998), Cohen (1998), and Bell (2002a) all assess the formal role groups play by testifying at confirmation hearings. The problem is that groups have not been allowed to testify in recent decades (Bell 2002a, 87). As a result, groups have turned to informal lobbying mechanisms. Bell (2002a) provides an overview of the different ways groups informally participate, as well as a case study of informal interest group activity in Frederica Massiah-Jackson's confirmation to the Eastern District Court of Pennsylvania in 1998. Caldeira, Hojnacki, and Wright (2000) examine the tactics used by groups to informally influence senators but do not address how groups decide initially to become involved in particular nomination fights.

The majority of extant studies focus on either the impact of interest group activity or the tactics groups use once they become involved in a judicial confirmation fight. What they do not do is provide insight into *how* and *why* groups make the decision to join in the battle. Since groups involved in confirmation fights use the same basic set of lobbying tactics (see, e.g., Caldeira, Hojnacki, and Wright 2000), this suggests that the crucial question is not what groups do once they join the fight but rather how they decide whether to become involved in the first place. This chapter seeks to answer this question by identifying the factors groups weigh when deciding whether to oppose a particular nominee.

Interest Groups in Judicial Selection Politics

The decision to object to a nomination is comprised of several important steps. First, groups must decide whether they wish to take part in the issue of judicial selection at all. Even with the increased scrutiny given to lower court selection in recent years, and judicial selection in general, most groups do not focus on this issue. This is not to suggest that these groups do not care about who sits on the federal courts but rather that they may feel their interests are best served by focusing their attention and resources elsewhere. Many groups focus primarily on policy development and on electing like-minded representatives, goals that can be realized fairly expeditiously. Comparatively, judicial selection is a more difficult issue to prioritize, for the potential gains and harms are much more abstract, indeterminate, and long term. As Nan Aron explained in a 2002 interview, "The fact is that most Americans have no interest and almost no knowledge about what judges do." Similarly, conservative activist Tom Jipping (2002b) stated, "To the extent that there is either a lack of understanding or a misunderstanding, among many of your activists, you may have a big education effort to go through, to get things straight. Frankly, a lot of conservatives, pro-life people and so on, mistake or misperceive what judges are supposed to do."

While group leaders may recognize the importance of judicial rulings on the issues their group supports, convincing their members to focus attention on the issue of judicial selection is difficult. In the same interview, Jipping stated, "Conservatives have an indirect relationship with the courts; we get our stuff primarily from legislatures and we just want courts to respect that. So simply the introduction of an additional step complicates [the process of convincing conservatives to pay attention to judicial selection]."

The creation of judicial watchdog umbrella groups is one solution to this problem. Umbrella groups such as Alliance for Justice (AFJ) on the left and the Judicial Selection Monitoring Program (JSMP) on the right focus almost exclusively on vetting judicial nominees. These umbrella groups represent literally hundreds of other, like-minded groups on the issue of judicial selection. Joining such an umbrella group offers smaller or more focused groups the ability to have a say in judicial selection without having to devote their own resources to this cause and away from other priorities.[4]

One exception to the question of whether a group's members understand the importance of judicial selection concerns those interested in the issue of abortion. These activists recognize that the battle over abortion rights is concentrated primarily in the courts. Elizabeth Cavendish of NARAL explained, "There's a real recognition that lower court judges hold vast power over women's reproductive lives" (2002). Similarly, Jipping, who at the time of the interview worked for Concerned Women for America (CWA), a conservative pro-family organization, commented, "People do have a general sense that in any of the cultural issues that we're concerned about, the damaging things that have happened from our point of view, have happened from the courts" (2002b).[5] However, these groups focus solely on these issues; in other words, they care only about how judges will rule on abortion. Their participation in judicial selection is limited, if not absent, when the issue of interest is not in play.

Thus, while interest in federal judicial selection is certainly increasing, the number of groups actively involved in lower court selection at present is quite small: the high hurdle to participation and the need to first explain why this issue even matters result in a few select groups on each side of the aisle leading the charge and conducting the bulk of the research presented to senators (discussed in chapter 4).

Once groups decide to pay attention to the issue of judicial selection, they must sift through the dozens of nominations pending at any one time and decide whether each nominee is acceptable or potentially problematic. Groups actively involved in monitoring lower court selection spend a great deal of time researching nominees, especially nominees to the circuit courts. This research allows the groups to assess each nominee. As Nan Aron of the AJF explained, "The most important thing we do here is review the record. . . . We pull out our full arsenal of research people here to basically gather as much information as we can to inform us and the Senate Judiciary Committee about these individuals. That is the most important piece of the process" (2002). Similarly, Tom Jipping (2002b) noted that "the Administration, the White House and the Department of Justice have lots and lots of money and lots and lots of people to do lots and lots of dealing. But when you're in opposition . . . you really are dealing with senators who have staffs that are stretched," so information about nominees becomes extremely important. Aron and others acknowledged, however, that they lack the resources to research every district court nominee. And since most groups are informally aligned with a particular political party, they generally do not research nominees when that party occupies the White House.

Different types of groups focus on gathering different types of information. The AJF, an umbrella group, reviews circuit court nominees' records; its staff reads any published opinions, articles, or speeches by the nominees and interviews lawyers who have worked with them. On the other hand, CWA, a membership group, relies on its members to identify nominees requiring a close vetting: "One of the benefits of a membership organization, we have a lot of people on the ground, and so you have people in the states, in these cities, in the areas where these nominees are from, people who know a lot about their background, who may know the things that they've done" (Jipping 2002b). Groups also gather information on the political implications of nominations. Since many of these groups work in coalitions with other groups, the various types of groups share information with each other. Based on the full range of information available to them, groups then determine whether they believe a nominee is potentially problematic, in terms of either the nominee's record or the groups' long-range policy goals. Only after groups have determined that a nominee is potentially problematic do they take the final step of deciding whether to publicly oppose the nominee.

Only one previous study investigates the decision by interest groups to publicly target a nominee for defeat. Through interviews with interest group leaders, Scherer (2003) finds that groups consider four factors in determining whom they will target: the nominee's ideology; whether the nominee has a detailed written record; for liberal groups, how recently they waged another confirmation fight; and the ideological balance of the circuit court where the vacancy exists. Unsurprisingly, the group leaders interviewed all noted that divided government makes the decision to oppose easier. Finally, these interest groups all agreed they had to pick their battles carefully, so the four factors enumerated by Scherer help groups determine which battles are necessary.

Still to be illuminated is the full range of considerations interest groups must weigh when deciding whom to target, and in particular the political, institutional, and environmental factors they must assess. The decision to oppose is multifaceted, and groups must be aware of how opposing a certain nominee affects them and other important actors in the process. In particular, the decisive player in the lower court confirmation process is the Senate. Accordingly, groups cannot defeat a nominee alone; instead, they must convince like-minded senators to join the fight and agree either to delay the nomination or to vote against it in committee or on the Senate floor. Without this crucial senatorial support, the nominee will be confirmed, and most likely confirmed easily. In essence, groups need to be "Senate specialists" in that they must understand how Senate norms and senators' personal relationships potentially influence each nomination. I therefore focus on identifying the totality of factors groups must be cognizant of when making the decision to object. Specifically, this chapter investigates five categories of factors interest groups must consider when determining whether to object to a nominee. In descending order of importance, these are (1) nominee-based factors, (2) nomination-based factors,[6] (3) interest group–based factors, (4) senator-based factors, and (5) factors related to the temporal political environment. My analysis recognizes that these factors are interrelated, and their relative importance may rise or fall when weighed by different groups. Finally, this assessment highlights the relative costs each factor has on the price a group pays to fight a particular nomination.

Because the decision to object reveals important information about interest groups more broadly, I explore whether different types of groups weigh different factors when deciding whom to oppose, and whether liberal and conservative groups consider separate factors when making these decisions. Given that different types of groups have distinct goals and represent divergent constituencies, it is likely that they also differ in their calculations when deciding whether to oppose a nominee. For example, do single-issue groups weigh the same factors as more broad-based interest groups? Does a group such as NARAL, which is concerned solely with the issue of reproductive rights, make the decision to oppose a judicial nominee in the same way as groups like the National Organization for Women (NOW) or CWA, which speak on numerous women's issues? Similarly, do issue groups and membership groups rely on the same decision calculi as umbrella groups? It is also likely that liberal groups may weigh certain factors more than conservative groups, and vice versa. As we saw in chapter 4, liberal groups play more of an information-transmission role, while conservative groups focus on public relations. These role differences may mean these groups also differ in how they make the decision to oppose a particular nominee and in what factors they consider.

Investigating the Decision to Oppose

To answer these questions, I interviewed the leaders of those interest groups on the left and the right most consistently involved in the current lower federal court selection process.[7] While the current process is marked by a high level of group activity, that activity is, for the most part, limited to a few groups. Through a comprehensive set of searches of newspaper archives, I identified the leading groups on the issue of lower court confirmations (see appendix A for more detail about the search methodology). I then interviewed the leaders of these groups. The groups represented here reflect those most often cited on the issue of lower court selection between 1985 and 2002.[8] I interviewed the following six people during the summer of 2002: on the right, Thomas Jipping, former head of the JSMP and then legal director for CWA;[9] and the then head of a leading conservative group, who asked not to be identified ("Conservative Activist"); on the left, Kim Gandy, then president of NOW; Nan Aron, president of the AFJ; Ralph Neas, former executive director of the Leadership Conference on Civil Rights (LCCR) and then president of the People for the American Way (PFAW); and Elizabeth Cavendish, then legal director of NARAL Pro-Choice America.[10] AFJ and PFAW on the left and JSMP on the right are large umbrella organizations that act on behalf of smaller groups on the issue of federal judicial selection. AFJ and PFAW are active on the issues of civil rights and women's rights and devote much of their attention to monitoring judicial confirmations. JSMP is part of the Free Congress Foundation, a leading conservative organization, and acts on behalf of more than 700 grassroots organizations solely on the issue of judicial selection. NOW on the left and CWA on the right are multi-issue membership groups active on the issue of judicial selection, and both these organizations pay particular attention to women's issues, family values, and abortion. Finally, NARAL is a single-issue abortion rights membership group. NOW, CWA, and NARAL work in concert with the leading umbrella groups, and they actively engage in judicial selection politics on their own as well. The interviews were conducted in Washington, D.C., between June and

August 2002, and each lasted between one-half hour and two hours, with most lasting approximately one hour.

The overarching question addressed in these interviews was how each interest group makes the decision to oppose a certain nominee. During the summer of 2002, liberal groups were on the offensive and conservative groups were working to support challenged nominees. Thus, I encouraged the conservative activists to talk about actions taken during the Clinton administration and actions they planned to take during a future Democratic administration.

The Meaning of an Interest Group Objection

Before assessing the specific factors groups consider, it is necessary to understand what the decision to object entails. Most notably, groups do not simply announce opposition to nominees; rather, a decision to object means the group will launch a campaign to try to defeat the nominee, decisively sending the nomination down the public partisan track. As Nan Aron explained, "We won't engage an extensive grassroots operation unless we have decided that there's a nominee we want to defeat." Even if groups dislike every nominee proposed by a particular president, they cannot expend the precious political capital—in terms of resources and reputation—necessary to fight every single nominee. To preserve limited resources, groups carefully choose which nominees they will actively oppose. The Conservative Activist explained, "It is a matter of strategy, of being practical, [of asking,] is it really worth it to go after this person, is it really worth it to go after that person? Is the person really worth going after anyway?" Similarly, Aron commented, "Obviously, just like everything else, we have to pick our battles and figure out which are the ones that we can engage the public [on] around a very high visibility discussion of a judicial nominee." The decision to object thus reflects a highly strategic decision about which nominees are the "most" problematic and the "most" important to defeat.

The crucial decision groups must make is thus not *whether to get involved* in a nomination fight, including in support of a nominee, but rather *whether to oppose* a particular nominee. Since nominees are usually confirmed easily to the lower courts, groups become involved in supporting a nomination only if it runs into trouble: "Well, that's determined by the opposition, not by the support. . . . Fights are determined by whether there's an opponent. . . . You don't need to put resources into an effort where it's not needed" (Jipping 2002b). By opposing a nomination and sending it down the public partisan track, opposition groups force supportive groups to become involved and expend precious resources.[11]

Moreover, groups may view many nominees as objectionable, but, given the costs of a public confirmation fight in terms of resources and political capital consumed, the decision to oppose a nominee reflects a high level of opposition. As discussed in chapter 4, groups have a multitude of lobbying strategies open to them. Groups therefore must answer two key questions: (1) Do we object to this nominee? and (2) *How much* do we object to this nominee? As Elizabeth Cavendish explained, "When you think about opposition, it would be well to think about a continuum of releasing a fact sheet showing something dangerous, to how much lobbying we are doing and how much money we're putting into it in terms of mobilizing grassroots folks and time and reputation."

This chapter focuses on the decision to mount a full-fledged fight against a nominee, the highest degree of opposition possible, rather than merely a finding by an interest group that nominees or their positions are "troubling" or "concerning."[12] Groups may dislike many of a president's nominees, but they will do very little to try to defeat most of these nominees, as they recognize the nominees will likely be easily confirmed. As Kim Gandy noted, "Well, certainly we're not fighting all fifty-six of the nominees . . . and those are the ones that just fly right through. There's not really anything you can do about it."

When groups do engage in full-force confirmation fights, they have a variety of reasons for it. The primary motivation is to defeat disliked nominees, but groups also keep in mind farther-reaching objectives: "I think our challenge is figuring out how you come up with a principled response and address the vacancy crisis, but also address the reality of what the right is trying to do. And how, from our perspective, do you force [George W.] Bush to the bargaining table. And I think the best way is to defeat some of the right-wing nominees he's sent up there" (Neas). Likewise, Jipping (2002a) explained that confirmation fights help "create an environment in which the political cost of a confirmation fight has to be taken into account at the nomination phase. . . . That's why, for example, we were talking about what's the value if you can't defeat someone, what's the value of still having a fight. That's one of those impacts. You create a climate in which the controversial nominee is going to be fought." Thus, groups on both sides of the aisle argue that sometimes confirmation fights are needed to influence future nominations.

This widespread view reveals an interesting issue with respect to judicial confirmation politics. Rational political actors usually oppose a bill or nomination only if they believe they have a strong probability of winning, because losing hurts their ability to be seen as a credible threat in the future. However, all of the activists interviewed stressed that sometimes the fight itself is important, even if the fight fails.[13] Thus, other considerations besides winning may exist. There are two reasons why fights against judicial nominees may realize gains regardless of their outcomes. The first is that presidents overestimate the probability of losing. A senior official in the George W. Bush administration explained in an interview in July 2002, "We have to assume no nomination will get a pass, so we prepare for every single one." He continued, "For interest groups on both sides, it is in their best interest to fight to the death on judicial nominations, especially before an election, to invigorate the base and fund-raise." Presidents thus recognize that groups may want to elevate the stakes of a nomination in order achieve broader goals. Furthermore, since groups only oppose those nominees whom they regard as most egregious, and since groups have successfully kept objectionable nominees off the federal bench, presidents must assume the opposition can gain broad public support and win.

A second reason why even unsuccessful fights against a nomination may realize important gains is that the fight itself is extremely costly, and so presidents attempt to mitigate the possibility of future fights. Presidents enjoy a limited amount of political capital, and fights over judicial nominees divert resources from other priorities. Because presidents want to see their policy goals enacted and need senatorial (and possibly interest group) support to do so, groups recognize that even the threat of a fight can lead to changes at the nomination and confirmation stages.[14] As Cavendish explained, "a strong [floor] vote [is] . . . part of the Washington world show of strength." Groups therefore sometimes launch a fight even when they know they will lose, as a way to force the president to the bargaining table. Groups recognize, however, that they cannot fight every nominee. How do groups make the essential decision of whom to oppose?

Making the Decision to Object: The Five Primary Factors

Several factors aid groups in distinguishing among the numerous nominations made every congressional term. These factors help groups decide which nominees are the "worst," and they also aid groups in weighing the costs and benefits of launching particular fights. The five categories of factors are (1) nominee-based factors, (2) nomination-based factors, (3) interest group–based factors, (4) senator-based factors, and (5) factors related to the temporal political environment. Different groups may weight these factors differently, based on their organizational missions and primary objectives.

NOMINEE-BASED FACTORS

All groups first consider factors related to the particular nominee, and these factors significantly influence groups' decision-making processes. Scherer (2003) discusses two such nominee-based factors, the nominee's ideology and the presence of a clear written record groups can rely on to prove the nominee is ideologically extreme. Groups must also be concerned with the following additional nominee-based factors: how "bad" the nominee is relative to other nominees, whether the nominee has personal ties to the Senate Judiciary Committee, and the character of the nominee's home-state support.

Not surprisingly, the most important factor groups rely on when determining which nominees to publicly oppose is the nominee's personal ideology or judicial philosophy. As discussed in chapter 4, groups first conduct research to determine the positions of each nominee and to help senators and their staffs begin to distinguish among the numerous nominations made every presidential term. Groups then oppose those nominees who hold the most extreme and troubling positions. As Elizabeth Cavendish noted, "There are times when a nominee is so outrageous right out of the box that it's not a lengthy process to decide to oppose. . . . Like Michael McConnell coming up, who's an academic with a very long record against *Roe v. Wade.* . . . Those [decisions] are really simple."

Most decisions are not so simple. Groups must judge whether they can prove to senators and the public that the nominee holds objectionable ideological positions. Thomas Jipping (2002b) explained, "We had to be able to articulate why we thought [the nominee] would be an activist judge. . . . And we had to be able to do so in writing. . . . Not just say it, but actually be able to articulate it. . . . You're sort of convinced in your gut that they're going to be an activist, but if you can't articulate it, if you can't put it in writing with a footnote or two or something like that, that's not credible."

Groups also need to be able make a strong case so they can commandeer crucial Senate support. As Jipping pointed out in the same interview, "Frankly, politically, United States Senators are not going to go out on a limb, unless you can give them something to work with, unless you can make a case." Similarly, Senator Howard Metzenbaum (2002) stated, "I think that if the XYZ group came in and said, 'We want you to be opposed to John Smith,' I think the first question any senator would say is 'Why?,' and they would have to justify their position. If they just said, 'Well, a lot of us just don't like him,' that would go out the window, that wouldn't fly." Groups must convince senators to vote against the nominee; otherwise the campaign will fail, and the nominee will be confirmed.

A key factor, therefore, is whether the nominee has a clear record that showcases his or her positions on controversial issues. "If we can't substantiate it, then we don't pursue it. But if it's something that can be substantiated, and it looks credible to use, then we pursue it, and see if it can be substantiated" (Gandy). If a nominee has not served as a judge or a law professor, two activities that usually produce extensive written records,[15] groups look to other aspects of a person's record: "You take people's record as you find it. You look at what's there to see whether it helps you answer the same question [of whether they hold extreme positions]. . . . Not the fact that they did public interest pro bono work, but what kind of cases did they choose to do? What kinds of arguments did they make? . . . Different people's records, depending on what people have done previously. You sift through what's there, but the question you're trying to answer is always the same" (Jipping 2002a).

Groups must therefore devote valuable resources to determining a nominee's positions and to proving to the other major players in the judicial confirmation process that these positions are so problematic as to deny the nominee confirmation. In light of this reality, another crucial factor arises: how bad the nominee is in relation to the other nominees.

Since groups know they cannot fight every nominee owing to limited resources and the traditional deference given to the president's nominees, they go after only the "worst" nominees. As the Conservative Activist stated, "You don't just blindly go after somebody, not just because they are nominated by Clinton. Presidents should still be able to get nominations through. . . . We would pick who we thought were probably the worst cases and try to mount some opposition. . . . It boils down to the decision is this worth it, is this person's record bad enough. Is this really something we should worry about or not?" Similarly, Gandy explained that NOW opposes only "whenever there's [a nominee] coming up that we think is really bad."

Groups must therefore be concerned with how the disliked nominee compares to the overall field of nominees, and they must gauge whether the fight is necessary or desirable. As the comments reproduced above emphasize, ideology is extremely important but not necessarily the sole determinant of whether a nominee will be opposed. Some major issues confront groups as they survey the field of judicial nominees. On the one hand, a nominee's ideology is not always easy to determine or show conclusively: "I'm confident that [all of George W. Bush's nominees are] bad, but most of them are really unknown. . . . We don't even know that we're not pleased with them. We don't know anything about them" (Gandy). The ability to prove a nominee's positions becomes paramount to a successful opposition. On the other hand, the sheer number of lower court nominees and the pressure on the committee to move nominees quickly can hamper efforts to learn about a nominee's positions, as Gandy's comments suggest.

Since groups are likely to dislike any nominee selected by an opposition president, much of their decision to oppose rests on other institutional and environmental factors that help groups distinguish between nominees and weigh the importance of the nomination against the costs of waging a fight. The first additional nominee-based factor that groups must weigh concerns the nominee's personal ties to the Judiciary Committee. A personal tie to the committee helps nominees by shielding them from opposition and increasing the costs of a fight. Nominees who have worked for the committee are known personally to the senators on the committee and are likely to have established good relationships with senators on both sides of the aisle. For example, Elizabeth Cavendish noted that Dennis Shedd was protected thanks to his previous job working for committee member Strom Thurmond: "It's certainly true with Shedd. That's where we really had a strong sense the fix was in. And Sharon Prost, who was Hatch's staffer on the Federal Circuit."[16] Having worked for the committee thus translates into strong personal ties, an advantage that is difficult for interest groups to overcome.

The second additional nominee-based factor concerns the nominee's home-state support. For some nominees, their connection to particular home-state senators affords them a greater chance of being confirmed, given the long-standing norms of senatorial collegiality and deference. Groups on both sides of the aisle recognize that while senators may hesitate to vote against a president's nominees, they may, in fact, be more worried about offending their Senate colleagues.

A number of activists on both sides emphasized that which senators support a nominee may heavily influence whether they will attack that nominee. This issue plays out in two ways: whether a fellow partisan supports the nominee and whether the nominee or home-state senators have ties to the Judiciary Committee. The first key issue is whether a Republican appointee has Democratic home-state support, and vice versa: "[The decision to oppose] very much depends on a whole range of factors. Who the nominator is. Who the senators are. . . . And [a supportive Democratic home-state senator] is a factor that we take into account" (Aron). Groups must therefore be wary of opposing such nominees. Groups do not want to undermine their claim that they only go after the most egregious nominees. Home-state support from a fellow partisan decreases the likelihood that groups can easily claim the nominee is "outside the mainstream." Kim Gandy explained how Democratic home-state support for Dennis Shedd muted NOW's ability to oppose him: "He's Hollings's guy. He's definitely a darling of the right wing. But Hollings is a Democratic Senator. [Shedd is] sponsored by both senators; one of them is a Democrat. Which makes it really, really difficult to do anything."

Additionally, senatorial collegiality plays a large role in judicial confirmation politics. Senators serve for six-year terms, and turnover in the Senate is lower than in the House; as a result, a norm of collegiality characterizes Senate relationships. Groups recognize that senators are more likely to listen to a personal appeal from a fellow colleague, even one from the opposite side of the aisle, than an attack by an outside group when determining how to vote. As Jipping (2002b) explained, "They all know each other . . . [and may give] in to the collegiality."

Groups also do not want to jeopardize future relationships with these senators. Groups that also actively pursue legislative agendas might need to call on these same senators to support or oppose bills related to the group's mission. While AFJ and JSMP are mainly judicial watchdog groups, issue-oriented groups such as NOW, NARAL, and CWA concurrently lobby senators on dozens of bills every congressional term and rely on good relations with senators to ensure that their concerns are heard. In sum, while home-state support may not always deter groups from publicly opposing a nominee, it certainly influences their decision and may minimize their ability to mount a successful opposition.

Second, some nominees' home-state senators serve on the Judiciary Committee. Because the fate of a nomination is often decided in committee rather than on the floor, groups believe home-state support on the committee provides a critical form of protection for nominees. This is so because collegial deference is the norm, and this deference is heightened by the fact that many of the committee members have worked together for decades and have developed strong relationships that transcend party lines. Nan Aron argued that D. Brooks Smith passed rather easily through the committee since he "was being strongly pushed by a powerful member of the Judiciary Committee," Republican moderate Arlen Specter.[17] Similarly, Ralph Neas acknowledged that "Senator Specter did a good job, and then they did a very fine grass-tops[18] strategy. . . . They did a great job of lobbying the Democratic members of the Judiciary Committee" in support of Smith. In Smith's case, not only did his home-state senator serve on the committee, his home-state senator was of one of the most respected moderates on the committee and in the Senate overall. On the conservative side, Tom Jipping (2002b) also noted the value of a Judiciary Committee patron: "It is critical for a controversial nominee; they have to have a patron. And they have to have not just someone who, in the case of Trent Lott, sends the name to the White House but someone who, [as] Jack Danforth did for Clarence Thomas, . . . will fight for the nominee, and [as] Specter, at a different level, did for [D. Brooks] Smith." In sum, groups all cited the importance of nominee ties to the committee and how such ties may undercut their ability to wage a successful confirmation fight.

NOMINATION-BASED FACTORS

Beyond factors related to the specific nominee, other institutional, political, and environmental issues also greatly influence groups' decision calculi. Three important factors about the nomination itself, rather than the actual nominee, also affect interest group decisions about whom to oppose. Scherer (2003) highlights the ideological balance of the circuit court on which the vacancy occurs, as well as the ideology of the states within that circuit. The third factor concerns whether the nomination was made as part of a trade.

Groups' analysis of the vacancy itself transmits valuable information to senators about the institutional importance of the nomination. As a result of the current ideological balance of a circuit court, certain vacancies might be more important than others. For example, many noted the close ideological divides on the Sixth Circuit and the D.C. Circuit during George W. Bush's first term (Berg 2003; Horn 2003; Maltzman and Binder 2000; Perine 2003). As a result, even one appointment may tip the ideological balance of these courts and thus the courts' decisions on important social and political issues.

Similarly, groups with concerns about particular issues identify certain states as key battlegrounds. For example, groups active on reproductive rights contend that certain states are more likely to pass laws limiting access to abortion. Appointments to the circuits that include these states may therefore have more of an impact because of the abortion cases these judges likely will hear. NARAL is particularly concerned about nominations to the Fifth Circuit, which represents three Deep South states—Texas, Louisiana, and Mississippi—NARAL believes are the most likely to pass restrictive abortion laws (Scherer 2003, 248). These groups closely monitor circuit court appointments, since the Supreme Court has reduced its caseload and increasingly left the final decisions on issues such as abortion to the circuit courts: "For the vast majority of important cases . . . literally 99 percent of them stop at [the circuit court] level. It's the court of last resort for 99 percent of the cases" (Gandy). Likewise, conservative groups focus on the liberal leanings of the Ninth Circuit and nominees from California.[19] Even if the actual nominee is not necessarily "the worst," nominees to these circuits are scrutinized more intensely than nominees to other circuits, and groups are more likely to mount attacks against nominees to these circuits.

A final, and additional, factor about the nomination itself that groups must consider is whether the nomination was made as a part of a trade. As chapter 3 showed, judicial nominations have become part of the normal politics that characterize the modern legislative process. A key component of the passage of legislation is the intense bargaining and negotiations necessary to create a bill that can garner bipartisan (or complete party unity) support in order to secure the required number of votes for passage. Such a bill may include provisions added to win crucial votes, including amendments that may mitigate the bill's impact or are unrelated to the main point of the bill. Similarly, the confirmation of judicial nominees is often the result of negotiation and compromise. It has become increasingly difficult for a president's nominees to move successfully through the judicial confirmation process (Hartley and Holmes 1997, 2002). Presidents and opposition senators may therefore enter into trades whereby a senator's favored candidate is nominated in return for the senator supporting some number of the president's nominees. Such trades can create a problem for groups aligned with the president's party, as they must decide whether to support the trade (and the guaranteed confirmation of nominees they support) or rally against a disliked compromise nominee. For example, Senator Slade Gorton blocked certain Clinton nominees during the 106th Congress until Clinton nominated his choice for a vacant Ninth Circuit seat. Liberal groups had to decide whether to support the trade, allowing stalled Clinton nominees to be confirmed, or oppose the trade, given their dislike of Gorton's choice, Barbara Durham.

One option is for groups to oppose just the disliked nominee; another option is to oppose the trade itself. Groups on both sides of the aisle expressed their general dismay over such trades. As Jipping (2002b) remarked, "I would rather the president get more vocal and more public about illegitimate tactics by the opposition, than a backroom deal that lets some nominations go forward." He said the following about the Durham deal in the same interview: "I don't like deals. I don't think that's a good way to pick judges because it ends up distracting from the central criterion. But also, the Republicans are notoriously bad dealers, and [Durham] is a great example. They didn't even end up with Barbara Durham.[20] . . . They were practically throwing nominees [at the Democrats]." Similarly, Cavendish said, in relation to a deal Clinton made with Senator Orrin Hatch, "There was a District Court nominee to Utah, Ted Stewart, and we made calls to the White House and made a bit of a fuss. We didn't put a huge amount of resources into it because the fix was in." NARAL recognized that the cost of fighting Hatch's choice outweighed the benefits of confirming a large group of Clinton nominees. And with a Republican Senate, NARAL's fighting the trade nominee was likely to be "a sure loss" and thus not worth expending the group's valuable resources.

Other activists acknowledged that trades are sometimes a necessary part of the process: "Oftentimes we'll oppose [the nominee] because that's what people count on us doing. But we also know that we won't be an obstacle to the possibility of a trade taking place. In fact, people might be relying on us to oppose a candidate to set up the trade" (Aron). The increasing politicization of the confirmation process means presidents and home-state senators look for ways to get their nominees confirmed, and activists also recognize that confirming like-minded nominees is crucial to their broader agendas.

INTEREST GROUP–BASED FACTORS

Beyond the important nominee- and nomination-based factors groups assess, interest groups must also look inward. When determining whether to publicly object to a particular nominee, groups must pay attention to key factors about their own organizations. Put simply, groups differ widely: some groups focus on a single issue, while others have a broad mission; some groups represent other groups, while others represent mobilized citizens. These variations not only affect how groups operate in general, but also influence the types of nomination fights each group may join. The internal factors groups must consider include their available resources, the likelihood of a coalition-led fight, and their organizational structures and missions.

First, an interest group must consider whether it has the resources needed to fight the proposed confirmation battle. Each group has a different perspective as to how many battles it can wage. As Elizabeth Cavendish of NARAL explained, "Interest groups with limited resources need to find those battles where there are enough persuadables that you can actually win. If it's a sure loss. . . ." For many groups, resource levels matter. Smaller, less well-financed groups must pick and choose their battles carefully. As the Cavendish quotation suggests, groups want to be sure their efforts will pay off.

Other groups, however, argue the egregiousness of the nominee outweighs the need to preserve resources. The Conservative Activist commented, "I think that it is a practical decision, but it is not just dictated by resources because . . . if we know about the person's record, we are still going to take steps, no matter what." The Conservative Activist also pointed out that his group opposed very few nominees during Clinton's two terms of office.[21] NOW's Kim Gandy similarly stated, "We do them all. Every single one. I think we're the only organization that does that, and we have a constant argument with our allies because they say, 'Well we have to target, we can't take on every nominee. We can just take on the worst ones.' And we're always saying, 'Well, of course, we can take on every nominee that's bad. How can we not. How can we say, here are six really bad nominees, and we're going to let three go through.' And so we just do them all."[22] However, Gandy was referring specifically to circuit court nominees. In reference to district court nominees, she said that even at the level of conducting research, "If we find that somebody really terrible is being nominated to any position, an appointed position, then we'll get involved. But we don't have the staffing to do them all." In other words, internal resource constraints matter.

Group resource concerns are somewhat mitigated if groups can form a coalition, the second internal factor groups consider: "We look at factors like is there going to be a good coalition to mount a coalition effort so that this is a winnable fight . . . where there could be a coalition if someone is consistently bad in his ruling or his or her practice and philosophy across a range of issues, or at least a significant number of issues where you can get people mobilized" (Cavendish). Gandy similarly commented that collaboration is "a huge part of it in many ways, because none of us has enough resources to do it on our own." Even though NOW says it will oppose every circuit court nominee it finds objectionable, this decision becomes much easier when other groups join the fight.

Coalition efforts not only solve resource constraint problems for individual groups, they also help groups mount a more successful campaign. A coalition fight allows each group to expend less of its own resources and decreases the cost of joining certain fights. Coalition efforts are especially attractive to smaller, less well-financed groups as they can then oppose the nominee without having to expend precious resources on the fight. Groups especially favor coalitions when they want to focus their resources on defeating other nominees. Cavendish explained, "We did fairly little on D. Brooks Smith. The coalition made a big effort on Brooks Smith. We participated, but it wasn't [for us] an all-out fight to the end." Coalitions also help single-issue groups gain more traction in the debate while allowing them to stay true to their missions: a nominee who can be opposed on many levels rather than on just one issue is more likely to draw crucial Senate opposition. Finally, coalition fights are more likely to win. A broad coalition increases the intensity of the opposition, and a coalition effort suggests the opposition to the particular nominee is widespread. For example, many argued that the broad coalition opposed to Robert Bork's nomination was the key to his eventual defeat (Bronner 1989; Pertschuk and Schaetzel 1989). A coalition fight allows more groups to participate by decreasing the costs for each group and by increasing the likelihood of success, as a coalition fight is more likely to win than an attack by only one or two groups.

Finally, groups must consider factors related to their organizational structure and mission. In particular, whether a group is an umbrella group, an issue group, or a membership group affects how each group makes the decision to oppose a particular nominee. Umbrella groups act as a formal coalition of different groups on a particular issue and speak on behalf of their member groups. Before taking positions on each nominee, umbrella groups must determine whether the groups they represent agree with the proposed position. Nan Aron explained, "When we issue a report or take a position on a particular nominee, we check with our members and solicit their views on what we should do. Obviously, if we are not in sync with our members, then we will not go forward and take a public position."

Umbrella groups must also tread carefully when there exists disagreement among the member groups. For example, the AFJ was very careful during Clarence Thomas's confirmation to "very publicly [indicate] on all of our press releases, reports, memoranda to the Hill, that several members, and we named them, were not in agreement with us" (Aron). Thomas Jipping (2002b) presented a similar picture of how the conservative JSMP operates: "When we did choose a nominee to formally oppose, we would draft a letter, circulate it to all of those groups, asking for their signature . . . We weren't specifically speaking for anybody, because we didn't want to do that." Umbrella groups must also be cognizant of not unilaterally making decisions for their members: "A lot of [our members] would not be comfortable with us telling them what to do" (Conservative Activist). Large umbrella organizations must therefore carefully balance the views of the activists in Washington with the concerns and positions of the groups they represent. This requirement may cause umbrella groups to stay out of certain fights or, as in the case of the AFJ's opposition to Clarence Thomas, to stipulate carefully who stands with them. In the latter cases, such divergent views can hurt a group's position, as the power of umbrella groups is their ability to speak for the many and present a coalition of opposition from the outset.

Issue-oriented groups, on the other hand, and especially single-issue groups, emphasize the need to stay close to their group's mission: "A group like NARAL really has to stick to its mission strongly. You'll notice that we're not opposing any of the people whose record is silent on choice" (Cavendish). Cavendish explained that NARAL did not oppose Jeffrey Sutton or Miguel Estrada as neither had a clear record on choice, even though NARAL members may have disliked other positions they held. Multi-issue groups have more leeway, but they must still show the nominee is extreme in relation to the issues they care about. Umbrella groups such as the AFJ recognize the constraints facing issue groups: "And there are some groups, obviously the choice groups, who will only look at issues related to choice" when deciding whether to join a particular fight (Aron). Issue groups must show that the nominee in question has articulated a questionable position on the specific issues of importance to them; otherwise, these groups stay silent in order to protect their organizational missions.

This requirement can also create an interesting counter-problem. Thomas Jipping, who at the time was legal director of CWA (2002b), expressed his concern that many of CWA's members focused too much on nominees' issue positions rather than on the broader question of whether the nominees would be activist judges: "Frankly, a lot of conservatives, pro-life people, and so on mistake or misperceive what judges are supposed to do. You find them saying, 'We want a pro-life justice.' . . . 'We want a justice for the conservative ideology.' . . . It's a more poignant challenge in a membership organization." He recounted a conference call about the Priscilla Owen nomination with other issue groups: "I was on a conference call with a number of conservative activists around the country. . . . And the state pro-life leaders were saying, 'What's her position on abortion?' And you try to explain, 'Look, she's not running for the legislature, she's a judge, and so her position on abortion is irrelevant.' And they're like, 'No, really, what's her position on abortion?' "

Jipping's comments highlight an additional concern for membership groups: whether their grassroots members will support the fight. Groups that rely on their ability to mobilize grassroots activists to persuade senators of the benefits of supporting their causes must first convince their members that the targeted nominee is worth the effort. Alternatively, group leaders without such active grassroots memberships have more freedom to decide whether to oppose a nominee. Since many membership groups are also issue-oriented groups, their leaders must frame their concerns about a nominee in terms amenable to their members. Thus, as Jipping noted in relation to CWA, since this group focuses heavily on abortion, its members want to know where the nominees stand on the issue of abortion. Without such information, these members may refuse to engage in the grassroots activities that give these groups their clout in the political process.[23]

Overall, groups must pay attention to how their decision will affect the group itself. Resource constraints and the need to protect the group's mission weigh heavily on groups' decision calculi. Coalitions and umbrella groups must ensure their member groups are in agreement before proceeding. Issue groups must not only show that a nominee holds extreme views but also prove that the nominee holds these views on their issues of interest. These calculations mean groups may sit on the sidelines if their opposition may in other ways harm the group itself or undercut its mission. As a result, understanding the role of interest groups in judicial selection also means understanding the influence of internal group characteristics and structure on groups' decisions and actions.

SENATOR-BASED FACTORS

Two senatorial factors also affect groups' decisions. The first factor is whether a nominee has strong home-state support. As discussed under nominee-based factors, strong home-state senatorial support can undermine a group's efforts and significantly raise the cost of a fight; this is especially true when a fellow partisan supports the nomination. Second, groups must also consider whether senators, particularly those on the Judiciary Committee, are willing to take up the fight and actually *oppose* the nominee. As Shapiro (1990) argues, groups recognize that a fight against a nominee is only as strong as the number of senators who are willing to join the battle. Thus, while group objections turn a nomination down the public partisan track, the ultimate outcome of the nomination depends on the actions of senators.

Groups need to determine whether senators will join the fight: "A lot of it is, is this someone we can actually get Republicans or Democrats persuaded on" (Conservative Activist). Senatorial disinterest provides an extremely strong deterrent against group fights. Senators may not be persuaded by the groups' arguments, or the senators themselves may be wary of launching a fight. Cavendish explained, "Did we just wage a huge fight? What's the mood of the Senators? . . . Do we need a few non-controversials between fights? Factors like that can go into [the decision], too" (see also Scherer 2003, 2005). Similarly, many group leaders voiced frustration that senators are unwilling to challenge nominees: "I think it's an obstacle that senators think and know these guys are bad but won't vote against them because there's no political price to be paid for it. . . . And they feel very deferential to presidential nominees" (Cavendish). Groups recognize that senators traditionally defer to a president's lower court nominees; only recently have senators been willing to closely vet lower court nominees on grounds other than qualifications or ethical complaints.[24] Cavendish also stated her belief that certain senators have "a pretty deep pocket full of no votes that they can use whenever without paying a political, collegial price, and the others have some sort of mental quota about how many they can vote against, and they're assessing 'Is this one of the worst ones, what do I gain, what do I lose by opposing?' And it may relate to collegiality as well as the merits of that particular nominee. Who wants this person?" Gandy likewise commented, "What [senators] keep saying is that they're under terrible pressure. They're under terrible pressure" to vote for a president's (and certain friendly senators') nominees.

Similarly, the Conservative Activist explained that his group wants "Republicans to begin taking this [issue] more seriously." He lamented that Republicans were not overly willing to fight a judicial nomination battle, and in fact, most of the Clinton nominees who drew objections were eventually confirmed. Thomas Jipping (2002b) had this to say about Republican opposition to Clinton's nominees: "No Republican senator opposed more than about 8–9 percent of President Clinton's nominees. No senator, no Jesse Helms, not anybody. So, every senator was at least

90 percent deferential to the president." In the same interview, Jipping complained about the lack of support for George W. Bush's stalled nominees: "Where have the floor speeches been? . . . Where have those Republican senators been? They've been AWOL." He acknowledged senators were beginning to pay attention to Miguel Estrada's nomination, but also noted that "very few" senators not on the Judiciary Committee cared about nominations other than those from their own state (Jipping 2002b). Groups must ensure they garner the necessary senatorial support to defeat the opposed nominees and do not waste the political capital senators are willing to expend on these confirmation fights.

Some activists suggested the issues surrounding the nomination may affect senators' willingness to join the fight. For example, Gandy believed the fight against Charles Pickering was successful because "the focus of the fight against Pickering was on race. The focus around D. Brooks Smith was around sex discrimination, and one's OK and one's not OK. Race discrimination is not OK. I think that Pickering didn't have a chance. Sex discrimination, unfortunately, is still OK. . . . It's not something the Democrats are going to get really up in arms about, and the Republicans know that. I think it's sad, but it's true." Alternatively, Jipping (2002b) highlighted the problems with a strict focus on abortion: "How do you get to 51 votes if the only thing anybody talks about is abortion? Not all Republican senators are pro-life. How do you get to 51?" Senatorial disinterest increases the amount of resources groups must expend. Groups also risk losing credibility if they pick fights with nominees other actors in the process support.

FACTORS RELATED TO THE TEMPORAL POLITICAL ENVIRONMENT

Finally, groups must assess the temporal political environment when deciding whom to oppose. The Conservative Activist explained, "Part of it is how good or bad [the nominees] are, and part of it would be the practical realities of the political situation. [The decision to oppose is] a kind of mix of those two things." Part of this "political situation" is whether the groups believe they can persuade senators to actively oppose the nominee. Persuading senators obviously becomes easier during divided government, when the opposition party can more easily win nomination fights. Two other political factors also influence groups' calculations. First, groups are wary of staging too many fights concurrently. Second, groups must consider the level of action the president is taking to defend his nominees.

Groups recognize that back-to-back battles may be politically precarious, especially as senators and groups both want to emphasize they are opposing only the most egregious nominees (Scherer 2003). Additionally, senators may be wary of future fights when previous fights produced extremely negative backlashes. Nan Aron explained that D. Brooks Smith's confirmation did not generate much senatorial opposition in part because "he came right after [Charles] Pickering. And after Pickering a lot of these Democrats went back to their states and received a lot of criticism generated by the White House. Edwards went back to North Carolina, and Karl Rove sent in money, battalions, generating negative press. Karl Rove did the same thing in Georgia [to Senator Max Cleland]. . . . It was interesting in Georgia, because Cleland doesn't sit on the Judiciary Committee. But it was a kind of a warning shot across the vote." Thus, while the Pickering fight was successful, for many senators the White House's response created an environment in which the next fight was more costly than usual. The concerted campaign in Georgia underscored the Bush (43) administration's stance: it would not sit idly by while its nominees were defeated, and it would pour considerable resources into criticizing senators who might oppose its nominees, even if they might be sympathetic to many other administration policies.

Consequently, as the above example underscores, a crucial component of the political environment is how hard the appointing president is willing to fight for his nominees. The president's degree of involvement affects the types of nominees he selects, the amount of resources he will expend to support his nominees, and the level of group activism needed to oppose nominees or to support beleaguered nominees. Liberal activists complained vigorously that Clinton did not strongly defend his judicial nominees. As Nan Aron commented, "Clinton wasn't all that interested in judgeships." In the same interview she lamented that he nominated moderates in an attempt to appease the Republican Senate: "He put on very moderate candidates. In fact, both his candidates to the Supreme Court were overwhelmingly endorsed by Orrin Hatch." Similarly, Ralph Neas had this to say when asked whether Clinton could have done more: "Yes. On two different levels. Number one, on the nominees themselves. Number two, you would probably find a consensus in the progressive community that the Clinton administration didn't accord the same priority to judicial nominations as has [the Bush (43)] administration— that is, fighting for them once they were blocked. . . . There were [some nominees] that were languishing for months and years, and the [Clinton] administration should've made a much bigger deal out of it." Many complained that Clinton capitulated on certain nominees. For example, it was widely noted that the nominations of Peter Edelman and Judith McConnell were scuttled owing to conservative reactions to their potential nominations (Acheson 2002).[25] Liberal groups were thus dissuaded from expending effort in support of nominees they believed the Clinton administration was unwilling to support.

Similarly, conservatives called the lack of presidential and senatorial support for George W. Bush's nominees "a failure of leadership by the administration and the Senate Republicans" (Jipping 2002b). Conservative group leaders expressed frustration that, by the summer of 2002, "There's not yet been a real meeting of the minds between the administration and the Senate Republicans as to whose job it really is to get the President's nominees confirmed" (Jipping 2002b). Jipping noted it took the Bush administration more than a year to react to Democratic opposition, and he had this to say about choosing one's fights: "There's also kind of an 'us versus them' perspective, in terms of the [Bush] administration and outside groups. 'We're us, you're them, we don't want to be perceived as messy and political and partisan and all this kind of stuff, so we are going to try to be above the fray.' . . . But I've got to get the job done [of confirming nominees], unfortunately. And the dynamic of the fight, and the job that's to be done, is defined by your opposition" (2002b).

The Influence of Group Characteristics on the Decision to Object: The Conundrum of Organizational Mission

The interviews thus illuminate five primary sets of factors groups consider when deciding whether to oppose a judicial nominee. The discussion above reveals important ways in which group characteristics influence group behavior. Perhaps most interesting, liberal and conservative groups do not seem to differ in how they make decisions. Even though liberal groups are more likely to focus on information gathering and conservative groups are more likely to engage in public relations campaigns, they all seem to rely on the same calculi when making the decision to become involved in a particular nomination in the first place. Rather, the differences revealed all link to the group's organizational structure and mission.

Put simply, the key differences are between umbrella groups and membership groups, and between multi-issue groups and single-issue groups. First, all groups must cater to their members and constituents, whether those members are other organized groups or mobilized citizens. This means that umbrella groups must ensure that their member groups agree with the umbrella group's positions. When disagreements exist, umbrella groups may choose to stay on the sidelines, or they may decide to carefully explicate who is with them and who is not. For example, many civil rights groups refused to oppose Clarence Thomas's nomination to the Supreme Court, so the leading liberal umbrella groups had to walk a careful line in explaining which of their members joined the opposition. The power of an umbrella group's objection may therefore be minimized, since its strength comes from its ability to speak for the many. This concern is magnified insofar as the two leading judicial watchdog umbrella groups, the AFJ and JSMP, respectively speak for basically all liberal and conservative groups active on the issue of judicial selection. Alternatively, membership groups must be careful to take positions their members support. Since membership groups draw power from their ability to mobilize their members and wage grassroots campaigns, membership groups must be sure their members will indeed join the fight.

This concern leads to the second key difference: issue groups must make sure their objections are related to their organization's central mission. As a result, the decision calculi differ for multi-issue groups as opposed to single-issue groups. Single-issue groups are especially concerned with sticking to their organizational mission. These groups must carefully cull nominees' records to see whether the nominee has taken a position on their issue of concern. If the nominee lacks a clear record on that issue, single-issue groups stay out of the fight, even when the nominee may hold views on other issues the group leaders are confident their members would dislike. For example, NARAL did not oppose Jeffrey Sutton's nomination during the 107th Congress. Sutton drew opposition from civil rights and disability activist groups, but his record did not clearly reveal how he might rule on abortion-related cases. Even though NARAL leaders assumed their members would also be opposed to a nominee who seemed hostile to the rights of the disabled, they declined to participate in the opposition to his nomination in order to stay loyal to their mission (Cavendish).

Multi-issue groups must also be concerned with their missions, but a broader set of goals gives them more ability to oppose a wide swath of nominees. Since NOW considers itself a "civil rights group," it is able to oppose nominees who do not have a specific record only on women's issues (Gandy). But even multi-issue membership groups must make sure they are taking positions their members support. Straying too far from the group's core concerns can cause members to leave the group or refuse to engage in the grassroots activities that give membership groups their power. Thus, while groups across the ideological and political spectrum generally weigh the same factors when assessing whether to oppose a particular nominee, important differences emerge when we look at groups in terms of their organizational structure and mission.

The question is whether the need for groups, especially issue groups, to stick to their core missions more broadly influences the lower court confirmation process. The interviews reveal that it does, in multiple ways. First, heightened activity by issue groups necessarily concentrates the discussion on a few core issues and on how nominees may rule on these core issues. As Jipping (2002b) explained, this focus can lead activists on both sides of the aisle to care more about a nominee's perceived view on *Roe v. Wade* rather than about the nominee's qualifications or potential to be an "activist" judge. It also means these groups launch more results-oriented campaigns. Groups focus on whether nominees will or will not possibly vote to overturn *Roe v. Wade,* or how they may vote in employment discrimination cases or cases about the death penalty, rather than whether the person is qualified. Not surprisingly, many of these issues resonate with voters and the media. As a result, battles over nominees frequently reduce to battles over how judges should rule in cases concerning abortion and the death penalty.

Second, since many of these issue groups have large and active memberships, senators must also be cognizant of how these issues will play with their constituents and mobilized party members. Scherer (2003, 2005) argues that senators listen to these groups because they bring considerable weight come election time. Membership groups can mobilize mass grassroots campaigns, raise money, turn out voters, and, in the end, influence senators' reelection chances. Cavendish explained, "[NARAL is] known for having really good lists and IDs of people who are pro-choice and who are willing to act on their beliefs that we can mobilize in a more targeted fashion . . . [through] campaigns that can generate really hundreds of thousands of calls." The leaders of these groups recognize their power: "NARAL is really powerful because we're a grassroots organization . . . Because they know we mobilize people at election time" (Cavendish 2002, quoted in Scherer 2005, 127). Similarly, Jipping (2002b) said this about the CWA: "We have almost 600,000 members. . . . We're able to take directly to the field . . . taking real action, doing real things." Jipping specifically mentioned that he can activate CWA's members to lobby their senators, and so CWA's main strength is its ability to mobilize these activists.

The conundrum is that many of these most mobilized voters and activists are motivated almost solely in response to a few issues. Senators on the Judiciary Committee must be mindful of this tension. As one Democratic committee staffer commented, "We have our institutional interest and [the groups] may have their institutional interest—say NARAL wants to stop every person that they even have an idea might be anti-choice. Well, that's fine, and their interest is in finding that out for every nominee. Well, that may not be my primary focus. So if they want to tell me about it, that's fine." Thus, senators who want to fight for "open-minded" judges or judges who will not "legislate from the bench" also have to be cognizant of how these issues play at home. When the bounty of calls and letters comes from groups who want judges with particular views on certain issues, it makes it very difficult for senators to focus on other issues.

In many ways, focusing on only one or two key issues is easier for senators. Resource constraints and a limited ability to find out about nominees means that clear evidence that a nominee is "problematic" on a particular issue provides important information for senators, especially senators not on the Judiciary Committee. While Jipping correctly noted that not all Republicans are pro-life or all Democrats pro-choice, it is also true that certain senators look for clear evidence of a nominee's position on *Roe* when making their decisions. Thus, a type of Catch-22 emerges: senators and group leaders want to evaluate nominees on whether they will be good judges, but such a determination is difficult and time-consuming. Instead, voters and group members often define a "good" judge as one who holds like-minded views on certain issues. Accordingly, groups with a central mission must vet judges in light of this mission in order to preserve the organization itself.

As a result, the current federal judicial confirmation process has become focused on the core issues that dominate political debates and play out in the judiciary as well. This landscape is unlikely to change soon. If national activists can indeed convince people to pay attention to the courts and who sits on the federal bench, it is likely that these citizens will also focus on the potential rulings of a nominee. This pattern is seen not only in the vetting of judges; American political debates and election fights are increasingly focused on particular issues as well. Whether a particular candidate for office is pro-choice or pro-life, supports the death penalty, or is a supporter of cutting taxes or of increased social welfare programs are the questions voters are most likely to ask. Issues drive American politics, and it is unsurprising that they drive assessments of judicial nominees as well. Since the way to convince citizens that courts matter is to show them the "dangers" of a "bad" judge, usually by bring-ing up specific rulings on specific issues, are we really surprised that sena-tors, activists, and citizens all want to know whether a judge will vote to uphold or overturn *Roe v. Wade*?

Conclusion

An interest group's decision to oppose a nomination, thereby send-ing it down the public partisan track, reflects a series of careful calcula-tions. Groups recognize they cannot attack every nominee and therefore must determine which nominees are worth the fight. Groups consider five categories of factors when making their decisions: nominee-based factors, nomination-based factors, interest group–based factors, senator-based factors, and factors relating to the temporal political environment. Of greatest importance are the nominee's ideological positions and other nominee-specific factors. Group objections also offer valuable cues about the importance of the nomination itself. Finally, groups must determine the cost of the fight to themselves and to like-minded senators. A costly fight is sometimes necessary, but groups are nothing if not pragmatic. In particular, the interviews reveal that if senators support the nominee, no matter how egregious, a confirmation fight may be more costly for the group than for the nominee or appointing president.

Interest group objections permanently divert a confirmation onto the public partisan track. Even though public partisan confirmations are relatively rare, they spark broad public attention and stimulate debates over key policy issues. But it is unclear what impact interest group objec-tions have on the outcome of opposed nominations. Do group objec-tions merely make a nominee's path to confirmation more contentious and costly, or do they translate decisively into a defeat for the nominee? More specifically, do senators heed the call of groups and vote against op-posed nominees? Scherer (2003) argues that groups are able to convince senators to oppose (and, by extension, vote against) nominees the groups find most egregious because of the electoral power these groups wield; when senators decline to listen to these groups, they run the risk that these same groups will oppose them when they are up for reelection. The question left to be investigated is how often senators in fact listen to the objections of like-minded groups and vote against opposed nominees. Simply put, do interest group objections matter? In chapter 6 I examine the impact of interest group objections on the ultimate fate of nominees in the Senate Judiciary Committee.

6

WHITHER NOMINEES?

The Fate of Nominations Sent down the Public Partisan Track

Chapters 4 and 5 outlined the important roles interest groups play in judicial confirmations. Chapter 4, based on interviews with Senate staff, highlighted groups' information-transmission role. Because senators and their staff lack the resources to conduct in-depth investigations of each and every lower court nominee, groups serve a vital purpose by helping to fill this information gap. This information-transmission role occurs early on in the process. Once nominees begin to move through the process, groups need to decide whether to formally oppose judicial nominees and launch a campaign to defeat them. Chapter 5 explicated, based on interviews with group leaders, how groups make the critical decision to turn a nomination down the public partisan track. Chapter 5 discussed five categories of factors groups assess when determining whether to oppose a nominee. But do interest group objections actually matter? Do they convince senators to vote against opposed nominees for a seat on the federal bench?

Although interest group objections decisively reroute nominations onto the public partisan track, groups alone cannot derail nominees. Rather, groups must convince like-minded senators to vote against the nominee. As a former Judiciary Committee staffer explained, "step one" is that groups must oppose the nominee, "and step two is that senators must agree." One former committee staffer even suggested that so-called controversy means little unless Senate opposition is strong: "D. Brooks Smith is really interesting because the groups are jumping up and down. . . . [T]hey got votes against Smith, but is that really 'controversial'? . . . Unless opposition is early, it is very hard to defeat nominees." Finally, senators must think about how to pitch the issue to their colleagues. A committee staffer argued, "If there is no smoking gun and generally vague concerns, that's a harder campaign to mount. What does [Senator X] say to his colleagues to get them to vote no?"

Relatively few studies examine whether interest groups influence judicial confirmation outcomes, and this lack of scrutiny is especially notable at the lower court level. Earlier studies focus on the effect of group lobbying at the Supreme Court level and find that the more groups lobby, the more likely it is that a nominee will receive negative votes on the Senate floor (Cohen 1998; Overby et al. 1992; Segal, Cameron, and Cover 1992). The majority of lower court confirmation studies analyze confirmation durations (Bell 2002b; Binder and Maltzman 2002; Hartley and Holmes 1997, 2002; Martinek, Kemper, and Van Winkle 2002; Nixon and Goss 2001), but to date, only one study has assessed the impact of group objections. Scherer, Bartels, and Steigerwalt (2008) find that group objections are the leading cause of confirmation delay and the primary reason nominees are not eventually confirmed. A subset of lower court confirmation studies examines group activity, but these studies primarily investigate the impact of formal group participation, that is, testifying at confirmation hearings (Bell 2002a; Cohen 1998; Flemming, MacLeod, and Talbert 1998). However, Judiciary Committee chairs have not permitted groups to testify since the mid-1980s. It seems useful, then, to measure the impact of informal group activity on confirmation outcomes.

The most powerful mechanism of informal interest group activity is the decision by groups to publicly oppose a nominee. Groups may investigate and write a report about every nominee, especially nominees to the circuit courts, but they publicly oppose only the most objectionable nominees. When groups oppose a nominee, they launch a campaign to defeat the nominee, and use all the resources at their disposal (Caldeira, Hojnacki, and Wright 2000). The decision to oppose is made only after careful consideration. The remaining question is what impact these groups' objections have on a nominee's fate.

Interest group objections can potentially influence a nominee's path to confirmation in several ways. First, group opposition may lead the chair of the Senate Judiciary Committee to refuse to schedule a hearing or vote on the nomination. Obviously, such influence is difficult to substantiate: chairs normally do not explicate why a nominee fails to advance through the committee, and media reports at best can only speculate as to why nominees are not considered. We do know some number of nominees are blocked because of objections from home-state senators (see chapter 2); as former committee chair Orrin Hatch explained, "There was no way to confirm those [nominees], no matter how much I would have liked to, without completely ignoring the senatorial courtesy that we afford to home-state Senators in the nomination process, as has always been the case."[1]

Such leadership responses to group activities obviously occur only when there is divided government and the committee chair is a member of the opposition party. As Binder and Maltzman explain in relation to the effect of divided government, the majority "takes advantage of its scheduling power to delay confirmation" (2002, 196). That said, since individual committee senators, including minority-party senators, can delay hearings for short periods, they could potentially do so in response to pressure from like-minded groups. There are also instances of minority senators asking for vote delays in order to gain more time to lobby for their preferred nominees. For example, Republican senators used this tactic prior to Charles Pickering's committee vote in March 2002 (Savage 2002).

In addition, systematically parsing the effect of group objections from other potential influences, such as lateness in the term, ethical or financial problems uncovered during the FBI investigation (which are traditionally kept confidential), or signals from the administration to move other nominations, is extremely difficult. Scholarly accounts suggest that Judiciary Committee chairs routinely slow down judicial nominations during presidential election years (Epstein and Segal 2005, 190; Scherer, Bartels, and Steigerwalt 2008). For example, the liberal People for the American Way (PFAW) suggested in an April 3, 2008, letter that then chair Patrick Leahy invoke the "Thurmond rule" against President George W. Bush's nominees and process only noncontroversial nominees for the rest of the presidential election year. Democrats did in fact slow down their processing of Bush's nominations, but it is unclear whether their actions were in response to PFAW's letter or in anticipation of a successful Democratic presidential campaign. As Senator Charles Grassley said, "The Democrats have employed a lot of fancy footwork to dance around their constitutional responsibility to give fair consideration of President Bush's judicial nominees. They are doing nothing more than burning down the clock, having dreamt up every stalling tactic in the book to prevent qualified Americans from serving on the federal bench."[2] Committee Republicans boycotted a committee business meeting on July 17, 2008, to protest the lack of progress on judicial nominations, arguing that Democrats were using the impending election as an excuse not to approve Bush's nominees. Outside commentators, such as Curt Levey, executive director of the Committee for Justice, alternatively suggested that these decisions were "spurred on by interest groups."[3]

Similarly, the slow pace of the Judiciary Committee's processing of Clinton's lower court nominations led then chief justice William Rehnquist to chastise the Republican-led Congress in his 1997 *Year-End Report on the Federal Judiciary* for its "action—or inaction" on judicial nominees (Rehnquist 2002). Ironically, conservative activist Jipping criticized then chairman Hatch at the same time for confirming too many Clinton nominees: "Orrin Hatch has been the chief lobbyist for a number of the most liberal Clinton nominees" (Associated Press 1997).

Bell (2002a, 79–81) recounts how groups historically influenced the committee directly by testifying at nominee confirmation hearing, but such testimony generally has not been allowed since 1995. In reference to this change in the formal status of interest groups, Bell quotes a Republican senator: "Just because [interest groups] don't testify doesn't mean they don't have influence. Most of the time, it's below the surface. It's like a duck or a swan, most of the activity is underwater, where you can't see it" (76). As a result, groups now work behind the scenes to push nominations either onto or off the committee's agenda. When opposition to a nominee arises, the committee may choose not to act, and thus "save face for the nominee" by preventing potential embarrassment (Bell 2002a, 79, quoting Michael Carrasco, a former nominations clerk for the Judiciary Committee).

The clearest example of possible collusion between senators and like-minded interest groups arose during "Memogate" in November 2003, when a Republican committee staffer leaked confidential strategy memos exchanged between committee Democrats to the *Wall Street Journal* and the *Washington Times*.[4] As described by the *Wall Street Journal,* these strategy memos from the 107th Congress (when Democrats were in the majority) outlined liberal groups' suggestions to delay hearings on nominees such as Miguel Estrada. Whether these suggestions were in fact followed is uncertain, but we definitely know that groups on all sides have attempted to convince like-minded senators to delay or block those nominees they find objectionable while the nominations are still in the Judiciary Committee.[5]

To systematically determine whether group objections influence their intended senatorial targets, this chapter assesses what factors influenced Judiciary Committee votes on nominees to the circuit courts between 1985 and 2006. Although groups may persuade senators to delay hearings or Committee votes, or even block such proceedings altogether, it is difficult to parse the effect of outside group activities as opposed to other potential influences.[6] In addition, I am interested in whether group objections successfully convince senators that a particular nominee is "extreme" and thus unworthy to sit on the federal bench. Studying the influence of group objections on senators' votes provides the most direct test of groups' influence on senators' decisions.[7] Since senators' default position is to vote yes on lower court nominations (Scherer, Bartels, and Steigerwalt 2008), a public no vote signifies true objection to a nomination. The question then becomes the degree to which group objections, as opposed to other factors, push senators to vote against the nomination.

Between 1985 and 2006, not one nominee was defeated on the Senate floor, but six nominees were defeated in committee; it is therefore at the committee stage where we can accurately gauge the degree to which groups influence confirmation outcomes and, in particular, senators' votes. Jeffrey Robinson, former chief counsel for Senator Specter, explained, "If there's media coverage about a problem, then at the [committee] hearing people are going to be asked about the problem. But if no Senator has been persuaded that it's really an issue, then those questions are quite perfunctory, a canned answer is given, and the nomination goes through [the committee]" (2002). If groups cannot convince the senators on the committee to vote against the nominee, the nominee will likely be confirmed.[8] Studying committee votes thus provides a strong test of whether senators are responding to group cues. One Democratic committee staffer explained, "It's harder to vote no in committee, because there is more attention, and your vote's more important. The spotlight is on you. Once you vote, people don't change their votes between the committee and the floor except in extraordinary circumstances. . . . And, so people who aren't on the committee don't face that. . . . If you're one of 35 or 40 no votes [on the floor] it's not as big of a deal as if everyone is looking to you, are you going to be the one who votes no [in committee]."

Group leaders also recognize the importance of committee votes: "Rarely does the Senate disagree with the decision by the Judiciary Committee. . . . The final decision reflects whatever the Judiciary Committee does" (Neas 2002). Examining committee votes therefore reveals whether groups are able to successfully convince senators to vote no on a nomination and even convince enough senators to defeat the nomination altogether.

Assessing Judiciary Committee Votes

A total of 272 circuit court nominations were made between 1985 and 2006. Two hundred twenty-two of these nominations received committee votes, and twelve of these nominations had two committee votes in two separate Congresses, for a total of 234 committee votes during this time period. Six of these twelve nominations were filibustered on the floor of the Senate during the 108th Congress, and then received new committee votes once the showdown over judicial filibusters was resolved in the 109th Congress. One nomination was stalled during the 108th Congress but not filibustered, and then sent back to the committee after the filibuster agreement was reached. The other five nominations concerned Clinton nominees, all of whom had committee votes in successive Congresses and were then confirmed.

To determine what impact, if any, interest group objections had on these 234 committee votes, two questions about group influence must be addressed. First, how much influence do groups have in making circuit court nominations "controversial"? In other words, do senators respond to the cues sent them by groups that a particular nominee is problematic by voting against that nominee? And if so, how often? Second, to what degree do group objections, relative to other factors, affect the percentage of negative votes a nominee receives in committee?

As discussed in chapter 5, interest groups try to influence the confirmation process informally, yet directly, by opposing egregious nominees and launching a campaign to defeat these nominees. If a nominee is opposed, groups utilize all of the tactics at their disposal (Caldeira, Hojnacki, and Wright 2000); if a nominee is unopposed, the groups stay quiet.

Scherer, Bartels, and Steigerwalt (2008) argue that interest group objections serve a special purpose in lower court confirmations, that of sounding a fire alarm and convincing senators to closely vet a particular nominee. Given the vast number of lower court nominations made every congressional term and the traditional deference given the president (and home-state senators) to choose lower court judges, senators cannot scrutinize each and every nominee. Rather, senators' default position—including senators in the opposite party of the president—is to vote yes on a lower court nomination unless a problem is brought to their attention. Group objections thus alert senators to a potential problem and sound a fire alarm that the nominee needs to be investigated carefully. But if no fire alarm is sounded, the nominee will most likely be confirmed swiftly and unanimously. Thus, the fire alarm theory argues that senators rely on groups to sound an alarm if a nominee is problematic, and otherwise assume a nominee is fit for the federal bench. This theory leads to the proposition that when interest groups sound an alarm by opposing a nominee, like-minded senators should be more likely to vote against the nominee in the Judiciary Committee.

To test this proposition, I determined whether each nomination made to the circuit courts between 1985 and 2006 was publicly opposed by an interest group. I conducted a comprehensive set of searches of newspaper archives for reports that a group publicly opposed a particular nominee. Nominees were counted as opposed if their nomination was objected to by at least two national interest groups.[9] Appendix A provides more information about the search methodology, while appendix B explains how group opposition was measured and coded. Appendix C lists all nominations to the circuit courts during this time period that were found to be opposed by at least two national groups. Fifty-four (19.9 percent) of the 272 nominations made during the time period under analysis were publicly opposed by groups. The following sections investigate what impact, if any, these group objections have on the fate of a nomination.

Do Interest Group Objections Make a Judicial Nomination Controversial?

First, does an interest group objection make a nomination "controversial"? In other words, does a group objection heighten the amount of controversy surrounding the nomination, decrease the likelihood of successful confirmation, and thereby succeed in diverting the nomination from the noncontroversial track onto the public partisan track? There are two ways to begin addressing this question. One, we can determine how many opposed nominees also received negative votes in committee. A high correlation between group objections and negative votes provides at least some evidence that senators are responding to the cues sent to them by groups and more intensely scrutinizing the opposed nominees. A lack of negative votes offers support for Shapiro's (1990) argument that senators may reject these cues, and if so, the nominations will proceed without impediment. We know that senators' default position is to vote for a nominee, and that senators are unlikely to vote against a nominee without sufficient evidence and prodding (Scherer, Bartels, and Steigerwalt 2008). A link between group opposition and negative votes thus indicates the groups may have succeeded in convincing senators to move away from this default position. Two, we can ascertain how many *unopposed* nominees also received negative votes. A finding that a number of nominees lacking group opposition also received negative votes in committee would suggest that groups exert little influence on senators' decisions of how to vote or that senators receive informational cues about

TABLE 6.1 Number of negative votes received by circuit court nominations in the Judiciary Committee, 1985–2006 (99th–109th Congresses)

VOTES RECEIVED	NOMINATIONS RECEIVING SUCH VOTES	%
Unanimously confirmed	183	78.2
1–3 no votes	9	3.8
4–6 no votes (and confirmed)	12	5.1
7–9 no votes (and confirmed)	24	10.3
7–10 no votes (and defeated)	6	2.6
Total number of committee votes	234	

Note: The number of senators serving on the Senate Judiciary Committee and the partisan composition change every Congress. In 1988, only thirteen senators served on the committee, and thus seven negative votes were all that were needed to defeat Susan Liebeler's nomination. However, in 1994, eighteen senators served on the committee, and so seven no votes were not enough to defeat Rosemary Barkett's nomination.

troublesome nominees from other sources as well. Finally, if we discover that unopposed nominees are confirmed with few or none no votes while their opposed counterparts encounter strong senatorial opposition, this suggests that senators do respond to the signals sent to them by groups and that group opposition heightens the amount of controversy surrounding a particular nomination and increases the likelihood of the nominee facing a rocky path to confirmation.

Overall, 222 nominees received committee votes; twelve nominees had committee votes in two different Congresses.[10] Of the 234 total committee votes taken between 1985 and 2006, 183 (78.2 percent) were unanimous (table 6.1). Nine nominations were objected to by three senators or less, and the other forty-two nominations received four or more no votes in committee. Six nominations were defeated in committee, and another twenty-three nominations were in danger of being defeated, as each received more than 40 percent negative votes.

Of the 222 nominees who received committee votes, forty-five nominees (20.3 percent) were publicly objected to by an interest group; table 6.2 lists all opposed nominees who received committee votes and the ultimate outcomes of their nominations. Figure 6.1 compares how opposed versus non-opposed nominees fared in committee; this graph reports only the first committee vote for those nominees subject to two separate committee votes. Thirty-eight of these opposed nominees received at least one no vote. The other seven nominees were unanimously passed out of committee. Thus, the treatment of these nominees shows that senators

TABLE 6.2 Outcomes of opposed circuit court nominations that received committee votes, 1985–2006 (99th–109th Congresses)

	COMMITTEE VOTE	FLOOR VOTE
99th Congress		
Daniel Manion	9–9, 11–6[a]	48–46, 50–49
Alex Kozinski	Voice vote	54–43
100th Congress		
Susan Wittenberg Liebeler	6–7, 8–5[a]	None
David Sentelle	14–0	87–0
Bernard Siegan	6–8, 7–7[a]	None
101st Congress		
Clarence Thomas	13–1	Voice vote
102nd Congress		
Edward Carnes	10–4	62–36
Andrew Kleinfeld	14–0	Voice vote
Kenneth Ryskamp	6–8, 7–7[a]	None
103rd Congress		
Martha Daughtrey	12–5	Voice vote
Rosemary Barkett	11–7	61–37
Lee Sarokin	12–5	63–35
104th Congress		
William Fletcher	12–6	None
105th Congress		
Marsha Berzon	10–8	64–34
Richard Paez	12–6	None
Timothy Dyk	14–4	74–25[b]
Margaret McKeown	16–2	80–11
William Fletcher	12–6	57–41
106th Congress		
Raymond Fisher	16–2	68–29
Richard Paez	10–8	59–39
107th Congress		
Charles Pickering	9–10	None
D. Brooks Smith	12–7	64–35
Lavenski Smith	19–0	Voice vote
Dennis Shedd	Voice vote	55–44
Priscilla Owen	9–10	None
Michael McConnell	Voice vote	Voice vote

(continued)

TABLE 6.2 (continued)

	COMMITTEE VOTE	FLOOR VOTE
108th Congress		
Jay Bybee	12–6	74–19
Deborah Cook	13–2	66–25
Miguel Estrada	10–9	Filibuster
Richard Griffin	10–9	Filibuster
Carolyn Kuhl	10–9	Filibuster
David McKeague	10–9	Filibuster
Priscilla Owen	10–9	Filibuster
Charles Pickering	10–9	Filibuster
John Roberts	14–3	Voice Vote
Henry Saad	10–9	Filibuster
Jeffrey Sutton	11–8	52–41
Timothy Tymkovich	10–6	58–41
D. Michael Fisher	12–0	Voice vote
William Pryor	10–9	Filibuster
William Myers	10–9	Filibuster
Janice Brown	10–9	Filibuster
William Haynes	10–9	None
Diane Sykes	14–5	70–27
109th Congress		
William Myers	10–8	None
William Pryor	10–8	53–45
Terrence Boyle	10–8	None
Priscilla Owen	10–8	55–43
Janice Brown	10–8	56–43
Thomas Griffith	14–4	73–24
Brett Kavanaugh	10–8	57–36
Richard Griffin	Voice vote	95–0
David McKeague	Voice vote	96–0

[a]Nominee had two committee votes on the same occasion; the first vote was to confirm, while the second vote was to send the nomination to the floor "without recommendation." A tie vote is considered a defeat.
[b]Floor vote occurred during the subsequent Congress.

FIGURE 6.1 Number of negative votes received by unopposed and opposed circuit court nominations in the Judiciary Committee, 1985–2006 (99th–109th Congresses)

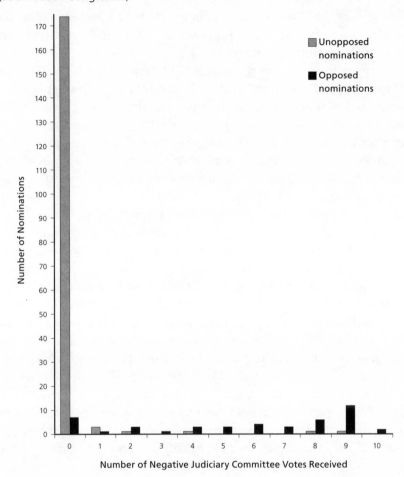

Note: Chart reflects a total of 222 nominations; for nominations that received two committee votes in successive Congresses, this chart reflects the nominees' first committee vote.

can and do unanimously reject the cues interest groups send them.[11] In addition, Richard Griffin's and David McKeague's nominations both received nine no votes during the 108th Congress, and both were then filibustered on the Senate floor. After the Gang of Fourteen resolution was reached during the 109th Congress, these two nominees were passed out of committee by voice vote and then confirmed unanimously by the full Senate. These results also clearly reveal, however, that senators rarely ignore these signals. Overall, 84.4 percent of nominees who were opposed by outside groups also faced at least some senatorial opposition in committee. Turning to the degree of opposition, thirty-three (73.3 percent) of these opposed nominees received four or more no votes, and twenty-three (51.1 percent) of these nominees received seven or more no votes in committee. Group objections thus substantially correlate with senatorial opposition in committee.

Comparatively, only seven nominees (3.9 percent) out of the 181 who were not opposed by interest groups also received negative votes in committee, and all were eventually confirmed (see figure 6.1). Three of these nominees received one no vote, one received two no votes, and one nominee received four no votes.[12] These results suggest that senators may object to particular nominees based on information or cues received elsewhere, but that this situation occurs very infrequently and the degree of opposition is extremely slight. Rather, the Judiciary Committee unanimously approves unopposed nominees more than 96 percent of the time.

Only two unopposed nominees (1.1 percent of all unopposed nominees) received a considerable number of no votes: George W. Bush nominees Randy Norman Smith (eight no votes) and Susan Neilson (nine no votes). Both instances reflect an institutional dispute in which the nominee was caught in the middle; in the end, however, both nominees were confirmed unanimously by the entire Senate. Susan Neilson was one of the four Michigan nominees blocked by senatorial courtesy by Senators Levin and Stabenow to protest the treatment of Clinton's Michigan nominees. When then chairman Hatch decided to allow Neilson's nomination to move forward over the home-state senators' objections during the 108th Congress, the committee Democrats voiced their opposition to this departure from Senate norms by voting against her nomination. However, once the dispute over the Michigan seats on the Sixth Circuit was resolved, Neilson was confirmed unanimously.

Randy Norman Smith's nomination was similar. Smith, who is from Idaho, was nominated to the Ninth Circuit during the 109th Congress. The two California senators argued, however, that the open seat actually belonged to California.[13] Senator Diane Feinstein threatened to place an institutional hold on Smith's nomination if it made it to the Senate floor. When Smith's nomination was brought to a committee vote, the Democrats banded together to vote against Smith's nomination. The situation was resolved when an Idaho Ninth Circuit vacancy opened. Smith's original nomination was withdrawn and he was renominated for the Idaho Ninth Circuit seat in the 110th Congress. Smith was then, like Neilson, confirmed unanimously.

FIGURE 6.2 Time to committee votes for unopposed and opposed nominations to the circuit courts, 1985–2006 (99th–109th Congresses).

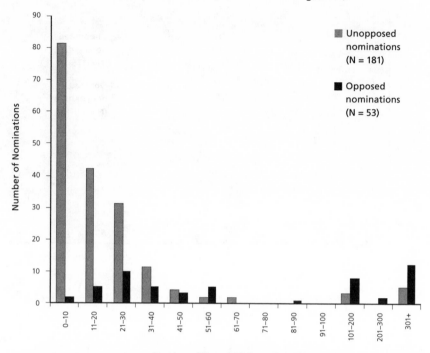

Number of Days until Committee Vote

Finally, nominations opposed by interest groups receive more scrutiny and face more senatorial opposition throughout the entire Senate confirmation process. Opposed nominations are significantly more likely to face considerable time delays on their path to confirmation (figures 6.2 and 6.3) as well as sizable senatorial opposition on the Senate floor (figure 6.4). While 61.7 percent of unopposed nominees had a floor vote within ten days of their committee vote, 48.5 percent of opposed nominees waited more than fifty days to be confirmed. And whereas 94.3 percent of unopposed nominees were confirmed unanimously by the full Senate, 63.6 percent of opposed nominees received more than twenty negative votes on the Senate floor.

Overall, group objections substantially correspond with an increase in the likelihood that a nomination will face (potentially considerable) senatorial opposition in committee and on the Senate floor. The Spearman correlation between whether a nomination is opposed by an interest group and the number of negative votes it will receive in committee

FIGURE 6.3 Time to Senate floor votes for unopposed and opposed nominations to the circuit courts, 1985–2006 (99th–109th Congresses).

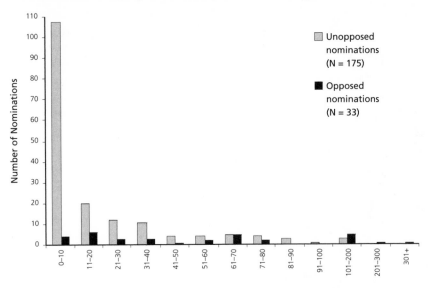

Number of Days between Judiciary Committee Vote and Floor Vote

is .8121, and this correlation is significant at $p < .001$. Alternatively, it is rare for senators to vote against nominations at either the committee or the floor stage that have not garnered group objections. These findings provide strong empirical support for the interview findings presented in chapter 4 that senators rely heavily on groups to provide them with needed information about judicial nominees. As senators and their staffs lack the resources to thoroughly investigate each and every nominee, groups fill this gap. Groups especially focus on pinpointing which nominees are ideologically extreme and worth a public battle to defeat. In sum, this preliminary analysis suggests that when groups sound an alarm by opposing a judicial nominee, senators indeed listen and respond accordingly.

These descriptive findings support the proposition derived from the Scherer, Bartels, and Steigerwalt (2008) fire alarm theory that interest group objections result in circuit court nominations becoming controversial and receiving negative votes in committee; alternatively, nominations lacking group opposition are likely to be confirmed easily. These findings do not definitively establish, however, *how much* influence group objections have on senators' committee votes. Are group objections a

FIGURE 6.4 Number of negative votes received by unopposed and opposed circuit court nominees on the Senate floor, 1985–2006 (99th–109th Congresses).

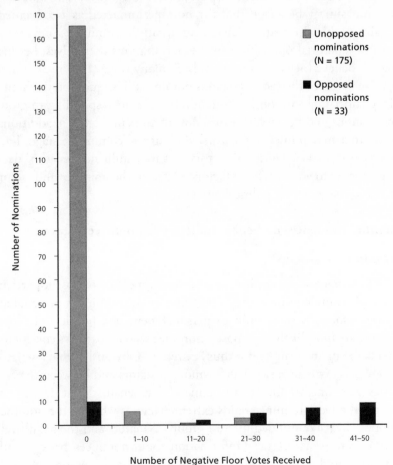

significant predictor of how a judicial nomination will fare in committee, or are senators actually influenced by other factors when deciding how to vote?

To answer these questions, I used regression analysis to determine what factors influence committee votes on circuit court nominations. Since most nominees are eventually confirmed, other scholars analyze what factors influence how long it takes for a nomination to move through the entire confirmation process (Binder and Maltzman 2002; Martinek, Kemper, and Van Winkle 2002; Scherer, Bartels, and Steigerwalt 2008). However, while longer confirmation durations may reflect potential controversy surrounding the nomination, chapters 2 and 3 showed that many nominations face lengthy waits because they are trapped by parliamentary procedures in unrelated disputes. Longer confirmation durations may thus simply be a sign that the nomination acted as a convenient bargaining chip. In contrast, analyzing negative committee votes clearly captures senatorial opposition to the nominations themselves; because senators believe they can vote no only so many times, they reserve their negative votes for the most egregious nominees. The question is whether this senatorial opposition is a function of senators responding to group objections or to other factors. I turn now to an examination of additional factors that may influence senators' votes at the committee stage. I am interested in two categories of factors that may influence senators' decisions on how to vote: personal factors related to the nominee and factors related to the temporal political environment.

Potential Influences on Senate Judiciary Committee Votes

PERSONAL FACTORS

When senators determine whether to support or oppose a particular circuit court nominee, they first consider the nominee's personal attributes, especially the nominee's personal views and political ideology. Senators are most likely to oppose a nominee who holds views considered outside the mainstream and is thus "extreme." Obviously, what a senator perceives as extreme varies widely among senators and between the two parties. A strong argument can be made that senators' best determination of whether a nominee holds extreme views is whether the nominee is opposed by like-minded interest groups. Senators and their staffs rely on groups to provide crucial information about nominees' backgrounds and views, and group objections signal like-minded senators and their staffs that a nominee holds ideologically extreme views. I therefore utilize the Interest Group Objection variable to capture both the impact of informal interest group activity on senators' votes as well as the influence of perceived ideological extremeness.

I also utilize an independent measure of nominee ideology. This second measure is based on the Giles, Hettinger, and Peppers (2002) scores. These scores take into account the fact that presidents and home-state senators from the president's party all play a role in selecting lower court nominees. When senatorial prerogatives are in play, the nominee's ideology is likely to be closely related to the home-state senators' ideologies; when there is a lack of senatorial courtesy, the nominee's ideology is more likely to reflect that of the appointing president. The Giles, Hettinger, and Peppers scores use the Poole-Rosenthal Common Space scores to create a measure of nominee ideology. This then allows us to compare the nominee's perceived ideology to the ideology of key senators. Such a comparison is necessary because nominee extremeness varies in relation to the political context. For our purposes, the most important relationship is the ideological distance between the nominee and the median opposition senator on the Judiciary Committee. Members of the president's party are highly unlikely to oppose the president's nominees, while opposition senators may be persuaded to vote against an objectionable nominee. I therefore measure the ideological distance between the nominee and the median committee senator in the opposition party. Since this measure accounts for who was serving on the committee at the time of each nominee's committee vote, it allows us to determine the effect of the nominee's ideology in relation to the temporal political environment. Nominees who are more ideologically distant from the committee's opposition median can be considered more extreme than other nominees, and thus more likely to encounter senatorial opposition. I use these two measures to test the following hypothesis:

Hypothesis 1: Ideologically "extreme" nominees are more likely to receive a higher percentage of negative votes in the Judiciary Committee than less ideologically extreme nominees.

As mentioned in chapter 4, during the summer of 2002 I interviewed twenty-one current and former Judiciary Committee staff members (see table 4.1). I asked each of the interviewees what they believed influenced whether a nominee ran into opposition in committee. The interviewees all agreed that having a patron on the Judiciary Committee greatly aided nominees on their path to confirmation.[14] As one senior committee staffer explained, "Overall, it matters who your patron is."

There are two ways to gain such a patron: the nominee may be from the home state of a senator serving on the committee or the nominee may have worked for a senator serving on the committee (and this job also likely played a part in this person being selected by the president). All of the committee staffers felt that whether a nominee has a personal connection to the committee plays an important role in how a nominee will likely fare in committee. For example, many of the interviewees mentioned the different outcomes for George W. Bush's nominees D. Brooks Smith and Charles Pickering. During the 107th Congress, both Smith and Pickering were objected to by interest groups. Smith was passed through committee and eventually confirmed, while Pickering was defeated in committee on a party-line vote. While some might assume Pickering's patron, then Senate minority leader Trent Lott, would be a powerful advocate, those on the committee believed Smith was confirmed because his patron, Arlen Specter, was a respected member of the committee. Numerous staffers said their senators were "not about to pick a fight with Specter." Thus, while senators may have opposed Smith, they refused to vote against him. Additionally, many felt Lott's role outside the collegial committee structure hampered his ability to shepherd his nominee through committee, especially as he used the media to garner support for Pickering rather than lobby committee members one-on-one, as Specter did quite successfully.

Similarly, many interviewees felt nominees who had previously worked for the Judiciary Committee held a distinct advantage. One committee staffer explained, "It's not that the staffer is substantively okay to the Committee members, but that they are personally familiar with the staffer. There is a real sense of collegiality in the Senate, for better or worse." These interview findings lead to our next two hypotheses:

Hypothesis 2: The presence of a patron on the Judiciary Committee will decrease the percentage of negative votes a nomination receives in committee.

Hypothesis 3: Nominees who have previously served as staffers on the Judiciary Committee will receive a lesser percentage of negative votes in committee than those who have not.

Duration studies illuminate two other personal factors that have been found to influence how quickly a lower court nominee is confirmed. These factors also likely influence whether a nominee encounters opposition in committee. The first is the nominee's American Bar Association (ABA) rating, and the second is the nominee's race and gender (Bell 2002b; Martinek, Kemper, and Van Winkle 2002).[15] Since the ABA evaluates a nominee's professional qualifications, a higher ABA rating suggests the nominee is more qualified for a seat on the federal bench. These nominees should consequently fare better in the confirmation process than nominees rated as less professionally qualified. Martinek, Kemper, and Van Winkle (2002) find nominees with higher ABA ratings are indeed more likely to be confirmed quickly. Similarly, a number of studies find race and gender influence a nominee's path to confirmation; for example, Bell (2002b) finds white males are more likely to be confirmed quickly, at least during periods of divided government. This leads to our next set of hypotheses:

Hypothesis 4: White nominees will receive a lower percentage of negative votes than minorities.

Hypothesis 5: Male nominees will receive a lower percentage of negative votes than female nominees.

Hypothesis 6: Nominees with higher ABA ratings will receive a lower percentage of negative votes than nominees with lower ABA ratings.

POLITICAL FACTORS

Beyond nominee characteristics, senators must be cognizant of the current political environment. The first potentially important political factor is whether key players in the process are facing reelection. Reelection concerns arise in two ways: first, nominees generally fare worse during a presidential election year than at other times in a president's term, as senators hope their party's candidate will win the election and the president is generally seen as politically weaker (Segal 1987; Segal and Spaeth 1986). End-of-term reviews also find the process slows down significantly during presidential election years (Goldman 1989; Goldman and Slotnick 1999).

Hypothesis 7: Nominees who undergo committee votes during a presidential election year will receive a greater percentage of negative votes than nominees whose votes do not take place during a presidential election year.

Second, whether it is a midterm election year may also affect how a nominee fares in committee, because out-party senators may be more willing to vote against nominees in the hope that their party will regain the Senate majority. In addition, senators themselves may be up for reelection and thus worried about their own reelection prospects.

Hypothesis 8: Nominees who undergo committee votes during midterm election years will receive a greater percentage of negative votes than those whose votes take place in a nonelection year.

Previous studies also find that opposition senators are more likely to vote against a Supreme Court nominee when their party controls the Senate, as the chance of actually defeating the nominee is much more likely (Ruckman 1993; Segal 1987; Segal and Spaeth 1986). However, senators have also become more and more willing to challenge potentially objectionable nominees, even during periods of unified government. For example, Senate Democrats successfully filibustered ten

nominees during the 108th Congress when they were in the Senate minority. Thus, due to the increasingly partisan environment in the Senate
and the increased attention paid to lower court nominations, divided
government may not act as a strong deterrent to senatorial opposition.
Alternatively, during divided government the chair of the committee
may be less likely to schedule potentially objectionable nominees for
a vote; rather, chairs have noted their desire to work on confirming as
many nominees as possible.[16]

Hypothesis 9: Divided government will influence the percentage of negative votes a nominee will receive in committee.

Finally, senators' ideologies have been found to be a crucial factor in
the rejection of Supreme Court nominees, and we can presume senatorial
ideology plays a role in committee votes on lower court nominees as well
(Cameron, Cover, and Segal 1990; Guliuzza, Reagan, and Barrett 1994;
Segal, Cameron, and Cover 1992). In general, more liberal senators are
more likely to vote against a more conservative president's nominees, and
vice versa. Partisan ties matter as well, as senators generally support their
president's nominees. When opposition committee senators are more
ideologically distant from the appointing president, they should be more
likely to challenge the president's nominees. I therefore constructed a
measure that captures the ideological distance between the appointing
president and the median opposition party senator on the committee.
When the president and the opposition committee members are ideologically close, the committee should be more inclined to approve the
president's nominees, while ideologically distant opposition committee
members should be more inclined to try to defeat a president's nominees.
My final hypothesis is the following:

Hypothesis 10: As the ideological distance between the committee's opposition party members and the president increases, a nominee will
receive a larger percentage of negative votes in committee.

The dependent variable used in the analysis below is the percentage
of no votes received by each nominee during his or her Judiciary Committee vote. Examining the percentage of no votes allows us to determine
which nominees encountered opposition in the committee, as well as the
degree of opposition these nominees faced.[17] I use the percentage of no
votes each nominee received rather than simply a count of the number of
no votes because the number of senators on the committee changes with
each Congress. Over time, the membership of the committee has ranged

from thirteen senators to nineteen members. Thus, in 1988, seven no votes meant defeat for Susan Liebeler's nomination, but in 1994, when the committee's membership rose to eighteen, seven no votes were not enough to defeat Rosemary Barkett's nomination. The percentage of no votes each nominee received was constructed based on the actual number of committee members who voted on each nominee, as not all members are present at each vote. Those nominees who were confirmed by unanimous consent or by voice vote were coded as receiving 0 percent no votes.

To test the above hypotheses, three models were constructed, one analyzing factors relating to the nominee, one examining the temporal political environment at the time of the committee vote, and an aggregate model that combines these two sets of factors. Appendix B explains how each of the variables was measured and coded, while table 6.3 summarizes the hypothesized effect of each of these variables. Since I created a continuous yet bounded dependent variable—the percentage of no votes a nominee can receive ranges from 0 to 100 percent—tobit analysis is used, as it allows us to estimate a model that reflects that the dependent variable is censored at zero as well as at 100. Tobit results can be interpreted in a similar manner as traditional ordinary least squares results. In each of the tables of results for the models, a positive coefficient means that the presence of the factor increases the likelihood of the nominee receiving negative votes, while a negative coefficient means that the presence of the factor decreases the likelihood of the nominee receiving negative votes in committee. I also provide information on the substantive impact of all significant variables on the percentage of negative committee votes a nomination is likely to receive for each of the three models to further illustrate the degree to which each factor influences a nominee's fate in committee. In all three models I used robust standard errors clustered on the nominee's year of nomination.

The Results: Factors That Influenced Senate Judiciary Committee Votes on Circuit Court Nominations between 1985 and 2006

PERSONAL FACTORS

Table 6.4 reports the results of the regression model testing personal factors about the nomination. Whether a group publicly objected to a nominee is by far the strongest determinant of whether a nomination will receive negative votes in committee. The presence of group opposition increases the percentage of no votes a nomination will receive by 73 percentage points; when we look at predicted probabilities, holding every-

TABLE 6.3 Summary of hypotheses

INDEPENDENT VARIABLES	HYPOTHESIZED EFFECT OF THE INDEPENDENT VARIABLE ON THE PERCENTAGE OF NO VOTES A NOMINEE WILL RECEIVE IN COMMITTEE
Patron	–
Former Senate Judiciary Committee staff member	–
Interest group objection	+
"Extreme" nominee in relation to the median opposition party senator on the Judiciary Committee	+
Race	–
Gender	–
American Bar Association rating	–
Presidential election year	+
Midterm election year	+
Divided government	±
Ideological distance between the median opposition senator on the Judiciary Committee and the appointing president	+

thing else constant, the model predicts that an opposed nomination will receive 27.1 percent no votes. Alternatively, an unopposed nomination is predicted to receive a negative percentage of no votes, and so is fully protected from defeat. Thus, while the nomination may not be defeated, the presence of an interest group objection ensures that the nomination will face a rough road to confirmation, while the absence of such opposition almost guarantees an easy ride to confirmation. In comparison, the coefficients on the other variables are all quite small, and thus these variables have relatively little influence on the overall percentage of negative votes received.

These findings also highlight how interest group objections serve a dual purpose. First, group objections are an extremely powerful informal lobbying tactic. Since groups are blocked from participating formally in the confirmation process, they have turned to informal lobbying campaigns to make their voices heard. These results conclusively show that senators are listening and responding to these group fire alarms. Second, group objections also transmit valuable ideological cues to the committee senators. Since senators lack the resources to investigate every nominee, and since a nominee's ideology can be difficult to ascertain, senators rely

TABLE 6.4 Tobit estimates: Impact of nominee-based factors on Judiciary Committee votes for circuit court nominations, 1985–2006 (99th–109th Congresses)

INDEPENDENT VARIABLES	B (SE)
Interest group objection	73.04***
	(7.53)
"Extreme" nominee in relation to the median opposition party senator on the Judiciary Committee	26.48
	(16.97)
Race	−2.86
	(6.57)
Gender	−10.43**
	(3.17)
Former Senate Judiciary Committee staff member	−174.28
	(unknown)
Patron	−1.53
	(4.28)
American Bar Association rating	2.45
	(1.81)
Constant	−65.68**
	(22.46)
N	234
Log likelihood	−264.77597
Cox-Snell R^2	.522

Note: Robust standard errors clustered on year of nomination.
#$p < .1$, *$p < .05$, **$p < .01$, ***$p < .001$, two-tailed tests.

on groups to alert them to potentially troublesome nominees. Group objections signal that a nominee's views are likely outside the mainstream, and thus worthy of scrutiny. Senators clearly rely on these group signals about ideology, as nominees without group opposition are virtually certain to be confirmed easily.

Most likely because of this dual aspect of interest group objections, the independent measure of nominee ideology is insignificant by conventional measures in a two-tailed test ($p = .120$), though it is in the expected positive direction. This finding does not mean nominee ideology is unimportant. Rather, it highlights the reality that ideology alone is not enough to explain why nominees run into trouble in the Senate. It also reinforces the observation that senators' default position is to confirm nominees. The predicted probabilities buttress this idea: regardless of the distance between the nominee and the committee opposition median, the model predicts a negative percentage of negative votes, thus illustrating that an extreme ideology does not lead directly to senatorial opposition. Finally, looking at just a simple bivariate correlation between extreme ideology and percentage of negative votes, the relationship is a mere .138 ($p < .05$); comparatively, the Spearman correlation between an interest group objection and negative votes is .814 ($p < .001$). In other words, interest groups objections provide additional information that a simple measure of ideology cannot. This finding mirrors that of Scherer, Bartels, and Steigerwalt (2008), who show conclusively that senators rely on groups to raise a fire alarm when a nominee requires increased attention; in the absence of group opposition, nominees will be confirmed and confirmed swiftly, even when ideologically extreme (1036–37). Senators therefore also look to group objections to alert them to which nominees are the most ideologically extreme *and* the most worthy of defeat. Since, as discussed in chapter 5, a necessary component of group opposition is extreme nominee ideology, the findings reported here inherently reflect the importance of both group activity and nominee ideology in persuading senators to vote no.

The only other significant variable in Model 1 is the nominee's gender. Males are less likely to receive negative votes than their female counterparts by 10 percentage points. The substantive effect is much smaller, however, than that of interest group opposition: being male has roughly one-seventh the impact of being objected to by an interest group. If we look at the effect of interest group opposition and gender in combination while holding all else constant, the model predicts that without interest group opposition, males and females will both be confirmed unanimously. When interest group opposition occurs, all else being equal, the model predicts male nominees will receive 25.3 percent no votes, while the percentage of no votes jumps to 35.7 percent for females, a difference of 10.4 percentage points. While race is in the expected negative decision, it is not significant. Thus, these findings partially echo previous studies that found that nontraditional nominees face increased scrutiny, generally because they are perceived to be more liberal than white males. It seems this reality is still true for females but not for minorities. Interestingly, ABA ratings are not found here to influence committee votes. This finding most likely reflects the reality that many of the George W. Bush nominees who faced opposition were also rated highly by the ABA.

The other important finding from this model is the effect of having worked on the Senate Judiciary Committee. As seen in table 6.4, this variable's presence in the model resulted in a highly irregular coefficient and no other values, such as standard errors or p values, for the variable. This odd result reflects the fact that only six nominees who served on the committee were nominated to a circuit court during the time period under review. Five of these nominees received a committee vote, and all five were voted unanimously out of committee, thus receiving 0 percent no votes.[18] Since being a former committee staffer perfectly predicts one's outcome—in other words, a former committee staffer will receive zero negative votes in committee—this variable is kicked out of the model.

A closer examination of Dennis Shedd's 2002 nomination reveals the enormous impact of being a former committee staffer. Shedd previously worked as a committee aide for Senator Strom Thurmond. Shedd's nomination drew fire from liberal interest groups but was passed out of committee by voice vote in deference to Senator Thurmond. Immediately after the voice vote was taken, however, all of the Democrats asked to have their votes recorded as a no in the hearing record. Shedd's nomination was therefore technically voted out of committee unanimously but it would have been defeated in a roll call vote. Shedd's personal ties to Senator Thurmond and the Judiciary Committee were crucial to his elevation to the circuit court.

Despite the opinions voiced in my interviews with both committee staff and interest groups, having a home-state senator on the committee was not a significant factor in how a nominee fared. Thus, home-state support on the committee does not in and of itself shield a nominee from opposition.

POLITICAL FACTORS

Table 6.5 reports the results of the temporal political factors tested in Model 2.[19] Strikingly, none of these variables significantly predicts Judiciary Committee votes for circuit court nominations. Divided government almost reaches conventional significance levels at the outermost boundary ($p = .125$) but, contrary to previous studies, is negatively signed.

The finding for divided government suggests nominations were *more likely* to receive negative votes during periods of unified government between 1985 and 2006. This result suggests senators may have become much more willing to oppose lower court nominations, and to do so even when the likelihood of defeating the nominee is lower, because they

TABLE 6.5 Tobit estimates: Impact of politically based factors on Judiciary Committee votes for circuit court nominations, 1985–2006 (99th–109th Congresses)

INDEPENDENT VARIABLES	B (SE)
Presidential election year	17.85
	(14.43)
Midterm election year	6.93
	(16.26)
Divided government	−27.12
	(17.63)
Ideological distance between the median opposition senator on the Judiciary Committee and the appointing president	82.16
	(128.25)
Constant	−96.89
	(103.60)
N	234
Log likelihood	−344.52748
Cox-Snell R^2	.054

Note: Robust standard errors clustered on year of nomination.
#$p < .1$, *$p < .05$, **$p < .01$, ***$p < .001$, two-tailed tests.

know they lack enough fellow partisans to successfully reject the nominee on a simple party-line vote. This result may also reflect the reality that opposition senators have other ways to block nominees when they are in the Senate majority. When the opposition party controls the Senate, the Judiciary chair may decide to move only uncontested nominees through committee. As a result, potentially objectionable nominees may face obstacles other than negative votes, including the possibility of never receiving a committee hearing or vote. During unified government, the Judiciary chair is likely to try to confirm as many of the president's nominees as possible, so the only option open to opposition senators is to vote against the nominee. This finding may also be driven in part by the judicial confirmation battles that occurred during the 108th and 109th Congresses, both of which were periods of unified government. The 108th and 109th Congresses were marked by a large number of bruising confirmation fights and a Senate minority willing to oppose nominees even when defeat through traditional means (i.e., votes in committee or on the floor) was highly unlikely. The question is whether these fights reflect a new era of judicial confirmation politics or whether the environment will again alter under President Obama.

PERSONAL AND POLITICAL FACTORS COMBINED

Table 6.6 reports the results of the aggregate Model 3, which includes all of the nominee-based factors along with the factors describing the temporal political environment. This aggregate model conclusively confirms the earlier descriptive findings that interest group objections are the driving force behind how a nomination will fare in committee. Whether a group has publicly objected to the nominee is by far the strongest predictor of whether a nomination will receive negative votes in committee: the presence of a group objection alone accounts for a 70 percentage point change in the percentage of no votes a nomination will receive. Holding all else constant, the model predicts opposed nominations will receive 26.2 percent no votes, a sizable degree of senatorial opposition. Although defeat is not guaranteed, group objections make a nominee's path to confirmation all the more difficult and ensure that the president will have to expend significant political capital to see the nominee successfully confirmed. Alternatively, the model again predicts that unopposed nominations will be unanimously confirmed. These results provide clear evidence that when groups sound a fire alarm, senators indeed listen and respond.

In addition, female nominees are still more likely to face senatorial opposition than male nominees. Overall, all else being equal, the percentage of negative votes decreases by 10 percentage points if the nominee is male rather than female. However, as in Model 1, this impact pales in comparison to the influence of interest group opposition. If we look at the effect of these two factors in tandem, the model predicts that, all else being equal, unopposed nominees will be confirmed easily regardless of gender. In contrast, the model predicts that an opposed male nominee will receive 25.4 percent negative votes but an opposed female nominee will receive 35.7 percent negative votes, an increase of 10.3 percentage points.

Finally, combining the personal and political factors in Model 3 reveals the influence of electoral factors on a nomination's fate in the Judiciary Committee. During a presidential election year, nominations are more likely to receive negative votes than during non-presidential election years. This finding mirrors earlier studies that found that as presidential elections approach, nominations are more likely to face longer delays or be denied confirmation altogether. Thus, one important effect of the temporal political environment is that when presidents are politically weaker, they must work harder to see their nominees con-

TABLE 6.6 Tobit estimates: Impact of nominee-based and politically based factors on Judiciary Committee votes for circuit court nominations, 1985–2006 (99th–109th Congresses)

INDEPENDENT VARIABLES	B (SE)
Interest group objection	70.0***
	(6.93)
"Extreme" nominee in relation to the median opposition party senator on the Judiciary Committee	17.44
	(12.78)
Race	–5.46
	(4.79)
Gender	–10.27**
	(2.96)
American Bar Association rating	2.59
	(1.72)
Patron	–1.57
	(4.75)
Former Senate Judiciary Committee	–164.95
	(unknown)
Ideological distance between the median staff member opposition senator on the Judiciary Committee and the appointing president	–2.27
	(50.46)
Presidential election year	10.94*
	(5.21)
Midterm election year	4.11
	(6.43)
Divided government	–6.07
	(4.50)
Constant	–54.46
	(42.59)
N	234
Log likelihood	–262.41188
Cox-Snell R^2	.531

Note: Robust standard errors clustered on year of nomination.
#$p < .10$, *$p < .05$, **$p < .01$, ***$p < .001$, two-tailed.

firmed. Much as for gender, the substantive effect of having one's committee vote during a presidential election year is much smaller than that for interest group objections. In general, we see an almost 11 percentage point increase in the percentage of negative votes received in presidential election years. When we combine the impact of electoral politics with that of interest group opposition, the model predicts that, all else being equal, unopposed nominees will be confirmed unanimously, regardless of any approaching elections. However, if the nominee is opposed, the model predicts that the percentage of negative votes received will increase from 25.9 percent in a non-presidential election year to 36.8 percent in a presidential election year.

Alternatively, in both Model 2 and Model 3, the variables indicating midterm election years and the ideological distance between the president and the opposition committee median were not significant predictors of committee votes. Including group objections and the president-committee opposition scores in the same model causes the president-committee opposition scores to become negative; this suggests once again that group objections signal both group opposition and ideological extremism. The lack of an effect for midterm elections suggests that while the political status of the president influences how senators vote in committee, committee members are not concerned about their personal electoral fortunes. This may be because few committee members face reelection each electoral cycle and most committee members hold relatively safe seats.

Finally, if we examine the effect of all three significant factors in Model 3, we uncover when it is most likely for a nomination to face extreme senatorial opposition. All else being equal, Model 3 predicts that unopposed male and female nominees receiving a committee vote in a non-presidential election year will both be unanimously confirmed. Alternatively, if the nominee is female and opposed by interest groups, and if her committee vote occurs in a presidential election year, the model predicts that she will receive 48.4 percent negative votes. This predicted probability highlights how the right combination of personal and political factors may lead to defeat, an important finding given that only six nominees were actually defeated in committee during the time period under analysis. These factors in part explain the defeat of Susan Liebeler's nomination during the 100th Congress.

In sum, interest groups decisively influence whether nominations are turned down the public partisan track. The informational and ideological cues offered by interest groups when they object to circuit court nominees are by far the most significant predictors of whether a nomination will receive negative votes in committee. Groups speak out loudly against nominees they find troublesome. Even more important, senators listen: these nominees will likely face a bruising battle for confirmation and negative votes in committee. In stark contrast, unopposed nominations are basically shielded from senatorial scrutiny.

While group opposition does not guarantee defeat, it does make the confirmation of ideologically extreme nominees all the more costly for presidents. Senators are becoming more and more willing to vote against nominees they find ideologically extreme, and to do so even when in the Senate minority. By making it clear that objectionable nominees will encounter a tough confirmation battle, groups (and the senators who heed their call) strategically utilize their power to oppose to influence presidential calculations about which nominations are worth fighting over. Groups thus play a crucial role in determining who will sit on the federal bench, and they have ensured that presidents and supporting senators must take their concerns seriously.

However, it is still true that the vast majority of nominees face little to no opposition. Nominees are much more likely to become ensnared in the private political fights discussed in chapter 3 than they are to be opposed by an interest group. Even when nominees are opposed by groups, senators must still agree to vote against the nominee. The results shown here highlight both that senators oppose nominees without group objections only in rare cases, but also that senators may reject group cues when other forces are at work. Most important, even intense group opposition cannot trump the institutional norm of collegiality among senators: as highlighted by Dennis Shedd's nomination, nominees who previously worked for the Judiciary Committee are all but guaranteed unanimous approval from the committee.

These results indicate that while group opposition sends a nomination down the public partisan track, groups still need to convince senators to vote no, and they must make a strong case to secure this necessary senatorial support. Groups are therefore waging louder and more organized public partisan campaigns in an effort to convince senators to vote against troublesome nominees. These campaigns amplify the amount of partisan and ideological tension surrounding the lower court confirmation process. These tensions reached a boiling point during the George W. Bush administration.

The Future of Public Partisan Battles

This chapter has so far examined the role of interest groups in making circuit court nominations controversial at the committee stage by convincing senators to vote against these nominations and potentially defeat them. The reality is that most nominees make it through the Senate fairly easily, and even opposed nominees are likely to be confirmed.

However, groups—and like-minded senators—can force the president and supporting senators to expend precious resources to ensure a contested nominee is eventually confirmed. As the increasing ideological and partisan polarization has affected the Senate more generally, it has in turn influenced how judicial confirmation politics play out on the Senate floor. During the 108th and 109th Congresses, this partisan battle reached its apex when the minority Senate Democrats successfully filibustered ten nominees on the Senate floor and blocked their confirmations.

A filibuster is the epitome of a public partisan battle: opposing senators take the drastic step of refusing to allow debate on the nomination to come to an end, and thus publicly bring the operation of the Senate to a halt. While filibusters and holds are closely connected, they are also quite different in nature. A hold tells the majority leader that a senator will object to bringing a piece of legislation or nomination to a vote; in theory, the senator placing the hold is implying he or she will stage a filibuster if the majority leader does not heed the senator's wishes. However, as shown in chapter 3, holds are generally used to conduct behind-the-scenes negotiations. Holds are a powerful private political tool rather than a public expression of opposition.

In stark contrast, filibusters are highly public and dramatic. To sustain a filibuster, senators must continuously speak on the Senate floor—and, in today's age, on television—an action that serves to suspend all other Senate business and, for all intents and purposes, shuts down the Senate. If a motion to end debate is brought to a vote, sixty senators must agree to invoke cloture; if the cloture vote fails, debate continues. Once cloture is invoked, the Senate must devote a maximum of thirty *more* hours of floor debate to the nomination or bill, and only then is a floor vote held (see Beth and Bach 2003; Davis 2007).[20] Thus, filibusters vividly reflect the power even individual senators possess to make their voices heard.

In 2003, the brewing battle over lower court nominations came to a head. The fight began during the Clinton presidency when conservative senators successfully blocked the confirmation of numerous Clinton nominees. The Republican senators argued the blocked nominees were ideologues who would tilt the federal bench in a liberal direction on issues such as abortion, crime, and affirmative action. Since Republicans controlled the Senate for all but two years of Clinton's administration, they could easily block the nominations; for example, the Judiciary Committee chair could simply not schedule a hearing or committee vote, and the majority leader could simply not schedule a floor vote or could strictly honor all holds.

When George W. Bush became president, Democrats scrutinized his judicial nominations closely. Democrats were upset with the treatment of Clinton's nominees, and they feared Bush would nominate what they viewed as conservative ideologues. Democrats also believed Bush was unlikely to adequately consult them about potential nominees. Since a Supreme Court vacancy seemed unlikely at the start of his administration, Democrats and liberal interest groups were ready to battle over Bush's lower court nominees. Once Bush announced his first set of nominations on May 9, 2001, liberal Democrats and liberal groups responded forcefully and negatively. In particular, they opposed the nominations of Priscilla Owen and Charles Pickering.

Then, in July 2001, the political environment changed dramatically: Jim Jeffords, a Republican senator from Vermont, announced he was becoming an Independent and would henceforth caucus with the Senate Democrats. His defection swung the Senate majority to the Democrats, as well as control of the Judiciary Committee. Both Owen and Pickering were subsequently defeated in committee on party-line votes, and a number of other nominees faced bruising battles on their path to confirmation.[21]

During the 2002 midterm elections, the Republicans regained the Senate majority. Bush promptly renominated a host of opposed nominees, including Owen and Pickering. This immediately drew vigorous complaints from Senate Democrats, who argued that Owen and Pickering had been legitimately defeated during the previous Congress.

Chairman Orrin Hatch first moved the nomination of Miguel Estrada to the D.C. Circuit; Estrada had not had any action taken on his nomination during the previous congress. Judiciary Democrats, who had voiced strong objections to Estrada's nomination, voted unanimously to reject his nomination; however, he was successfully passed out of committee. When Estrada's nomination was brought up for a floor vote, Democrats decided to mount a protest against Estrada's nomination and Bush's nominees more generally. This protest culminated in a filibuster on March 6, 2003. The filibuster reflected the Democrats' willingness to fight a nominee solely on ideological grounds, and their continued complaint that Bush was not adequately consulting Democratic senators on his lower court nominations.

The fight did not end there. While Estrada's filibuster was ongoing,

Hatch brought the Owen and Pickering nominations up for new committee votes. This time, both passed successfully out of committee, again on party-line votes. When they were brought up for votes on the Senate floor, Senate Democrats vehemently and publicly objected, and they filibustered both nominations. By the end of the 108th Congress, the Senate Democrats had mounted ten successful filibusters of Bush's circuit court nominees, and tensions between the parties had reached an all-time high.

Ironically, Senate Democrats were aided in this endeavor by then Senate Majority Leader Bill Frist. Usually filibustering senators must take to the Senate floor and literally talk continuously to prevent consideration of the opposed measure (or any other). Frist decided, in the interest of ensuring the Senate could complete its other legislative business, to engage in a process known as "dual tracking." In the Senate, bills are placed on the Legislative Calendar and nominations on the Executive Calendar. Typically, the Senate deals with only one calendar at a time. Frist, however, allowed the two calendars to run simultaneously. Consequently, the Democrats could filibuster the nominations without actually having to bring the Senate to a halt. Frist's decision meant important legislative work was completed, but it also minimized, if not erased, the political costs of staging these filibusters. Since Democrats did not actually stop the Senate's operation, it was much more difficult for Republicans to levy charges of obstructionism against them. The actual filibusters were much less public and noticeable because senators did not have to publicly continue floor debate on the nominations. Thus, it was only the extremely educated citizen who was likely to comprehend the fact that the Democrats were indeed filibustering a record number of nominees.[22]

All of these factors worked to make these filibusters highly successful and the partisan tensions extreme. By 2005, the strains were evident, and more and more actors called for exercise of the so-called "nuclear option." The nuclear option proposed altering Senate Rule XXII to allow judicial filibusters to be ended merely by a majority vote, rather than a supermajority.[23] However, this action would directly undercut an important institutional goal of the Senate, namely, the notion that even a small minority of senators in vigorous opposition should be heard. On May 23, 2005, the Gang of Fourteen came to the rescue. A group of seven Republicans and seven Democrats banded together to end the stalemate. To prevent the nuclear option from being invoked and to resolve the existing disputes, these senators agreed a number of highly contested nominees, including Priscilla Owen, would receive a floor vote. They also stipulated that future filibusters against judicial nominees could occur only in "extraordinary circumstances."

The Gang of Fourteen in many ways saved the Senate and the lower court confirmation process. Nominees who had long been stalled were confirmed, and certain highly controversial nominees were withdrawn by the White House. And, since May 2005, while there have been public fights over circuit court nominees, the process has proceeded relatively smoothly: the Democratic majority in the 110th Congress continued to use its powers of scheduling to impede certain nominations, but consideration of Bush's nominations on the floor was reasonably trouble-free in comparison to the drama of earlier Congresses.

Conclusion

What do this story and the findings reported above suggest? First, while interest groups play an important role in the lower court confirmation process by identifying ideologically extreme nominees, it is still senators who must agree to vote against these nominees. Without crucial Senate support, nominees are almost guaranteed confirmation. Senators are also willing to ignore group objections when other important factors arise, such as with former Judiciary Committee staffers. Second, some senators are more willing than in past years to publicly fight against ideologically objectionable nominees, and to do so even with a measure of last resort, the filibuster. The increased number of attacks on nominees and the increased rate at which senators are responding favorably to these attacks suggest that lower court confirmation politics have the potential to erupt if relations between the president and the Senate are again stretched to a breaking point. One question for the Obama administration will be the degree to which President Obama collaborates with home-state senators, including Republican senators, to try to forestall such scuffles. Third, and perhaps most important, the final pages of this story also reveal that historical deference in favor of a president's lower court nominees is still alive and well. The deal brokered by the Gang of Fourteen ensured that nominees who had been the source of incredible conflict between President Bush and Senate Democrats were confirmed to the federal bench. Rather than necessarily granting Democratic senators an increased role in the selection process, the Gang of Fourteen focused on diffusing tensions and, ultimately, confirming as many nominees as possible. In the end, the norm of Senate collegiality trumped partisan and ideological concerns.

In sum, interest group objections decisively turn judicial nominations down the public partisan track, and these objections send valuable cues to senators as to which nominees are potentially troublesome. However, senators can and do reject these cues, and without crucial Senate support, even opposed nominees will eventually be confirmed. Thus, the future of judicial confirmations seems to be one in which senatorial deference to lower court nominees still exists, and only in "extraordinary" situations will nominees be defeated.

CONCLUSION

What the Future Holds for Lower Court Nominations and the Senate Confirmation Process

This book tells the story of how presidents, senators, interest groups, and concerned citizens battle over who sits on the federal courts. In one sense, it is the story of how individual senators possess enormous power over the operation of the Senate and the fate of judicial nominees; in another sense it is the story of how mobilized activists and citizens play a significant role in determining who will be confirmed to the federal bench. In both cases, it is the story of how the key actors in American politics have all realized the enormous power federal courts wield and that *who* sits on the bench many times determines the legal and political decisions these courts will reach.

Many of today's most important political debates are actually debates over legal policy. Whether women have a right to choose to have an abortion and what restrictions may be placed on that right are decisions ultimately made by the federal courts. So too are decisions about the rights of criminal defendants and suspected terrorists, the regulation of guns, and whether public school districts may pursue voluntary integration plans or voucher programs involving parochial schools. The legislative and executive officials at both state and national levels must thus pay close attention to the legal boundaries that define their ability to pass new legislation on these issues.

While many draw attention to decisions handed down by the U.S. Supreme Court, the reality is that the lower federal courts deal almost continually with the types of issues listed above. For example, between October 2007 and September 2008, the twelve geographically based circuit courts handled more than 5,000 cases dealing with civil rights and liberties and more than 3,500 cases dealing with prisoners' civil rights (Duff 2008). In comparison, during the 2006 term (October 2006–April 2007), the U.S. Supreme Court heard only twelve cases that contained any type of civil rights and liberties issue. The Supreme Court's decisions are important because they apply nationally, but 99 percent of cases adjudicated in the federal system—including those involving state laws—go no farther than the circuit courts. It is the judges on the circuit courts who ultimately decide thousands of important cases every single year, and so these judges also have an enormous impact on American public policy. Why? Because every time an appeals court judge interprets a law, he or she creates legal precedent and, in effect, makes policy.

As a result, presidents, senators, interest groups, and citizens have turned their attention to the staffing of the lower federal courts. Each of these important actors in the American political process has begun to realize that *who* sits on the federal bench has an enormous impact on *what* decisions are made in these courts. Judges are not robots who mechanically apply the law to the cases they hear; as Judge Robert Posner famously remarked, judges are not "potted plants" (Posner 1987). Judges make decisions based on the case facts, existing case law, and at times their own personal preferences.

Why do personal preferences ever come into play? Because the law is not always clear, and many legal issues are, to put it mildly, difficult and complex. Corley, Steigerwalt, and Ward (2008) find that more legal ambiguity and complexity increases the likelihood of disagreements among the justices as to the "correct" legal answer to the question at hand. When the constraining force of law is at a minimum, personal policy preferences are likely to determine the ultimate outcome in the case. For example, the Fourth Amendment of the U.S. Constitution protects against "unreasonable search and seizures." However, what does "unreasonable" mean? Is it unreasonable for the police to enter a house when they believe someone may be hurt, even if they lack a warrant? Is it unreasonable for police to chase a robbery suspect into a private building, even if they lack a warrant? What about a murder suspect, or a child accused of skipping school? Reasonable people—and, by extension, reasonable judges—differ as to the answers to these questions for which the law does not provide a clear answer. Judges who believe police need to be free to do their job in order to keep their communities safe are more likely to uphold warrantless searches, while judges who believe we need to protect innocent citizens against police abuses of power are more likely to closely scrutinize these searches. When the law is not clear, and thus the legal answer is not clear, judges' personal preferences will inherently influence their decisions. Since judges, and especially appellate court judges, are asked to decide cases without a clear-cut legal answer every day, the staffing of the federal appeals courts takes on enormous import.

This book therefore has focused on understanding the process by which judges are confirmed to the lower federal courts. But to understand who sits on the court, we need to first understand how they get there. By examining the path nominees follow from nomination to confirmation, we can discover who is being successfully confirmed and, just as important, which actors directly influence who is confirmed. I argue for conceptualizing the judicial confirmation process as a set of interconnected train tracks and each nomination as a train moving along these tracks from nomination to confirmation, occasionally being diverted from one track to another at different points in the confirmation process. This conceptualization of the confirmation process reveals how senators and interest groups may take actions that cause nominations to switch tracks, actions that may delay or even derail confirmation.

The four tracks framework provides a comprehensive analytic framework for understanding why some nominees are easily confirmed while others face a long, hard path to confirmation. This framework highlights the different confirmation environments nominations may face, as well as the fact that nominations may confront more than one of these confirmation environments as they move through the confirmation process. It also reveals how senators and interest groups both exert enormous influence over confirmation outcomes. Senators use potent parliamentary procedures to delay and possibly defeat nominations. Senators use these parliamentary tools for a variety of reasons, however, and not just to block objectionable nominees. Interest groups fill a sizable resource gap by providing detailed information about nominees and their views, as well as identifying which nominees senators should closely vet. Groups then work to defeat objectionable nominees and to secure the necessary senatorial opposition. The four tracks framework therefore helps us appreciate the implications of the structural components of the confirmation process as well as the roles performed by key actors, and thus aids in understanding who gets successfully seated on the federal bench.

The empirical overview presented in chapter 1 revealed that the overwhelming majority of circuit court nominations are confirmed relatively quickly and without resistance, thus following the noncontroversial track. Even as headlines are dominated by concerns about the increasing politicization of the lower court confirmation process, it is still true today that most nominations encounter little scrutiny or opposition. Out of 272 total nominations made to the circuit courts between 1985 and 2006, only fifty-four encountered concerted campaigns by interest groups to defeat their nominations. More broadly, the Senate confirmed

208 nominees to the circuit courts during this time frame, and 175 were confirmed unanimously by the full Senate.

However, this overview also revealed that even so-called noncontroversial nominations may encounter impediments on their path to confirmation. Examination of the senatorial courtesy and private political tracks highlighted senators' increasing use of parliamentary procedures to delay nominations in order to gain leverage in unrelated disputes with other senators or the current administration. Simply put, the reality is that nominations are indeed being routinely delayed, but not necessarily for the reasons commonly assumed.

Chapters 2 through 6 provided an in-depth empirical investigation of the senatorial courtesy, private political, and public partisan tracks to determine what motivates senators and interest groups to push a nomination off the noncontroversial track and onto one of the three other tracks. Chapters 2 and 3 focused on two parliamentary tools senators may use to delay, and possibly defeat, judicial nominations: senatorial courtesy and holds. These chapters systematically identified when these parliamentary tools were utilized against circuit court nominations, and why the particular nominations were blocked.

I found that senators use these two tactics, especially holds, because judicial nominations have become convenient, if not favored, bargaining chips in the modern-day legislative process. As the old adage states, no one likes to see how sausages or laws are made, because neither process is particularly pretty. In order to see their preferred bills passed and their home-state nominees confirmed, senators engage in a tit-for-tat game of bargaining and compromise. When the president or their colleagues seem unwilling to grant their requests, senators may pursue a strategy of hostage-taking, with judicial nominations as the captives. Senators trap judicial nominations to gain leverage in other, often wholly unrelated, disputes.

Judicial nominations provide an advantageous target for private partisan tactics because relatively few people care about whether each nominee is confirmed, and because in general, lower court nominations garner little media attention. Furthermore, the use of rather arcane and complicated Senate parliamentary procedures attracts even less attention and notice by the media or the public. Senators increasingly capture judicial nominations in holds as a way to see their goals fulfilled. In almost every case, the nominations are trapped for convenience. They are convenient because they are important to the person the senator is feuding with or because they are at the right point in the confirmation process at the right (or rather wrong) time. For example, Senator John McCain blocked progress on all of George W. Bush's nominations awaiting Senate floor votes in 2002, including seventeen judicial nominations, because he wanted Bush, a fellow Republican, to nominate his choice for the Federal Election Committee. McCain did not oppose any of the blocked nominees themselves. In fact, McCain eventually voted to confirm all of these nominees, but not until Bush responded to his demands. McCain realized, as have his Senate colleagues, that judicial nominations make extremely powerful bargaining tools.

Chapters 2 and 3 highlighted how individual senators can exert enormous power over both the outcomes of judicial nominations and the entire operation of the Senate. The Senate was originally created as an antidote to the anticipated problems of a publicly elected House of Representatives, in which passions might flare and temporal emotions might overtake reasoned debate. The Senate's rules encourage extended debate, and give more power over Senate functions to individual senators than to House members. Senators' longer terms of office (six years, versus two years in the House) were intended to elevate debate over passion. These longer terms also encourage a heightened degree of collegiality among senators. As a result, informal customs have developed and become institutionalized over time that reflect these Senate norms of debate and collegiality.

Senatorial courtesy and holds are two such informal, institutionalized customs. Senatorial courtesy allows senators to block objectionable home-state nominees. It developed as a mechanism of reprisal for home-state senators who believed they were not adequately consulted by the president as to who should be nominated from their home state. Senators would call upon their colleagues to grant them the "courtesy" of blocking the president's preferred nominee. In its modern-day incarnation, senators are allowed to block objectionable home-state nominees from the outset by returning a negative blue slip; negative blue slips generally prevent nominees from even receiving a Judiciary Committee hearing.

At its core, senatorial courtesy reflects the ongoing institutional struggle between the Senate and the executive branch over who rightfully holds the power to select nominees to the federal courts. Chapter 2 examined in detail each instance of senatorial courtesy between 1985 and 2006 and the motivation behind the senator's use of senatorial courtesy. Overall, senators block nominees through the use of senatorial courtesy in order to gain leverage in ongoing institutional disputes over nominee selection power or to exact retribution for the treatment of past favored nominees. Senatorial courtesy blocks nominees from progressing through the confirmation process, and it is but one tangible way in which we see the continuing fight over what the Senate's constitutional power of "advice and consent" means play out. Furthermore, given the prevalence of senatorial courtesy as a tool to exact leverage or retaliation, senators now frequently invoke senatorial courtesy as a temporary block rather than a permanent blockade. In eight of twenty instances of senatorial courtesy, the nominees were eventually confirmed; in each case, the nominees were confirmed once the administration had reached an agreement with the blocking senators. This finding provides further evidence of how historically straightforward objections to particular nominees have been transformed into devices through which senators can manipulate judicial nominations to pursue their own goals.

Senators can also ask the majority leader to put a hold on a bill or nomination once it has reached the Senate floor. By placing a hold, the senator signals the majority leader that he or she will stage a filibuster if the bill or nomination is brought up for a vote. Since floor time is limited, majority leaders generally support senators' holds to ensure that other bills and nominations are acted on. Holds thus grant individual senators enormous power by allowing them to halt the progress of bills and nominations. Since holds on nominations are extremely powerful, senators use them to gain leverage in unrelated disputes. Lower court nominations fly below the radar for most political elites and citizens; few people pay attention to who is nominated to each lower court vacancy, and what happens to each nominee. Senators can therefore place holds on judicial nominees, bringing their nominations to a halt, with relatively little political cost. Nominees may wait for floor votes for a variety of reasons, and so a delay due to a hold is unlikely to draw broad attention. On the other hand, the president or the home-state senators may care deeply about the nominees caught in these holds. Presidents want to see their nominees confirmed, and home-state senators may have strong personal or political ties to the nominee. Senators therefore place holds as a way of forcing the president or their colleagues to the bargaining table.

As discussed in chapter 3, these tactics work well: blocking senators usually achieve their desired outcome, and the political cost to them is generally low. Congress works through bargaining and compromise, and holds are a powerful tool senators can use to see their policy goals enacted and their nominees confirmed. Since all measures require at least majority support, holds allow individual senators to gain traction when conflicts over legislation or other issues arise. By conducting behind-the-scenes negotiations—and using a truly "inside the Beltway" mechanism to do so—senators can attain their goals at relatively little expense. While these holds may seem to belie the Senate norm of collegiality, they are viewed as an accepted cost of doing business. The fact that nominees are caught in the middle is but one more way in which judicial nominations have become part of the "normal" politics of the Senate.

However, this analysis of parliamentary procedures and behind-the-scenes negotiation does not tell the entire story of what happens to lower court nominees once their nominations are sent to the Senate. Beginning with chapter 4, I investigated what happens when nominations are forced onto the public partisan track. This section of the book focused on both senators and the third key player in lower court confirmation politics: interest groups.

Senators face enormous resource constraints on the issue of lower court selection; they especially lack the time and staff to investigate fully the hundreds of lower court nominations made each presidential term. As explicated in chapter 4, interest groups play a crucial role in investigating nominees and alerting senators to which nominees are potentially problematic. This information allows senators to differentiate among the dozens of nominations pending at any one time and determine who needs to be carefully scrutinized and who can be easily confirmed. Since the vast majority of nominees are confirmed easily and without opposition, groups help identify problematic nominees by sounding a fire alarm (Scherer, Bartels, and Steigerwalt 2008). Chapter 5 detailed through interviews with group leaders how groups decide which nominees they should try to defeat. Finally, chapter 6 showed that when groups raise fire alarms about lower court nominees, senators listen. They listen because they lack the resources to identify potentially extreme nominees on their own, and they listen because they risk political retaliation if they do not (Scherer 2003, 2005). When groups publicly object to a nominee, the nominee is destined to face a long, hard road to confirmation and a bruising confirmation fight. Although interest group opposition does not ensure defeat, it does decisively raise the stakes for all the players involved. Presidents and home-state senators must now divert precious political capital away from other important priorities, and the Senate must now devote valuable committee and floor time to vetting the nominee. Interest group objections raise the battle flags and ensure a concerted effort will need to be mounted to see these nominees successfully confirmed.

Interest groups recognize the long-term consequences of their objections. Groups fight nominees to prevent objectionable nominees from

being confirmed, but they also fight nominees in order to influence future nomination choices. Groups want presidents (and home-state senators) to recognize that extreme nominee choices will force them to divert resources away from legislative priorities in order to battle for their
favored nominees. Groups also want to remind these elected officials
that mobilized citizens and voters are increasingly scrutinizing who is
being confirmed to the federal bench and who votes for and against each
nominee. For example, pro-life and pro-choice groups pay close attention to who stands with them not just on legislative votes, but also on
judicial nomination votes. D. Brooks Smith, a George W. Bush nominee, was opposed by the National Organization for Women (NOW) in
part because of his opposition to the Violence Against Women Act and
membership in a male-only club. After Senators Joseph Biden and John
Edwards voted for Smith in committee in 2002, NOW issued a press
release claiming that the list of potential 2004 Democratic presidential
candidates "was significantly narrowed today."[1] NOW leaders wished
to make clear that they and their members were paying close attention
to whether senators stood with them in their fights against nominees.
Nomination politics may also bleed into electoral politics. One factor
attributed to Senator John Ashcroft's 2000 reelection defeat was his role
in the defeat of Ronnie White, an African American, to a district court
seat in Missouri (Scherer 2005). Black civil rights leaders and civil rights
groups launched a highly emotional campaign to oust Ashcroft from the
Senate. These accounts show that senators disregard the wishes of interest
groups at their peril.

In sum, judicial nominations have become part of the normal politics
of the Senate. Bargaining and negotiation, ideology and interest group
participation all characterize the modern-day judicial confirmation process. As senators work to see their policy goals become reality, judicial
nominations make useful bargaining chips. Furthermore, fights over
ideology and policy play out daily in the Judiciary Committee and on
the Senate floor as senators, the president, and outside groups all battle
over who gets to sit on the federal bench. Nominees' past issue positions,
public speeches and writings, and judicial opinions are scrutinized by
people on all sides of the debate. Senators' positions on nominees and
votes are closely watched. And in the modern era, even potential senatorial candidates' views on judicial nominees are investigated and used as
reasons to support or oppose possible candidates.

What does all this mean for the future of the lower court confirmation
process? The findings presented throughout this book lead to a few pre-

dictions. First, given the increased ideological and partisan polarization in American politics, judicial confirmation fights will likely continue. As more and more issues move from the legislatures to the courts, and as more and more people recognize the policy implications of even seemingly routine statutory interpretation decisions, debates over the views of judges will only increase. Groups on both sides of the aisle, along with politicians and concerned citizens, recognize that legal decisions and personal policy preferences are many times intertwined. Put simply, the more legally ambiguous and complex an issue, the more likely a judge's personal views will play a role. Central actors will thus turn more attention to trying to uncover how potential judges will rule on these issues. Candidates for office (including the two presidential candidates) in 2008, along with opinion leaders and group leaders, regularly highlighted the types of judges they thought should be appointed to the federal bench. The issue of judicial selection is moving more and more into the mainstream political arena, and in response, judicial confirmations will likely become even more debated and divisive.

Second, the role of interest groups in influencing the outcomes of judicial confirmations will likely grow stronger. The very real resource constraints senators confront are unlikely to be mitigated anytime soon. Groups that are able to invest time and resources in vetting potential federal judges will continue to be listened to by senators on both sides of the aisle, and the potential electoral consequences of not listening to these groups loom large as well.

While solving the issue of resource constraints seems simple—the Senate could merely hire more staff devoted to vetting judicial nominees—such a solution is both unlikely and potentially flawed. Hiring more staff is expensive, and the public and elected officials alike routinely complain about the costs of running Congress (see, e.g., Greenberg 1994; Thompson 2006; Updegrave 1992; Yehle 2009). For example, in 1994, Newt Gingrich's Contract with America strongly advocated decreasing the size of government. Immediately after the 1994 elections, the new House Republican leadership moved to reduce the number of legislative staff, concentrating primarily on cutting committee staff—which is what this proposal involves—as opposed to personal staff (Thomas 1994). Thus, while Judiciary Committee staff increases may solve the information gap and decrease reliance on interest group–provided information, such solutions are not always politically palatable.

Furthermore, increasing the number of committee staff may not solve the inherent bias problem associated with interest group–provided information. Outside groups vet nominees with an eye to their organizations' agendas and interests, and their evaluations reflect these concerns. Ironically, however, the seeming neutrality of committee staff may compound these bias concerns. Committee staffers are hired for their expertise in the committee's area of specialization. Senate (and House) committee staff work explicitly, however, for either the majority or minority party. As a result, while staff evaluations of nominees may be objective, they also likely reflect the issues and concerns of their respective parties. Thus, adding more committee staff—especially if the staff is concentrated in either the majority or minority office—may not solve the concerns that motivate many critiques of interest group–provided information.

Finally, the underlying question is whether increasing staff resources will lead to differing conclusions and outcomes. Hiring more staff and devoting more Senate resources to independently vetting each nominee is advantageous only if these investigations noticeably alter nominee evaluations. If Senate staffs produce reports that mirror the conclusions of outside groups, increased Senate resources may not solve the implicit bias concerns and would suggest that such resources could be better spent elsewhere. While chapter 6 found that nominations opposed by interest groups face a much more difficult path to confirmation, it also highlighted the corresponding realities: in the end, even opposed nominees are usually confirmed, and senators can (and do) ignore these group cues and confirm opposed nominees with little fanfare. These findings suggest that senators filter the information they receive from groups. Consequently, a potential concern is whether increasing staff resources may actually result in more scrutiny of judicial nominees and thus *more* confirmation fights. Senators do not currently oppose judicial nominees without sufficient prodding. However, if their opposition is based on Senate-led investigations, senators may become more willing to oppose nominees, since such decisions would not be as open to criticisms of undue outside influence.

Recent events also suggest *more* groups are likely to become involved in lower court confirmation politics. In particular, conservative groups are increasingly scrutinizing judicial confirmations, especially with the recent election of Barack Obama. Conservative groups now play a more principal role in the process as they have switched from merely supporting the president's nominees to opposing nominees they view as problematic. Conservative, rather than liberal, opposition will also likely mean a change in the central issues of concern. Beyond abortion, liberal groups focused on vetting whether George W. Bush's candidates held, in their view, extreme positions on race, sex, and disability discrimination, environmental issues, and the rights of workers. Conservative groups are likely to shift the focus to whether, in their view, nominees possess extreme positions on issues of law and order, such as opposition to the death penalty and due process complaints, as well as gay marriage and issues of religion in public life. Thus, while the level of intensity will likely stay the same—if not become greater—the shift to the Democratic Obama administration will likely lead to a major shift in the types of debates elected officials and interest groups have over who is fit to sit on the federal bench. The responses to Obama's first Supreme Court nominee, Judge Sonia Sotomayor, suggested this shift is occurring; she drew fire, for example, for being too "empathetic" and for joining a Second Circuit opinion that dismissed a reverse discrimination claim.[2]

Third, even as the level of public scrutiny over lower court appointments has risen, it is still low, so senators will likely continue to use judicial nominations as convenient bargaining chips in unrelated disputes. The need for a majority, if not a super-majority, to pass legislation in the Senate and see presidential nominations confirmed means senators continuously need leverage to see their goals enacted. Blocks on nominations offer a relatively expedient and low-cost mechanism to secure this leverage and commence negotiations.

The concern is that using nominations as bargaining chips further hampers the ability of the Senate to act expeditiously on lower court nominations. This in turn affects the ability of the lower federal courts to operate effectively, and in particular the ability of the circuit courts to efficiently hear and process cases. Nemachek (2008b) highlights how the circuit courts are becoming increasingly reliant on district court judges to help handle their caseloads. District court judges may sit by designation on circuit court panels to help the circuit courts hear more cases. District court judges, however, are vetted not for the job of handling appeals but rather for the job of presiding over trials—which is both substantively and legally distinct. The biggest difference is that appellate judges focus on addressing questions of law rather than questions of fact; put another way, trial judges resolve disputes and determine facts such as guilt or innocence, while appellate judges interpret and apply legal doctrine. The question left unanswered is how the use of district court judges on circuit court panels is influencing case outcomes and legal policy. When a district court judge sits on a circuit court panel, does it matter that these judges are not vetted as closely as circuit court judges and are vetted for a qualitatively different job? If the amount of time it takes for circuit court nominees to move through the process continues to lengthen, these concerns will need to be addressed.

Fourth, the increased divisiveness and growing length of time it takes to be confirmed in the present era may create problems for the nominees themselves (see Holmes 2008b). Nominees may be subjected to waits of months, if not years, and these waits can cause real hardships for the nominees and their families. For nominees in private practice, a long-pending nomination may be harmful to their livelihood. These nominees may feel pressure not to take on new cases, as complications or conflicts of interest may arise as their nomination progresses; as a result, nominees may lose substantial income while waiting for their nominations to wind through the Senate. Concerns have arisen that many potentially good candidates are removing themselves from consideration because they do not want to put their lives on hold during the nomination process. In his *2001 Year-End Report on the Federal Judiciary*, Chief Justice Rehnquist expressed his concern that long confirmation delays (along with inadequate pay) might scare off potential nominees: "The combination of inadequate pay and a drawn-out and uncertain confirmation process is a handicap to judicial recruitment across the board, but it most significantly restricts the universe of lawyers in private practice who are willing to be nominated for a federal judgeship. . . . [F]or lawyers coming directly from private practice, there is both a strong financial disincentive and the possibility of losing clients in the course of the wait for a confirmation vote" (Rehnquist 2002).

During a May 2002 Judiciary Committee hearing entitled "Ghosts of Nominations Past," former unsuccessful nominees all related at least some personal and professional harm. More recently, Charles Pickering (2006) argued in a *Washington Times* op-ed that "it is not surprising the 'brightest and best' young lawyers are deciding to direct their legal careers away from a judicial tract. They simply are unwilling to subject themselves and their families to such a humiliating process where they are viewed as mere pawns in a bitter, highly partisan political fight, and not as flesh-and-blood human beings with feelings and pride in their records." One broad impact of the findings presented throughout this book may be that the number of willing and able nominees will decrease in the future as potential candidates weigh whether they can withstand the personal and professional burdens a lengthy confirmation process entails.

Finally, what do these findings suggest more broadly about the future of our federal courts and judicial independence? The founders created a federal judiciary that was to be insulated from political pressures by appointing (rather than electing) judges and granting them life tenure. But increasingly political fights over who should sit on the bench dominate the modern-day lower court confirmation process. These fights are the result of presidents seeking to create a lasting policy legacy through judicial appointments, as well as senators and interest groups working to ensure their favored views are represented. The increased presence of interest groups ensures that more ideologically based factors are considered as these groups focus on making sure the confirmed judges reflect their policy concerns. Many interest groups—especially issue groups—seek judges who they believe will rule a certain way on certain issues. For those groups engaged in the fight over reproductive rights or gay marriage, the central question is how these potential judges will rule in such cases once on the bench. However, such a narrow-minded focus on particular issues can cloud reasoned debate. As several noted during the Supreme Court confirmations of John Roberts and Samuel Alito, debates over federal judicial nominees often seem reduced to the question of how the different sides believe the nominees will rule on cases involving *Roe v. Wade.*

Who sits on the federal bench is of tremendous importance, and debate over nominations is healthy. In fact, robust debate is most likely what the founders intended. Many debates over judicial nominations reflect the ongoing struggle over the fact that the Constitution requires both the president and the Senate to play a role in selecting federal judges. The Constitution deliberately splits this power between the president and the Senate by giving the president the authority to nominate and the Senate the duty to provide advice and consent. Earlier eras of trouble-free lower court nominations reflected, in part, presidential deference to senators in nominating lower court judges. However, as presidents began to recognize the policymaking implications of lower court selection, they worked to reclaim their nomination powers. Increased presidential nomination powers have in turn led to increased senatorial oversight at the confirmation stage. If senators are not allowed to offer advice in selecting judicial nominees, then they have determined that their consent must be won.

Neither branch was given complete power over judicial selection because the founders wanted to ensure that the voices of the many would be heard. However, it is also likely that the founders never anticipated the degree of public participation in the modern judicial confirmation process. Interest groups today perform the critical function of transmitting nominee information and citizen views to senators and presidents. While those who drafted Article III did not conceive of the role of interest groups—or even a publicly elected Senate—in the federal judicial confirmation process, our political system has continually evolved, and evolved in favor of increased input from all sides. As a result, we should be suspicious of attempts to make the process less transparent, and of efforts to limit whose voices are heard. We must also be vigilant to protect against a desire to conflate professional qualifications with the requirement that nominees hold certain policy positions. If we have learned no other lesson from American history, it is that a robust and inclusive debate—whether among citizens, legislators, or judges—is the best form of protection for the interests of all.

APPENDIX A

Data Collection Methodology

The empirical analysis undertaken for this book is based on a data set with information on all circuit court nominations made during the 99th through 109th Congresses (1985–2006). This unique data set contains information not just on nominees' backgrounds, progress through the confirmation process, votes, and ultimate outcomes but also on whether each nominee was subjected to a number of parliamentary procedures and whether he or she was publicly opposed by an interest group.

The data collection for this project was intensive, as much of the information needed for the study is not easily obtained from outside sources or governmental sources. For example, the Senate leadership does not keep records on holds that are placed on nominations or bills. Similarly, there is no central collection of information concerning whether nominees have been objected to by interest groups. Therefore, to collect the data, I conducted a series of comprehensive searches of newspaper archives.

I began with multilevel searches of Lexis-Nexis's General Newspapers database and Westlaw's All News database to find articles that mentioned any of the circuit court nominees included in this study and which were written during the period their nomination was pending. I then scrutinized each article mentioning a nominee for information about either (1) an interest group objection to the nomination, or (2) senatorial courtesy being used against the nomination, or (3) a hold being placed on the nomination. I noted (1) which groups, if any, opposed each nominee and the date that opposition was announced; (2) whether the two home-state senators invoked senatorial courtesy, and possible motivations for this use of senatorial courtesy; and (3) information on all holds placed against the nominee, including who placed the hold, how long it lasted, the reason for the hold, and whether it affected any other nominations.

Any additional information about the progress of the nomination or delays mentioned in the article was also recorded.

To ensure that all interest group objections lodged against circuit court nominees were captured, I also conducted a series of multilevel searches in the same archives for articles about, or press releases by, interest groups that are consistently involved in the judicial confirmation process. These articles were read to see whether they announced opposition to specific nominees in order to ensure all possible group objections were recorded. Finally, to verify the comprehensiveness of these searches, I compared the press releases announcing opposition to George W. Bush's judicial nominees archived on the Web sites of the Alliance for Justice and People for the American Way—the two leading liberal judicial watchdog groups— to my list of opposed nominees created through the above searches. Unfortunately, none of the leading judicial watchdog groups, liberal or conservative, has an archive of press releases prior to 2001. However, for those nominations made between 2001 and 2006, my list of opposed nominees matched the list of opposed nominees found on these two Web sites. Thus, given the fact that group opposition to a nominee necessarily sparks the public interest and media attention, and given the reliability of the post-2000 archive searches, my search method provides the most reliable manner of identifying nominees opposed by groups prior to 2001.

Next, to ensure that all instances of senatorial courtesy were recorded, I conducted a series of searches for any articles during the time frame under study that mentioned either "senatorial courtesy," "blue slips," or some type of "block" by a home-state senator. These articles were then read to determine whether a home-state senator had used senatorial courtesy against a circuit court nominee, and if so, why.

To identify all possible holds placed on circuit court nominees, I searched for any articles published during the time period under study that mentioned "holds" or "blocks" applied to any type of nomination; this search therefore captured articles about holds placed on other executive nominees to ensure that holds that were broadly applied were counted. I read each of these articles to determine whether a hold was placed, and if so, whether it affected any judicial nominations. In some instances I found reports of holds placed on particular nominations, but many times holds were placed on a group of nominations. In such cases the articles did not report whom the hold specifically captured but instead simply related that the hold applied to, for example, all judicial nominations awaiting floor action. Such articles were examined to determine, first, whether any judicial nominees were included in the hold;

second, whether all or some pending judicial nominees were included in the hold; and third, how long the hold lasted. I then calculated the dates the hold was in effect and determined which nominees were affected by the hold by looking at the dates when each nominee had a committee vote and/or floor vote. This search method thus captured not only holds placed on specific nominations but also holds placed on groups of nominations.

Finally, to identify the leading interest groups on the issue of lower court judicial selection for the interviews conducted in chapter 5, I searched Westlaw's All News database for any editorials, op-eds, and newspaper reports published between 1985 and 2006 that were written by or mentioned a member of an interest group. I double-checked this list against the list of groups that were identified as opposing each nominee to create a list of groups most consistently active on the issue of judicial selection. The groups selected represent those groups and group leaders most often cited or publishing on the issue of judicial selection during the time period under analysis. While in recent years more and more groups have become involved in judicial selection, many of these groups actively participate on only a few nominations during each congressional term, and rarely on lower court nominations. In contrast, the groups interviewed for this study were and are actively involved on almost every lower court nomination.

APPENDIX B

Variable Descriptions and Measurements for Tobit Regressions

Dependent Variable

The dependent variable is the *percentage of no votes* each nomination received in the Senate Judiciary Committee, and this variable has a potential range from 0 percent (i.e., unanimously confirmed) to 100 percent (i.e., unanimously rejected). Because of the bounded range of this variable, tobit analysis was used to estimate the models. Ordinary least squares (OLS) regression is usually preferred for continuous dependent variables, but the dependent variable used here is narrowly bounded and the observed values of the dependent variable are not normally distributed. Following Austin, Escobar, and Kopec (2000), tobit performs more robustly than OLS when the dependent variable is not normally distributed. However, the results using OLS were similar, both in terms of statistical significance and substantive effects, and the OLS results are available upon request from the author. This dependent variable was calculated based on how many senators participated in each committee vote, since commonly not all senators are present for every vote. I used the percentage of no votes rather than a count of no votes because the size of the committee has varied over time. Thus, during some Congresses seven no votes were enough for defeat, but in other years nine no votes were not. While a number of nominations were unanimously passed out of committee, only six nominations received less than a majority of yes votes and were defeated. Finally, to correct for any potential heteroskedasticity, I use robust standard errors clustered on the year of nomination.

Independent Variables

Patron—This variable designates whether the nominee has a home-state senator serving on the Judiciary Committee. This variable is coded 1 if a nominee's home-state senator served on the committee, regardless of the party of the senator or the nominee, unless the senator invoked senatorial courtesy. This is because senators use their home-state allegiances to help nominees through committee regardless of party, unless they oppose the nomination and decide to block it by invoking senatorial courtesy. For example, all of the Ohio nominees who were nominated by President Clinton are counted as having a patron in Senator DeWine, who took great pleasure in trying to make sure all of those nominees were confirmed quickly. Alternatively, Carolyn Kuhl is not counted as having a patron since her home-state senator, Diane Feinstein, blue-slipped her nomination. All other nominees are coded 0.

Former Senate Judiciary Committee Staffer—This variable denotes whether a nominee served as a staff member on the Senate Judiciary Committee. Former staff members are coded 1, and all others are coded 0.

Race—This variable is coded 1 if the nominee is white, and 0 otherwise.

Gender—This variable is coded 1 if the nominee is male, and 0 otherwise.

American Bar Association Rating—This variable reflects the nominee's ABA rating as to the nominee's level of professional competence for the federal bench. Nominees may be rated either "not qualified," "qualified," or "well qualified." They may also receive a split rating (e.g., majority "well qualified"/minority "qualified"). During the 100th and 101st Congresses a nominee could receive a rating of "extremely well qualified." However, the use of this rating was then discontinued, so those few nominees (five) who received an "extremely well qualified/well qualified" rating are coded as having received a unanimous "well qualified" rating. There were no nominees in this data set who received a unanimous "extremely well qualified" rating. The scale thus ranges from 1, unanimously "not qualified," to 7, unanimously "well qualified."

Divided Government—This variable is coded 1 for Congresses in which the Senate and the presidency were controlled by different parties, and 0 otherwise.

Midterm Election Year—This variable denotes whether the committee vote took place during a midterm election year. Votes during midterm election years are coded 1, and 0 otherwise.

Presidential Election Year—This variable denotes whether the committee vote took place during a presidential election year. Presidential election years are coded 1, and 0 otherwise.

Interest Group Objection to the Nomination—This variable denotes whether at least two national interest groups publicly opposed the nomination. As explained in more detail in appendix A, a multilevel search through Lexis-Nexis for Law Schools' General Newspapers database and

Westlaw's All News database was conducted looking for any mention of opposition to each circuit court nominee under examination. Searches focused on finding public statements by groups that they opposed a particular nominee and would therefore launch a campaign to defeat his or her nomination. Additional searches were conducted to find articles and press releases by groups (and their leaders) consistently involved in the judicial confirmation process in which they announced opposition to specific nominees, to ensure all possible objections were recorded. Specifically, searches were done on the following groups and their leaders: on the left, People for the American Way (Ralph Neas and Elliot Mincberg), NARAL Pro-Choice America (Kate Michelman and Elizabeth Cavendish), the National Organization for Women (Kim Gandy), and the Alliance for Justice (Nan Aron), and on the right, the Judicial Selection Monitoring Project (Tom Jipping and John Nowacki), Concerned Women for America (Thomas Jipping), and the Family Research Council (Kenneth Connor).

Interest Group Objection is coded dichotomously rather than as a count, as the threshold for interest group objections is usually one: if one group objects to a nominee, many others usually follow suit; it is rare that only one group objects to a nominee. Additionally, a single objection might actually represent multiple objections, as many of the leading judicial watchdog groups are umbrella organizations that represent a wide range of smaller groups and speak on their behalf. For example, the conservative Judicial Selection Monitoring Program represents more than 700 different conservative grassroots organizations on the issue of federal judicial selection, while the liberal Alliance for Justice represents numerous groups concerned with civil rights and women's rights. Similarly, groups on both sides of the aisle also acknowledge they work in coalitions to determine which nominees are egregious enough to mount a vigorous opposition campaign against; thus, a dichotomous variable (opposed/not opposed) better captures the reality of lower court confirmation politics in that nominees usually face no opposition or considerable opposition.

To ensure that this variable captured sustained and strong group opposition to a nominee rather than the opposition of a single, rogue group, evidence of two national groups opposing a nominee was needed for the nominee to be coded as "opposed." There was only one instance in which a nominee was opposed by only one group; almost every nominee coded as "opposed" was opposed by more than two groups, with some nominees opposed by literally dozens of groups. The analysis was run, however, using a count of how many groups opposed each nominee, and the results were statistically and substantively similar.

An alternative measure of interest group opposition is whether a group testified against the nominee during his or her Judiciary Committee hearing; Bell (2002a) and Flemming, McLeod, and Talbert (1998) both examine group activity in lower court confirmations in this manner, while Segal, Cameron, and Cover (1992) use this method to study Supreme Court confirmations. The issue for this study is that groups have not been allowed to testify in recent decades (Bell 2002a). But while groups no longer engage formally in the process by testifying, as Bell (2002a) notes, they do participate informally. Thus, the method used here to code for group opposition directly captures the influential informal role groups play in the current lower court confirmation process.

"Extreme" Nominee in Relation to the Median Opposition Party Senator on the Judiciary Committee—This variable measures the ideological distance between the nominee and the median opposition party senator on the Judiciary Committee. Senators' default position is to confirm all nominees, including those nominated by a president of the opposite party. Further, senators of the president's party do not oppose the president's nominees, except in the special instance where senatorial courtesy is applied. Thus, the key question is not the nominee's ideological distance from the committee writ large but rather the nominee's ideological distance from the median opposition committee senator. I hypothesize that the more distant the nominee is from the median opposition committee senator, the more "extreme" the nominee and the more likely it is that opposition senators may oppose the nominee on ideological grounds. To create this variable, I first used the methodology described by Giles, Hettinger, and Peppers (GHP, 2002) to determine the ideology of each circuit court nominee. GHP scores reflect the very real influence of senators on the selection process by taking into account the norm of senatorial courtesy. GHP scores utilize the Poole-Rosenthal Common Space scores and thus allow the nominee's ideology to be compared with that of key senators (Poole and Rosenthal 1998). To determine each nominee's ideology score, the first question is whether any of the nominee's home-state senators are from the same party as the president. If so, senatorial courtesy is presumed to influence the selection process, and so the home-state senators' ideology scores are used as the nominee's ideology score. If both home-state senators are from the president's party, the average of the two senators' Common Space score is used. If only

one of the home-state senators is a member of the president's party, that senator's Common Space score is used. If neither home-state senator is a member of the president's party, senatorial courtesy is presumed not to operate, and the nominee's ideology score is equal to the appointing president's Common Space score. Nominees to the D.C. Circuit and the Federal Circuit do not have home-state senators; the president's Common Space score is used for these nominees. I then determined for each Congress the ideology score for the median opposition party senator on the Judiciary Committee. Finally, I calculated the absolute value of the distance between each nominee's ideology score and the score for the median opposition committee senator during the Congress in which the nominee had his or her committee vote.

Ideological Distance between the Median Opposition Senator on the Judiciary Committee and the President—This variable measures the ideological distance between the median opposition party senator on the Judiciary Committee and the nominating president for each Congress under examination. I again utilized the Poole-Rosenthal Common Space scores to create this measure. I determined the ideology score for the median opposition party senator on the Judiciary Committee for each Congress. I then calculated the absolute value of the distance between this senator's ideology score and the appointing president's ideology score for each Congress. Since I am interested in what leads to nominees receiving negative votes in committee, the most important president-Senate relationship is the ideological distance between the president and the median opposition senator on the committee.

APPENDIX C

Circuit Court Nominations Opposed by Interest Groups,
99th–109th Congresses (1985–2006)

An asterisk indicates that the nominee was confirmed.

99th Congress (Court)
  Alex Kozinski (9th)*
  Daniel Manion (7th)*
100th Congress (Court)
  Susan Liebeler (Federal)
  David Sentelle (D.C.)*
  Bernard Siegan (9th)
  David Treen (5th)
101st Congress (Court)
  Clarence Thomas (D.C.)*
  Kenneth Ryskamp (11th)
102nd Congress (Court)
  Lillian BeVier (4th)
  Edward Carnes (11th)*
  Francis Keating (10th)
  Andrew Kleinfeld (9th)*
  Kenneth Ryskamp (11th)
103rd Congress (Court)
  Rosemary Barkett (11th)*
  Martha Daughtrey (6th)*
  H. Lee Sarokin (3rd)*
104th Congress (Court)
  James Beaty (4th)
  William Fletcher (9th)
  Margaret McKeown (9th)
  Charles Stack (11th)

105th Congress (Court)
  James Beaty (4th)
  Marsha Berzon (9th)
  Timothy Dyk (Federal)
  William Fletcher (9th)*
  Margaret McKeown (9th)*
  Richard Paez (9th)
106th Congress (Court)
  Marsha Berzon (9th)*
  Bonnie Campbell (8th)
  Timothy Dyk (Federal)*
  Raymond Fisher (9th)*
  Richard Paez (9th)*
107th Congress (Court)
  Terrence Boyle (4th)
  Deborah Cook (6th)
  Miguel Estrada (D.C.)
  Carolyn Kuhl (9th)
  Michael McConnell (10th)*
  Priscilla Owen (5th)
  Charles Pickering (5th)
  John Roberts (D.C.)
  Dennis Shedd (4th)*
  D. Brooks Smith (3rd)*
  Lavenski Smith (8th)*
  William Steele (11th)

Jeffrey Sutton (6th)
Timothy Tymkovich (10th)
108th Congress (Court)
 Claude Allen (4th)
 Terrence Boyle (4th)
 Janice Brown (D.C.)
 Jay Bybee (9th)*
 Deborah Cook (6th)*
 Miguel Estrada (D.C.)
 D. Michael Fisher (3rd)*
 Richard Griffin (6th)
 Thomas Griffith (D.C.)
 William Haynes (4th)
 Brett Kavanaugh (D.C.)
 Carolyn Kuhl (9th)
 David McKeague (6th)
 William Myers (9th)
 Priscilla Owen (5th)
 Charles Pickering (5th)

William Pryor (11th)
John Roberts (D.C.)*
Henry Saad (6th)
Jeffrey Sutton (6th)*
Diane Sykes (7th)*
Timothy Tymkovich (10th)*
109th Congress (Court)
 Terrence Boyle (4th)
 Janice Brown (D.C.)*
 Richard Griffin (6th)*
 Thomas Griffith (D.C.)*
 Brett Kavanaugh (D.C.)*
 William Haynes (4th)
 David McKeague (6th)*
 William Myers (9th)
 Priscilla Owen (5th)*
 William Pryor (11th)*
 Henry Saad (6th)
 Michael Wallace (5th)

A list of all nominees opposed between 1985 and 2004 previously appeared in Nancy Scherer, Brandon L. Bartels, and Amy Steigerwalt, "Sounding the Fire Alarm: The Role of Interest Groups in the Lower Court Confirmation Process," *Journal of Politics* 70 (2008): 1026–39, in the online Web appendix.

NOTES

INTRODUCTION

1. Most states require pregnant minors either to notify their parents or to obtain parental consent (or both) before obtaining an abortion. However, since some minor women may have strong reasons for not wanting to notify their parents or obtain their consent (such as in the case of incest), these state laws, as required by *Hodgson v. Minnesota* (497 U.S. 417 [1990]) and *Planned Parenthood of Southeastern Pennsylvania v. Casey* (505 U.S. 833 [1992]), must also provide a mechanism by which minors can turn to the courts for the necessary approval. This procedure for gaining judicial consent in lieu of parental consent is commonly referred to as a "judicial bypass."

2. Most state courts are similarly comprised of three levels of courts, trial, intermediate appeals, and highest appeals, though states are free to design their judicial system however they choose. States are also free to decide the method by which their state court judges are selected. Many states utilize some type of elective system. Some states hold traditional elections, whether partisan or nonpartisan, and potential judges run as candidates for the judicial office and serve for a set term of office; these elections may be contested. At the end of each term the judge must run for reelection. Other states use a system whereby the judge is initially appointed to the bench, usually by the governor, but then must sit for a "retention" election after a set period of years. The question for the voters in these uncontested elections is simply whether the judge should retain his or her seat. If the judge receives a majority of yes votes, the judge will serve for the term of office; if the judge receives a majority of no votes and is defeated, the appointment process begins anew. Many states also have mandatory retirement laws for judges. For more information on the variety of state court systems and selection systems and the impacts of these different design choices, see, e.g., Baum (2008), Bonneau and Hall (2003), Brace and Hall (1995), Hall (1992, 2001), Langer (2002), Lovrich and Sheldon (1983), and Tarr and Porter (1990).

3. Article II, Section 2 similarly gives the president the power to appoint, with the advice and consent of the Senate, ambassadors, other public ministers and counsuls, and all other executive branch officers the Congress creates and designates as requiring Senate confirmation. However, since these other officials serve "at the pleasure of the president," rather than for life terms, the Senate views its advice and consent role for such nominations as qualitatively different from its role in confirming nominees to the federal bench.

4. Kennedy gave this speech on the Senate floor on July 1, 1987. It was quoted in the *Wall Street Journal,* July 8, 1987, 18, and in Abraham (1999, 298).

5. This practice is discussed in detail in chapter 2.

6. For more information on Carter's Nominating Commission, see Berkson and Carbon (1980).

7. By 1979, thirty-one states had formed such merit-based nominating commissions (Maltese 1995; Neff 1981).

8. "Original intent" refers to a mode of constitutional and statutory interpretation. Practitioners of original intent engage in a textual reading of the Constitution or statute in question; when questions arise, they turn to an analysis of the intentions of those who wrote or ratified the constitutional provision or statute. The overarching idea is to ensure that one's interpretation of the Constitution (and statutes) reflects the values and intentions of those who wrote these provisions. Practitioners argue against both nontextualist readings of the Constitution as well as modern interpretations of constitutional provisions. Supreme Court Justice Clarence Thomas is a proponent of original intent, as is Judge Robert Bork (see, e.g., Bork 1990). Original intent is not, however, the same thing as being an "originalist": as Justice Antonin Scalia stated in a speech in 1996, "You will never hear me refer to original intent, because as I say I am first of all a textualist, and secondly an originalist. If you are a textualist, you don't care about the intent, and I don't care if the framers of the Constitution had some secret meaning in mind when they adopted its words" (Scalia 1996). For further discussion of original intent and its justifications, see Whittington (2001).

9. For example, the Supreme Court declared in *Gideon v. Wainwright* (372 U.S. 335 [1963]) that in order for indigent criminal defendants to receive a fair trial under the Sixth Amendment, states were required to provide them with a lawyer if they could not afford one. Similarly, the Supreme Court expanded Fourth and Fifth Amendment protections against interrogations without legal representation (*Escobedo v. Illinois,* 378 U.S. 478 [1964]), forced testimony (*Miranda v. Arizona,* 384 U.S. 436 [1966]), and unreasonable searches and seizures (*Katz v. United States,* 389 U.S. 347 [1967]).

10. In 1971, in *Reed v. Reed* (404 U.S. 71), the Supreme Court struck down an Idaho state law that, all else being equal, preferred men over women when determining who would be the executor of an estate, and in 1973, in *Frontiero v. Richardson* (411 U.S. 677), the Court overturned a federal law that required female military members to prove their husband's dependence, while assuming the dependence of the wives of male military members. The final step came when the Court determined in 1976 that sex-based classifications would be considered under "heightened scrutiny" for equal protection purposes (*Craig v. Boren,* 429 U.S. 190); treating sex as a "quasi-suspect" class meant the Court would now more closely scrutinize laws that primarily classified people according to sex in order to determine whether such sex-based classifications were justified based on real differences between the sexes or merely furthered stereotypical notions about differences between the sexes.

11. Tremendous opposition from southern states greeted the decision in *Brown.* In perhaps the most infamous incident, President Kennedy was forced to federalize the Alabama National Guard in order to physically remove Governor George Wallace from the steps of the University of Alabama and thus let the first African American students enter and register for classes.

12. Scherer's elite mobilization theory contends that as the party system in the United States changed in the 1950s and 1960s from two rather heterogeneous parties to two ideologically polarized parties, the increase in ideologically motivated partisans also led presidents to nominate candidates for the federal judiciary who reflected the views of these elites as part of an elite mobilization strategy (2005, 11–27). Presidents thus responded both to the desire to see the courts reflect their policy goals and to the need to appease party elites, who were now driven more by ideology than by traditional patronage concerns, by appointing like-minded judges to the federal bench. Scherer argues that presidents heeded the calls of these elites because of fears of electoral retribution.

13. The Free Congress Foundation was originally named the Free Congress Research and Education Foundation.

14. A *Congressional Quarterly Weekly Report* commented, "Since 1987, when President Ronald Reagan nominated Robert H. Bork to the U.S. Supreme Court, outside groups such as the Free Congress Research and Education Foundation and People for the American Way have gained prominence on Capitol Hill, making their voices heard both on particular nominations to the federal bench and on the broader issue of the judicial confirmation process" (quoted in Maltese 1995, at 137–38, and Bell 2002a, at 51).

15. Throughout this book, in order to differentiate between the two President Bushes, I occasionally refer to George H. W. Bush as "Bush (41)" and George W. Bush as "Bush (43)."

16. The twelve other nominees were associate Supreme Court justice nominee William H. Rehnquist, circuit court nominee Stephen G. Breyer, circuit court nominee J. Harvie Wilkinson, district court nominee Sidney A. Fitzwater, circuit court nominee Daniel A. Manion, Supreme Court chief justice nominee William H. Rehnquist, circuit court nominee Edward Earl Carnes Jr., circuit court nominee Rosemary Barkett, circuit court nominee H. Lee Sarokin, district court nominee Brian Theodore Stewart, circuit court nominee Marsha L. Berzon, and circuit court nominee Richard A. Paez.

17. The Supreme Court's original jurisdiction, as specified by Article III, Section 2, of the U.S. Constitution, includes disputes between states and cases involving foreign diplomats. Such cases arise only rarely.

18. Data come from the 2007 *Annual Report of the Director on the Judicial Business of the United States Courts.* The 1997 through 2007 reports are available online at http://www.uscourts.gov/judbususc/judbus.html.

19. In 2006, the Supreme Court also decided another 280 cases without hearing oral arguments (2007 *Annual Report of the Director on the Judicial Business of the United States Courts*).

20. With the confirmation of President Obama's first nominee to the Supreme Court, Justice Sonia Sotomayor, this tradition continues, as Sotomayor was previously a judge on the Second Circuit Court of Appeals.

21. Two other nominees, John Roberts and D. Michael Fisher, were opposed by outside interest groups but confirmed by voice vote on the Senate floor.

22. A line of related studies concerns whether confirmed lower court judges reflect the ideological leanings of the appointing president (Carp and Rowland 1983; Haire, Humphries, and Songer 2001; Scherer 2000, 2001). In general, these studies find that Democratic appointees are more liberal than their Republican counterparts, and vice versa. A number of studies have also examined the lower court nominating process (as

opposed to the confirmation process) (Goldman 1997; Hall 1979; McFeeley 1987). These topics have also been studied extensively in connection with the Supreme Court (Nemacheck 2008a; Yalof 1999).

1 WHAT MAKES A NOMINATION RUN INTO TROUBLE?

1. While Supreme Court nominations technically must pass through the same stages on their way to Senate confirmation, similarities between the Supreme Court and lower court Senate confirmation process end there. As highlighted by Scherer, Bartels, and Steigerwalt (2008), lower court nominations are generally nonsalient unless a "fire alarm" is sounded. Comparatively, all Supreme Court nominations are highly salient to the president, senators, interest groups, and the public, and all Supreme Court nominations garner a substantial amount of media attention. For example, the news of Justice David Souter's retirement on May 1, 2009, led to almost immediate admonishments to President Obama to pick a moderate justice, as well as discussions of whether conservatives would be able to mount an effective opposition to a potentially disliked nominee and whether Obama would select a minority or female nominee (see, e.g., Fox News 2009; McConnell 2009; Stern 2009; Wilson 2009). Thus, for all intents and purposes, all Supreme Court nominations follow the public partisan track discussed in detail in chapter 6. In addition, many of the parliamentary procedures available to senators with regard to lower court nominations are not applicable to Supreme Court nominations. For example, Supreme Court nominees lack home-state senators, and so senatorial courtesy is not an option. Therefore, the four tracks framework explicated here is intended to apply only to lower court nominations.

2. The power of the president to remove executive branch nominees at his discretion was reinforced by the Supreme Court in *Myers v. United States* (272 U.S. 52 [1926]): "Article 2 grants the President the executive power of government—i.e., the general administrative control of those executing the laws, including the power of appointment and removal of executive officers" (164). In 1935 the Supreme Court narrowed *Myers* by clarifying that while the president has the power to remove executive branch officers at his discretion, quasi-legislative officers or quasi-judicial officers, such as members of the Federal Trade Commission, can only be removed in accordance with the statutory removal conditions enacted by Congress (*Humphrey's Executor v. United States,* 295 U.S. 602 [1935]). Thus, any executive branch nominee who works under the command of the president in an executive function serves only at the pleasure of the president.

3. Rejections of executive branch nominees are few and far between. As of 2002 the Senate had rejected only nine cabinet nominees out of more than 700 cabinet-level nominations (Gerhardt 2003). Lower executive branch nominees are rejected more frequently, but the rate of confirmation is still consistently above 95 percent (McCarty and Razaghian 1999).

4. Lower court judges have always been vetted as to qualifications and ethical issues (Goldman 1997). While more attention is paid to circuit court nominees, district court nominees are also thoroughly investigated. In relation to ideological vetting, while the confirmation of federal judges was rather routine prior to Carter's presidency, with every presidential administration since, the contentiousness of the confirmation process has grown (Goldman and Slotnick 1999; Hartley and Holmes 1997, 2002).

5. Other than the nominee, who testifies at a confirmation hearing is determined

solely by the chair of the Senate Judiciary Committee. While interest groups and others might ask to testify, the chair retains complete power over granting such requests. Additionally, chairs have at times solicited certain witnesses to provide testimony on certain subjects related to the current nominee (such as asking Anita Hill to testify at Clarence Thomas's Supreme Court hearings in 1991). Historically, outside witnesses have been invited to testify at Supreme Court confirmation hearings, and only sporadically at hearings for nominees to the lower federal courts. That said, the current practice by the recent committee chairs has been to disallow any outside testimony at lower court confirmation hearings, especially from outside interest groups. The one general exception is the American Bar Association, which plays a unique—and somewhat controversial—role in the process (Vining, Steigerwalt, and Smelcer 2009). The ABA rates each judicial nominee as to his or her professional qualifications. The ABA is usually invited to testify whenever it gives a nominee a "not qualified" rating. For example, the ABA testified at Roger Benitez's hearing (nominated to the Southern District Court of California) on February 25, 2004, as well as at Dora Irizarry's (nominated to the Eastern District Court of New York) hearing on October 1, 2003, concerning each of their majority "not qualified" ratings. The Judiciary Committee also asked three members of the New York legal community to testify concerning Irizarry's temperament, and the chief judge of the Southern District of California to testify in favor of Benitez. More recently, the ABA was invited in May 2006 to testify at Brett Kavanaugh's (nominated to the D.C. Circuit Court) second hearing to explain why the ABA lowered his original rating. Listings of those who have appeared at recent confirmation hearings (sometimes along with a link to the witness's testimony) are available online at the Judiciary Committee's Web site, http://www.judiciary.senate.gov.

6. The Judiciary Committee may then decide to vote to forward the nomination to the entire Senate with a negative recommendation or with no recommendation, to allow the entire Senate to have the final say. For example, the committee voted during the 100th Congress, after rejecting Susan Liebeler's nomination 6–7, to send her nomination to the floor without a recommendation; however, she never received a floor vote.

7. Technically, Senate Rule XXXI stipulates that whenever the Senate adjourns or recesses for more than thirty days, and at the end of every congressional session, all pending nominations are sent back to the president. The president then must decide whether to renominate each of these returned nominations and thus send the nomination back to the Senate. In practice, however, nominations that are returned due to long breaks (such as the August recess) or between sessions are treated by the Senate as though they were not returned (i.e., a nominee who had a hearing is not generally asked to have a second hearing, and so on). At the start of a new Congress, presidents may decide not to renominate returned nominations. For example, Clinton chose not to renominate James Beaty and Robert Raymar at the start of the 106th Congress after their nominations were returned at the end of the 105th Congress. More recently, Terrence Boyle made public his disagreement with George W. Bush's decision not to renominate him at the start of the 110th Congress, stating that he did not withdraw voluntarily (Barrett 2007).

8. While groups may ask to testify at a nominee's confirmation hearing, such participation is allowed only at the discretion of the chair of the Judiciary Committee. Since the mid-1980s, chairs have permitted only the nominees themselves to testify at lower court confirmation hearings (Bell 2002a). See note 5 for additional information.

9. The idea of presidents "going public" stems from the seminal work of Samuel Kernell. Kernell (1997) defines going public as "a strategy whereby a president promotes himself and his policies in Washington by appealing to the American public for support" (1). Kernell also highlights how going public inherently contradicts the traditional political activity of bargaining and negotiation by potentially undercutting the possibility of future compromise.

10. Alternatively, Johnson and Roberts (2004) find that public support by the president improves the confirmation prospects of Supreme Court nominees. In contrast to Holmes (2007), who modeled whether or not a circuit court nominee was confirmed, Johnson and Roberts compared the actual number of votes a nominee received in the Senate to Segal and Spaeth's (2002) predicted number of votes cast in opposition to each nomination.

11. The use of holds and the length of such track diversions are investigated in more depth in chapter 3.

12. These numbers can be found online at http://www.uscourts.gov/vacancies/ summary.html. The number of judgeships can only be changed by an act of Congress. There are also three territorial courts, for the territories of Guam, the Northern Mariana Islands, and the Virgin Islands. These judgeships are not, however, Article III judgeships; rather, they are appointed by the president and serve for terms of ten years. In addition, territorial courts exercise both federal and local jurisdiction. The U.S. District Court for Puerto Rico was a territorial court from 1900 until 1966, when Congress determined that judges on this court would be considered Article III judges with life tenure.

13. In this study, nominations are counted by the person and not the Congress, if the nominee is renominated by the same president. For example, Sandra Lynch was nominated during the 103rd Congress and renominated during the 104th Congress, but her nomination is counted only once, since she was nominated both times by President Clinton. Conversely, Pamela Rymer was nominated first by President Reagan and then renominated by President George H. W. Bush, so she is counted twice in this study. The only exceptions to this rule are Priscilla Owen and Charles Pickering. Owen and Pickering were nominated by Bush (43) at the beginning of the 107th Congress, and their nominations were both defeated in the Judiciary Committee on party-line votes during that Congress. After the Republicans regained control of the Senate in the 2002 midterm elections, Bush promptly renominated Owen and Pickering in 2003. Their 108th Congress nominations were thus completely new nominations and are treated as such in this study.

14. Another six nominees received two no votes or fewer on the Senate floor, bringing the total to 181 (87.0 percent) confirmed nominees who faced minimal or no opposition. If we examine all 272 nominations, 64.3 percent were confirmed unanimously.

15. While the increasing political polarization of the Senate and the increased scrutiny given to lower court nominees have both contributed to lengthier confirmations, other factors may also delay the processing of nominations. For example, the Bush (43) administration determined in 2001 that it would not send the names of potential nominees to the American Bar Association for evaluation prior to presidential selection. The Senate Judiciary Committee decided it would send the names of nominees to the ABA once the nomination was received in the Senate, and would wait to hold hearings until the ABA ratings were received; this practice was followed during the entirety of Bush's

administration. As a result, the time from nomination to hearing was lengthened for all Bush nominees. Chapter 3 provides a detailed overview of the various reasons why the time between a nominee's selection by the president and the nominee's confirmation hearing is usually at least a few months.

16. It should be noted that many times the senator did not actually have a specific complaint about the chosen nominee, other than that the senator supported another candidate. However, since senators want to retain the right to nominate candidates from their home states, it was to their advantage to support their Senate colleagues over the president during such disputes (Harris 1952).

17. During a particularly nasty dispute between President Franklin Roosevelt and the two senators from Virginia, Roosevelt wrote a letter that was subsequently published in the *Washington Star* on February 8, 1939, arguing that the Constitution did not support the practice of senatorial courtesy (quoted in Harris 1952).

18. Not surprisingly, as the amount of ideological and partisan polarization has increased in the Senate, Judiciary Committee chairs' willingness to honor home-state objections from members of the opposition party during unified government has correspondingly decreased. For example, then chairman Orrin Hatch scheduled a hearing and committee vote for Ninth Circuit Court nominee Carolyn Kuhl over the strong objections of both California Democratic home-state senators once the Senate switched hands at the beginning of the 108th Congress in 2003.

19. I use the term "private" to refer to actions and fights that take place primarily out of the public eye rather than to denote fights or actions that are personal in nature. A "private political fight" occurs when senators use parliamentary tactics open only to them that are generally utilized out of the public or media's view and may even be used anonymously, highlighting their "hidden" nature. Private political fights contrast starkly to the public partisan track, on which senators (and interest groups) take public positions on nominees and publicly fight over the nominee's confirmation.

20. Goldman et al. (2001) surmise that Senate Republicans (who controlled the Senate during the 106th Congress) were attempting to stall judicial nominations, especially to the D.C. Circuit Court and the Fourth Circuit Court, at the end of Clinton's second term, in the hope that a Republican president would take his place and fill these slots with more conservative nominees.

21. Enrique Moreno was nominated to the Fifth Circuit, Elena Kagan to the D.C. Circuit, and James Wynn to the Fourth Circuit. Helene White was not confirmed during Clinton's tenure. However, she was renominated by George W. Bush (and ultimately confirmed) as part of a deal between Bush and the Michigan senators in 2008; this deal is discussed in greater detail in chapter 2.

22. As a Republican nominations counsel explained in December 2003, "the usual practice of the Committee" was to wait until they received a rating on a nominee from the ABA before scheduling a hearing (and he could think of no hearings that were scheduled before an ABA rating was received), though he noted this was "not a hard-and-fast rule" (telephone interview by the author). The staffer further commented that many senators not on the committee rely heavily on the ABA's ratings as well; it was thus not uncommon for home-state senators during the George W. Bush administration to wait to return their blue slips until the ABA's rating was received, further delaying the confirmation process. Currently, the Senate Judiciary Committee's Web site states that

the ABA's rating is needed before the committee will schedule a hearing on a judicial nomination (http://judiciary.senate.gov/about/faq.cfm#Nominations, accessed October 31, 2009).

23. In 2007, anonymous holds were restricted with the passage of Section 512 of the Honest Leadership and Open Government Act of 2007 (Public Law No. 110-81), which required senators, no later than six sessions days after placing their hold, to submit a statement of intent to object in the *Congressional Record.* However, a Congressional Research Service report by Oleszek (2008) noted a number of potential loopholes in the new policy, including the facts that the law was neither a change in Senate rules nor a standing order of the Senate and that compliance was the responsibility of each member, given the lack of a stated enforcement mechanism (2).

24. For example, on Tuesday, February 11, 1997 (a date chosen at random), the *Senate Daily Digest* reports that eight bills and two resolutions were introduced and twelve nominations were received, Bill Richardson was confirmed as ambassador to the UN, the proposed balanced budget amendment to the U.S. Constitution was debated on the floor, and four different committees held hearings or closed sessions (*Congressional Record,* "Daily Digest Highlights," February 11, 1997, D101–D104).

25. As a Democratic staffer explained (the full quotation can be found in chapter 3), senators and their staffs may not know why a nomination is stalled, including whether the delay is due to a hold. And even if they know a hold has been placed on the nominee, they may not be able to determine who has placed it.

26. For example, a hold on a major piece of legislation will be immediately noticed by those senators and interest groups interested in the legislation, and will likely garner national media attention. Conversely, a hold on one lower court nominee will be noticed almost exclusively by the nominee and her home-state senators. With dozens of nominations made each congressional term, outside groups and even the administration are unlikely to be concerned with a hold on just one nomination. It is when holds capture multiple nominations that interest increases. But even then, a hold is usually an inside-the-Beltway concern rather than an issue capturing national attention. More broadly, judicial nominations garner little media attention in general; many of the nominations examined in this study lacked even a single mention in the media of their nomination or the events surrounding the nomination.

27. Holds are counted in relation to the number of circuit court nominations blocked. For example, Senator John McCain placed a hold on five nominations during the summer of 2002. This was coded as five leverage holds placed on five separate nominations.

28. Holds were applied to 25.0 percent of all nominations made during this time frame.

29. Any citizen may also express opposition to a judicial nominee. However, these expressions of opposition are usually done in conjunction with a particular interest group or follow as a result of public positions taken by interest groups. Alternatively, the media may express opposition to a nomination through editorials and op-eds. At the lower court level, such media opposition occurs rarely, and usually only after there is intense opposition from interest groups and senators.

30. As the district courts are the federal trial courts, they do not answer questions of law but rather questions of fact. On the other hand, the circuit courts routinely

consider questions of law, including determining how the U.S. Constitution should be interpreted and applied. Chapter 5 explains in detail the perception by leading interest groups of the importance of circuit court nominations.

31. David Souter's nomination to the Supreme Court in 1990 is the quintessential example of a "stealth" nomination. Souter had little record on controversial subjects and was easily confirmed. However, such a strategy may backfire: numerous conservatives have publicly expressed their dismay with Souter's general alignment with the more liberal justices on the Supreme Court; an example is Gary Bauer, who called Souter's nomination "a colossal mistake" (*NewsHour* 2000). Upon the announcement of Souter's retirement in May 2009, discussion began in earnest about the relative merits of President Obama selecting a stealth nominee to replace Souter (see, e.g., Rosen 2009; *Star-Ledger* 2009).

32. For example, many argue that Reagan's nomination of Robert Bork to the Supreme Court failed in part because of Reagan's low levels of public and Congressional support in the wake of the Iran-Contra scandal (Ackerman 1988; Hodder-Williams 1988; Lichtman 1990; Silverstein 1994). Presidents have also been found to be weaker during the fourth year of their terms (Segal 1987; Segal and Spaeth 1986). Studies examining the causes of delay in lower court confirmations have produced similar findings (Binder and Maltzman 2002; Hartley and Holmes 1997, 2002; Martinek, Kemper, and Van Winkle 2002; Scherer, Bartels, and Steigerwalt 2008).

33. See, e.g., the report put out by People for the American Way, a liberal organization that monitors judicial confirmations, "The Dissents of Priscilla Owen: A Judicial Nominee Who Would Make the Law, Not Interpret It," available at http://www.pfaw.org/pfaw/dfiles/file_30.pdf. Additionally, media accounts of Owen's nomination noted committee Democrats' opposition to her record on abortion (Lewis 2002).

34. *In re Jane Doe*, 19 S.W.3d 346, Texas Supreme Court, June 22, 2000. See also Lewis (2002).

35. In comparison, between 1985 and 2002, only 12 (1.7 percent) of 715 district court nominations were opposed by interest groups, highlighting the increased scrutiny given to circuit court nominations.

36. The nominations of Priscilla Owen and Charles Pickering are counted twice in this study, and in both cases, each of their two nominations was opposed. During the 107th Congress, both were defeated in committee on party-line votes. Once the Republicans regained control of the Senate at the beginning of the 108th Congress, Bush (43) renominated both Owen and Pickering, and the Senate considered their nominations anew.

37. Five nominations were filibustered but never confirmed during the showdown over President George W. Bush's nominees in 2004 and 2005. Miguel Estrada's nomination and Carolyn Kuhl's nomination were both filibustered during the 108th Congress, and they both subsequently withdrew from consideration. Charles Pickering's nomination was filibustered during the 108th and 109th Congresses. Pickering did receive, however, a recess appointment in January 2004; recess appointments offer a way to circumvent the traditional confirmation process by allowing presidents to unilaterally appoint nominees during Senate recesses (see, e.g., Howard and Graves 2009). The filibuster continued against Pickering's nomination to a permanent seat on the bench, and he eventually withdrew. William Myers's nomination and Henry Saad's nomination

were both filibustered during the 108th and 109th Congresses. These two nominees were specifically excluded from the Gang of Fourteen agreement reached in May 2005, and both eventually withdrew.

38. Under the Senate rules, in order for debate to come to an end so that a floor vote on a bill or nomination can proceed, a cloture motion must be filed (see Beth and Bach 2003; Davis 2007). The Senate generally relies upon unanimous consent agreements to achieve cloture. However, if a senator or groups of senators object to the measure, they can require the Senate to vote formally on cloture as a successful cloture motion requires a supermajority of sixty votes (or three-fifths of duly sworn members if vacancies exist). If the cloture vote fails, then the measure cannot be brought to a vote of the full Senate; the Senate rules permit unlimited attempts to gain cloture. This is thus one more way in which nominations (and bills) can be defeated through the use of private political tactics.

39. The decision to support a nominee is much easier than the decision to oppose a nominee. Opposing a nominee entails a significant expenditure of resources, while supporting a nominee is relatively cost-free. Additionally, as discussed by Scherer, Bartels, and Steigerwalt (2008), while confirmation of lower court nominees is not presumed, it is still true that senators are hesitant to oppose a president's judicial nominees in general, and so the burden is on the opposition to make the case that resistance is warranted.

40. This slogan originally appeared on a sign made by Senator Charles Schumer and referred to the fact that the Senate had confirmed 168 Bush (43) nominees by that point, and the Democrats were filibustering only four (Hoppin 2003). By the end of the 109th Congress, the number of filibusters would reach ten.

41. Pickering was given a recess appointment to the Fifth Circuit on January 16, 2004 (King 2004). Recess appointments are temporary and last only until the end of the next Congressional session (i.e., the end of the next calendar year), since they do not require Senate confirmation (Howard and Graves 2009). Pickering was thus also renominated by Bush for a permanent seat on the Fifth Circuit Court. Faced with continued opposition to his pending nomination for a permanent seat on the circuit court, Pickering announced in December 2004 that he was withdrawing his name from consideration as a nominee and retiring from the federal bench (Liptak 2004). William Pryor was also granted a recess appointment while his nomination was being filibustered, but he was confirmed to a permanent seat on the Eleventh Circuit Court as part of the Gang of Fourteen agreement.

2 DEATH TO NOMINEES

1. For example, the Oklahoma City bombing took place on federal property, so Timothy McVeigh was tried by a federal judge from the Western District Court of Oklahoma.

2. While presidents may pay attention to regional ties when selecting justices for the Supreme Court (Daniels 1978), Supreme Court nominees do not have home-state senators, so the use of senatorial courtesy is not an option.

3. Such arrangements may be one-time deals or long-standing arrangements. In situations where the home-state senators are from different parties, senators may decide the out-party senator gets to name a fraction of the appointments. For example, New York senators Patrick Moynihan (D) and Alfonso D'Amato (R) struck a deal whereby

D'Amato chose one district court judge for every two that Moynihan selected during the Clinton administration (Lewis 1998). During the Bush (43) administration, Nevada senators John Ensign (R) and Harry Reid (D) agreed Reid would chose one district court judge for every three selected by Ensign (Tetreault 2001). In situations where both home-state senators are not from the president's party, other arrangements might be made. For example, Democratic senators Herb Kohl and Russ Feingold, along with Republican representative F. James Sensenbrenner Jr., announced in July 2001 the formation of an eleven-member bipartisan nominating commission for lower court vacancies occurring in the state of Wisconsin (press release announcing the commission's formation available online at http://www.senate.gov/~kohl/press/072301.html).

4. Attorney General William D. Mitchell, radio speech, April 26, 1929, in Justice, Press Releases, Attorney General, 1929–30, WHCF Box 25, HHPL (quoted in Maltese 1995, 121).

5. Senators have at times, though more rarely in the past two decades, invoked senatorial courtesy and then allowed the nominee to move forward after their concerns were addressed; see Slotnick (1980a) for a discussion of senatorial courtesy prior to 1980 and its use as a delaying tactic.

6. A 1979 Judiciary Committee staff memo stated: "In fact, no hearing has been scheduled on a nominee in the absence of a returned blue slip, thus institutionalizing senatorial courtesy within the committee as an automatic and mechanical one-member veto over nominees" ("Senatorial Courtesy" memo prepared for Senator Kennedy by the staff of the Senate Judiciary Committee, January 22, 1979, 2, quoted in Slotnick [1980a] at 63).

7. Letter to President Barack H. Obama from the Republican Senatorial Conference, March 2, 2009. The letter also emphasized that the selection of federal judges is a "shared constitutional responsibility." Interestingly, the letter was signed by all forty-one Senate Republicans; however, on April 28, 2009, Senator Arlen Specter announced he was joining the Democratic Party. A copy of the letter is available online at http://repub lican.senate.gov/public/index.cfm?FuseAction=Blogs.ViewandBlog_Id=3c522434 -76e5-448e-9ead-1ec214b881ac.

8. Carolyn Kuhl eventually withdrew in December 2004.

9. Michigan senator Spencer Abraham returned negative blue slips against Clinton nominees Helene White and Kathleen McCree Lewis. Their nominations were stalled for four years and a year and a half, respectively, and neither received so much as a committee hearing during Clinton's presidency.

10. Since nominees to the D.C. Circuit and Federal Circuit Courts lack home-state senators, this means they also lack home-state support. For example, John Roberts's nomination to the D.C. Circuit in 1992 never received a hearing; this might have been a result of the fact that he lacked a home-state senator to shepherd his nomination through the Senate. The opposite may be true as well: in 1983, Reagan successfully nominated Kenneth Starr to the D.C. Circuit Court after home-state opposition arose to his potential nomination for the Fourth Circuit, and Bush (43) used this tactic to seat Peter Keisler on the D.C. Circuit Court after similar home-state opposition surfaced to his proposed nomination to the Fourth Circuit (Biskupic 2001a).

11. A detailed explanation of the search methodology used to identify instances of senatorial courtesy between 1985 and 2006 can be found in appendix A. Newspaper

archives as well as White House reports were searched to determine which nominees, if any, were blocked through the use of senatorial courtesy.

12. Carolyn Kuhl and Terrence Boyle were eventually granted Judiciary Committee hearings and votes; neither was ultimately confirmed. However, Carolyn Kuhl's nomination was forwarded over the objections of her two home-state senators, and her nomination was filibustered for this reason on the Senate floor. Terrence Boyle's nomination moved forward only after the objecting home-state senator, John Edwards, left the Senate and was replaced by Republican Richard Burr in 2005.

13. Because nominees who were renominated by the same president in successive Congresses were counted only once, the numbers listed here reflect how many new nominations were made each term.

14. Goldman et al. (2003) contend that Bush (43) exercised much more control over the nominating process than previous presidents. Their review of Clinton's nominations argues that Clinton frequently allowed Republican senators to pick nominees, and his administration attempted to select moderates in order to avoid costly confirmation fights (Goldman et al. 2001; also see Acheson 2002).

15. Leahy eventually released the block on Julia Smith Gibbons of Tennessee and John Rogers of Kentucky, and both were then easily confirmed.

16. This was the only instance in the period under study that clearly follows the pattern of using senatorial courtesy merely to delay nominees (see also Slotnick 1980a).

17. There are thirteen circuit courts: twelve geographic circuit courts (including the D.C. Circuit Court) and the Federal Circuit Court. However, nominees to the D.C. Circuit and Federal Circuit Courts do not have home-state senators.

18. On the other hand, a potential California Ninth Circuit Court nomination during the 107th Congress was derailed by early home-state senator opposition, that of Representative Christopher Cox. Both California senators expressed their strong objections to his nomination to the Bush (43) administration, and his name was consequently withdrawn from consideration (Holland 2001a). This is also a clear instance of a president engaging in strategic selection (and honoring the tradition of senatorial courtesy) by considering the preferences of opposition party home-state senators prior to selection.

19. The Texas senators sent a letter on May 5, 2000, to then chairman Orrin Hatch stating that Moreno "simply had not achieved the level of experience necessary to be fully engaged and effective on a court one notch below the United States Supreme Court" (Hight 2000).

20. Boyle did not receive a floor vote during the 109th Congress because allegations emerged that he had presided over cases involving corporations in which he held investments; the federal Judicial Code of Conduct prohibits judges from hearing a case if they hold any stock in one of the parties (Evans 2006).

21. The four nominees from Michigan were Susan Neilson, Henry Saad, Richard Griffin, and David McKeague.

22. Tragically, Susan Neilson died three months after her confirmation, and her death created a second Michigan vacancy on the Sixth Circuit.

3 "HERDING CATS"

1. Developed in the medical literature, duration or hazard models explore what factors influence how long it takes for a person to experience the "hazard" of interest. In this case, the hazard is a successful confirmation by the full Senate.

2. This chapter does not discuss delays during the nomination phase. In general, the White House investigates a potential nominee (a process that usually takes two to three months) and then submits the nomination to the FBI and IRS for background checks. Beyond the time it takes for potential nominees to be vetted, more systematic delays in the nominating process are also common. For example, in late 1991 many observers noted that the Bush (41) administration took almost eleven months on average to make nominations to federal judicial vacancies (Nichols 1991).

3. Orrin Hatch was criticized by Democrats in January 2003 for breaking with this tradition and scheduling three circuit court nominees, Jeffrey Sutton, Deborah Cook, and John Roberts, to testify during the same hearing on January 29, 2003 (Holland 2003). Senator Edward Kennedy argued, "Scheduling any three Circuit Court nominees for a hearing on one day makes it difficult to perform adequately our constitutional duty. Doing so for three controversial nominees makes it impossible" (quoted in Holland 2003). However, unless problems arise, between four and six district court nominees are generally scheduled to testify at each hearing, a necessity given the large number of district court nominations made each congressional term.

4. The FBI focuses on uncovering illegal activities or potential conflicts of interest. For an overview of the ABA's review process, see *The Standing Committee on Federal Judiciary: What It Is and How It Works*, available online at http://www.abanet.org/scfed-jud/federal_judiciary07.pdf. Chapter 4 provides additional information about these investigations.

5. The FBI's investigation may be shortened if the nominee has previously been subjected to an FBI background check; for example, many circuit court nominees are being elevated from district court seats. Alternatively, the ABA rating process takes longer if the primary investigator awards a rating of "not qualified." If such a rating is given, another member of the Standing Committee will be asked to conduct an additional independent investigation and provide his or her own rating of the nominee (telephone interview with author, April 2004).

6. Previously, all presidents beginning with Eisenhower sent names of prospective nominees to the ABA to be rated on their professional qualifications, and nominations would (usually) be made after a nominee was deemed "qualified" or better by the ABA. George W. Bush's decision not only affected the Senate's confirmation process, it also significantly altered the selection process. Vining, Steigerwalt, and Smelcer (2009) provide a historical overview of how different presidents utilized the ABA and when in the selection process they sent the names of potential nominees to the ABA for review.

7. The first batch of ratings by the ABA was received by the Judiciary Committee in June 2001. This timing coincided with the surprise announcement that Vermont Senator James Jeffords was defecting from the Republican Party and becoming an Independent, throwing the Senate majority to the Democrats. Thus, a full-scale reorganization of the Senate took place, further delaying the processing of judicial nominees.

8. Only two nominations carried over from the 105th Congress had already had some sort of committee action, and both nominees were confirmed in January 1999.

9. This process was established in 1917 with the passage of Senate Rule XXII (De-Nardis 1989).

10. The Congressional Research Service has also produced reports that explain Rule XXII, filibusters, and the process of gaining cloture and their usage (Beth and Bach 2003; Carr and Bach 2002; Saturno 2003).

11. In 1984, Senator Edward Kennedy staged a filibuster against J. Harvie Wilkinson III, who was nominated to the Fourth Circuit Court.

12. DeNardis's dissertation primarily provides a detailed examination of the development of the filibuster. He refers to holds as "silent filibusters" and focuses on explaining how they, along with the filibuster in general, have changed the nature of the Senate.

13. One of the few scholarly works on judicial confirmations to mention holds is a 2001 law review article by Denning (2001) that mentions the hold as a tactic that highlights the growing ability of individual senators to impede judicial nominations but does not address systematically when, how, or why it has been used. Gerhardt (2003) provides a few recent examples of holds placed on nominations in order to further a discussion about log-rolling tactics in the realm of judicial appointments (140–43). Finally, Epstein and Segal (2005) discuss instances of holds against judicial nominees in their overview of the judicial confirmation process; they utilize data from an earlier version of this study (Steigerwalt 2004).

14. Filibusters per se are not found in the Senate rules, either. Rule XXII provides a mechanism "to bring to a close the debate upon any measure, motion, other matter pending before the Senate" and can be used to cut off any debate over a matter being debated on the floor, even a nonfilibuster. However, to end debate, a supermajority of senators (sixty) is needed.

15. This phrase became the title of his autobiography, *Herding Cats: A Life in Politics* (New York: HarperCollins, 2005). I first heard this term used in relation to the Senate during an interview with Lott's then chief of staff in June 2002.

16. DeNardis (1989) quotes former Senate majority leader Mike Mansfield that the Senate's rules "magnify the views strongly held by a single member of the Senate" rather than emphasize freedom of expression or minority rights (originally quoted in the *Wall Street Journal*, November 11, 1977, 14).

17. For a bill or nomination to be brought up for consideration on the Senate floor, unanimous consent agreements are many times utilized. Unanimous consent agreements circumvent the rather unwieldy rules of the Senate (and usually require senators to yield some right they possess under the rules, such as the right to unlimited debate or the right to offer an unlimited amount of floor amendments) and thereby accelerate the Senate's ability to deal with the multitude of bills and nominations pending at any one time. As Walter Oleszek (1996) explains, "The fundamental objective of unanimous consent agreements is to limit the time it takes to dispose of controversial issues in an institution noted for unlimited debate. These agreements, therefore, expedite action on legislation and structure floor deliberation" (210).

18. Statement of Senator Exon in the *Congressional Record*, October 5, 1984, S13779.

19. Since 1997, Senators Charles Grassley and Ron Wyden have engaged in a concerted bipartisan campaign to amend the Senate rules to prohibit anonymous holds.

20. In fact, a number of circuit court nominees included in this study were not mentioned in a single newspaper article, including even cursory reports announcing their nominations or subsequent confirmations.

21. Certain nominees get doubly penalized: nominees to the D.C. Circuit and the Federal Circuit lack home-state senators, so they have no one to lobby for action on their nominations.

22. One of Dole's 1996 presidential campaign platforms focused on curbing judicial activism and appointing more "law and order" judges (Burn 1996).

23. The strategic hold placed by Larry Craig in the summer of 2003 on more than 800 Air Force promotions is a perfect example of a hold where the blocking senator unconditionally supported the nominees in question but used them as a bargaining chip in an unrelated dispute. Craig placed the hold to force the delivery of four Air Force C-130 cargo planes to the Idaho Air National Guard, as had been promised seven years before. Craig's leverage hold was memorialized on the television show *The West Wing* when an Idaho Democratic senator placed a hold on hundreds of military promotions to gain funding for a long-promised missile defense system ("Constituency of One," aired October 29, 2003).

24. A striking example concerns the nomination of Richard Holbrooke to be U.S. ambassador to the UN in 1999. Numerous senators were on record praising his nomination and qualifications, but his nomination was blocked for months by three senators attempting to gain leverage in unconnected disputes: Charles Grassley's leverage hold was placed to protest the treatment of a whistle-blower at the UN who had no ties to Holbrooke, and Senators Trent Lott and Mitch McConnell blocked Holbrooke's nomination to force Clinton to nominate Bradley Smith to the Federal Election Commission (Raum 1999).

25. As a fascinating side note, Attorney General Meese decided against a special prosecutor because Whittlesay lacked "criminal intent" and had instead merely exercised bad judgment. This judgment led Congress to amend the independent counsel statute such that the attorney general may not take the target's "state of mind" into account when deciding whether to launch an independent counsel investigation (Mackenzie and Hafken 2002, 50).

26. This hold was originally placed only on then associate attorney general Stephen Trott's circuit court nomination; Trott was not involved with the Whittlesay investigation. A day later, the hold was extended to five more nominations, one circuit court nomination, and four district court nominations.

27. Part of Bush's delay in naming a nominee stemmed from the fact that he was required to fill the vacancy with a Democrat.

28. McCain's hold is also interesting in that then minority leader Trent Lott took to the Senate floor to criticize McCain (a fact made even more interesting since Lott had placed a hold on a nominee to the Federal Communications Commission), stating, "I'm not mad at him about it. But you can't have one senator holding up 60 nominations, including 16 judges, because he's got his lip stuck out over one commission appointee. You can't do that" (Kuhnhenn 2002). And, as politics indeed makes strange bedfellows,

when Lott attempted to force through fifteen nominations when McCain was not on the Senate floor, Senator Harry Reid took to the floor to object on McCain's behalf.

29. Shelby's hold almost resulted in another retaliatory hold when Black's two home-state Florida senators, Graham and Mack, threatened to block other pending judicial nominations as well as legislation supported by Shelby because of their ire that he chose their home-state nominee to block.

30. After Shelby placed his hold on Black, three other senators placed an anonymous hold on three female district court nominations and all future nominations that might be sent to the Senate floor. A battle then erupted after four Republican white male nominees were easily confirmed on June 26, 1992, while the female nominees remained blocked (McQueen 1992).

31. Helms's hold was a leverage hold to try to force the State Department to alter its policy of not negotiating with the Mozambique Anti-Communist Resistance Movement (RENAMO) and the Reagan administration to change its overall policy toward the Marxist government in power in Mozambique (Thurman 1999).

32. A third possible institutional dispute exists: the home-state senator dislikes the chosen nominee or believes he or she was not adequately consulted. In these instances, however, a senator will block the nominee through senatorial courtesy, and block the nominee from the outset, rather than wait for the nomination to be sent to the Senate floor. Recent uses of senatorial courtesy, as well as the reasons why senatorial courtesy has been utilized, are discussed in chapter 2.

33. Judge Silberman testified at a hearing chaired by Senator Grassley that the D.C. Circuit Court's caseload was not large enough to support twelve active judges (Biskupic 1995). A study found D.C. Circuit Court judges each handled approximately 124 cases per year, much less than the average number of cases handled by judges on other circuits. However, supporters argued that the cases the D.C. Circuit Court handled were so complex that these numbers did not adequately capture the court's workload, including D.C. Circuit Court Chief Judge Harry T. Edwards (Biskupic 1995). For an overview of these different arguments, see the *Congressional Record,* March 19, 1997, S2515–S2537.

It should also be noted that Grassley's opposition to a twelfth seat was not merely a mask for partisan complaints: Grassley has repeatedly introduced bills to permanently remove a seat from the D.C. Circuit Court, including during George W. Bush's administration. Congress has not, however, eliminated a permanent federal judgeship since the nineteenth century, while it has created more than 200 district court seats in the past few decades with the Omnibus Judgeships Acts of 1979 and 1990.

34. Garland received twenty-three no votes when his nomination finally received a floor vote, and they were all based on whether there was even a need for an eleventh seat on the D.C. Circuit Court.

35. *Congressional Record,* March 19, 1997, S2530.

36. Statement of the chairman, June 17, 2003, available online at rules.senate.gov/hearings/2003.

37. Many of these holds also applied to district court and executive branch nominations. My focus, however, is on determining how many holds affected circuit court nominations, and the motivations behind these holds. Appendix A details the search methodology used to find and verify these holds.

38. There were 272 separate nominations but only 263 separate nominees. Terrence

Boyle, John Roberts, Roger Gregory, Pamela Ann Rymer, Franklin Van Antwerpen, Jacques Wiener, and Ferdinand Fernandez were all nominated by two different presidents for the same position. Boyle was nominated in 1991 by Bush (41) and again in 2001 by Bush (43). Roberts was nominated in 1992 by Bush (41) and again in 2001 by Bush (43). Van Antwerpen was nominated in 1991 by Bush (41) and renominated by Bush (43) in 2003. Fernandez, Wiener, and Rymer were all nominated in 1988 by Reagan and renominated by Bush (41) in 1989. Roger Gregory was nominated in 2000 by Clinton and then renominated by Bush (43) in 2001. Additionally, Priscilla Owen and Charles Pickering were both defeated in the Judiciary Committee during the 107th Congress and were newly nominated during the 108th Congress; they were thus both nominated two distinct times by Bush (43).

39. The nominations of Susan Liebeler and Daniel Manion were both defeated in the Judiciary Committee during the 100th and 99th Congresses, respectively. The committee then voted to send each of their nominations to the floor without a recommendation. Liebeler never received a floor vote, while Manion was eventually confirmed by the Senate on a 50–49 vote. Since each of their nominations was sent by the committee to the Senate floor, they too could be subjected to holds.

40. Holds are counted in relation to the nomination. For example, Senator John McCain placed a hold on five nominations during the summer of 2002; this action is counted as five holds on five separate nominations. Additionally, a single hold reported as being placed by multiple senators is counted in reference to the number of nominations blocked by the hold, rather than how many senators placed the hold.

41. For example, Susan Black and Edward Carnes were caught in an institutional hold placed by Senator Larry Pressler over federal judgeships in South Dakota. Additionally, a number of senators placed an ideological hold on Carnes, which caused one of his home-state senators, Richard Shelby, to retaliate by placing a hold on Black's nomination. Thus, their nominations were subjected to two very different types of holds. William Fletcher, William Myers, and Richard Paez were each subject to distinct holds in two successive Congresses.

42. One of these holds was based on ethical questions about the nominee rather than ideological objections. James Dennis had a hold placed against him during the 104th Congress after allegations surfaced that his son might have improperly received a legislative scholarship to Tulane Law School.

43. Many articles reported rumors of anonymous holds placed at the committee stage, especially during the Clinton years. Technically, however, holds can only be placed once a nomination reaches the Senate floor, so such reports were not counted as holds for the purposes of this study.

44. William Fletcher was blocked by ideological holds during the 104th and 105th Congresses. Richard Paez was subjected to ideological holds during the 105th and 106th Congresses.

45. However, to further complicate matters, other unrelated holds may continue blocking a nomination's progress. The best example occurred in relation to Robert Byrd's institutional hold in 1985: Byrd's institutional hold affected seventeen judicial nominations, including that of Alex Kozinski. At the same time, Senators Levin, Kennedy, DeConcini, and Metzenbaum placed an ideological hold on Kozinski's nomination. When Byrd lifted his institutional hold, the agreement allowed the other sixteen judi-

cial nominations to be promptly confirmed, but Kozinski was still blocked due to the simultaneous ideological hold.

46. For example, Edward Carnes was blocked by Howard Metzenbaum in an ideological hold starting in July 1992. He was then also caught in Larry Pressler's strategic hold on thirty-one judicial nominations over judgeships in South Dakota. When Pressler's strategic hold was lifted two weeks later, Metzenbaum's ideological hold on Carnes still stood (and Carnes was confirmed only after a successful cloture vote).

47. Holds are only as strong as the majority leader allows them to be. If the majority leader decides not to honor a hold, he can schedule a bill or nomination for a vote and risk the opposing senator attempting to filibuster the measure. Such a filibuster attempt can be overridden if the majority leader is able to garner the sixty votes needed for cloture (Senate Rule XXII; see also Beth and Bach 2003).

48. Numerous reports state that after Summit continued to publicly criticize the ethical behavior of then attorney general Edwin Meese, key administration officials told Democrats that Summit's nomination could expire. And, as Summit's nomination was made by a fellow Republican, it is rather unlikely that D'Amato objected to Summit's nomination on ideological grounds.

49. Thomas Ambro was confirmed after a successful cloture vote in 1999. Merrick Garland's nomination was brought to a vote over the strong objections of Senator Charles Grassley; however, Grassley did not attempt to filibuster his nomination but rather mounted a strong campaign to defeat the nomination on the floor (see the *Congressional Record*, March 19, 1997, S2515–S2537).

4 INTEREST GROUPS AND JUDICIAL CONFIRMATIONS

1. During the 107th Congress, Charles Pickering and Dennis Shedd were asked to provide copies of any unpublished opinions they had written as district court judges (Democratic staffer 2002).

2. The report is available to all members on the committee. The minority staff may prepare a separate report, but during the 107th Congress, this occurred rarely (Republican staffer 2002).

3. On May 12, 2005, a minor scandal erupted when Minority Leader Harry Reid stated during the floor debate over Sixth Circuit nominee Henry Saad that "there is a problem there" in his FBI file; Republicans argued that these comments unfairly maligned Saad (Hulse and Lewis 2005; Hurt 2005; York 2005).

4. The ABA testified at Roger Benitez's hearing (nominated to the Southern District Court of California) on February 25, 2004, as well as at Dora Irizarry's hearing (nominated to the Eastern District Court of New York) on October 1, 2003, concerning their respective majority "not qualified" ratings. Both nominees were eventually confirmed.

5. There have been numerous complaints over the years that the ABA's ratings are not impartial, especially for more conservative nominees (Bronner 1989b; Lindgren 2001; Seckora 2001; but see Saks and Vidmar 2001). These allegations gained power when Robert Bork received a split rating of "well qualified/not qualified" by the ABA when he was nominated to the Supreme Court in 1987 owing to his "judicial temperament" (Greenhouse 1987; Stuart 1987). To many, the addition of judicial temperament as a criterion allows the ABA to make political judgments about the views nominees hold, rather than merely assessing professional qualifications. More recently, Vining,

Steigerwalt, and Smelcer (2009) find evidence of bias against more conservative nominees, at least with respect to whether a nominee will receive a "well qualified" rating.

6. There is considerable debate over what types of questions are suitable to pose to the nominees and whether nominees must answer questions that delve into their personal political views or views on issues they may confront once on the bench. This issue arises especially with the nomination of so-called stealth nominees who lack public records on key controversial issues. D.C. Circuit Court nominee Miguel Estrada's refusal to answer questions about certain issues posed by Democratic senators was a key reason for the filibuster mounted against his nomination during the 108th Congress (Stolberg 2003).

7. Staff commented that the nominee's answers to written questions were a significant source of information. One committee staffer interviewed in 2002 said, "Hearings are not always the most useful exercise, as there is not enough time to question nominees thoroughly and it takes a lot of work to get a Senator fully prepped such that he can do a back-and-forth dialogue with the nominee, especially on subtle legal points."

8. All interviews took place in Washington, D.C., between June and August 2002. Interviews with current staff took place in the office in which each worked, while interviews with former staff took place at their current places of business. The interviews were semistructured and lasted approximately one hour, with the longest lasting three hours and the shortest thirty minutes.

9. Given the other duties of the committee staff, preparation rarely begins before the week of the hearing. Hearings on judicial nominees usually occur no more than twice a month, and the general practice is for one circuit court nominee to testify, along with four to six district court nominees. In addition to judicial nominations, the committee also has jurisdiction over many other issues, such as changes to criminal laws, terrorism, and immigration, as well as appointments to be U.S. attorneys, non-career lawyer Department of Justice positions, and judgeships on the "local" District of Columbia courts.

10. In fact, a rift emerged between Republican committee members and leading conservative activists over whether Republicans did enough to stop Clinton nominees and to support George W. Bush's nominees. Thomas Jipping wrote a number of articles criticizing Orrin Hatch's stewardship of the committee during the Clinton administration ("Democrats Fight for Activist Judges, GOP Caves" 2000, liberally quoting Jipping as to the failings of the Lott and Hatch's leadership; see also Jipping 2000).

11. "The spontaneity of the grassroots gets replaced by Astroturf. . . . Some citizen contacting is in response to carefully organized campaigns with little spontaneity" (Verba 1993, 679). "Astroturf lobbying" refers to individuals or groups who do not directly lobby themselves but rather generate grassroots lobbying campaigns. Thus, for example, NARAL often does not have its Washington staff lobby but instead encourages its grassroots members to contact their representatives.

12. For a firsthand account of the Robert Bork Supreme Court confirmation fight, see Gittenstein (1992).

13. Many have discussed the suspected role played by conservative groups in George W. Bush's selection process, especially the Federalist Society, a conservative-leaning organization of law students and lawyers (Lichtblau 2002; Nemacheck 2008a, 23–24; see Volokh 2001 for an insider's description of the society and its beliefs). The Federalist Society attracted attention because of the number of executive and judicial

nominees Bush selected who were believed to have belonged to the organization (Lewis 2001). However, as DeParle (2005) highlights, even this simple statement of fact is difficult to confirm, as many of these same nominees have tried to distance themselves from the society or have denied belonging (see also *New York Times* 2005). Scherer and Miller (2009) explore whether Federalist Society members are more conservative on the bench than their non-society counterparts; one issue they confronted was how to accurately identify society members. The Federalist Society did, however, play a prominent public role in helping confirm George W. Bush's Supreme Court nominees John Roberts and Samuel Alito (Savage 2005).

14. This question was asked only of staffers who indicated they received information from interest groups.

15. The leading conservative activist, Thomas Jipping, attested that he would research Clinton nominees when others (including senators and staff) brought them to his attention.

16. This same staffer also wished for more conservative media outlets: "Democrats are more successful at projecting their message because the press helps them, and their groups are better organized and funded. . . . There is no question that the three conservative media outlets are the *Washington Times, Wall Street Journal,* and Fox News, and they help tremendously, but their circulation is much lower. Even more important is television—we have Fox News, but the Democrats have the rest."

5 INTEREST GROUPS AND THE DECISION TO OBJECT

1. Once on the public partisan track, nominations primarily follow this track. Because all nominations awaiting floor action can be subjected to holds, nominations on the public partisan track can be temporarily rerouted to the private political track (chapters 1 and 3 elaborate on the fluid nature of the private political track). However, once the hold is resolved, the nomination will return to the public partisan track.

2. See also "Rehnquist Battle Set, But Is Scalia's Role Overlooked?" (1986).

3. If Rehnquist's elevation was defeated, Scalia could then have been nominated for the vacant chief justice position, but that nomination would have required the confirmation process to begin anew.

4. For additional information about umbrella groups, in particular umbrella groups active in judicial selection, see Scherer, Bartels, and Steigerwalt (2008).

5. Concerned Women for America also focuses on marriage, pornography, and religion in public life, three notionally cultural issues that are battled over primarily in the courts as well.

6. "Nomination-based issues" are factors that affect the vacancy or seat the nomination was made to fill (i.e., whether the vacancy is on an ideologically balanced circuit court) or factors that affect the making of the nomination itself (i.e., whether the person was nominated as part of a trade).

7. All of these groups are aligned with the political party that traditionally reflects their views. Thus, liberal groups generally support Democratic nominees and oppose Republican nominees, and vice versa.

8. I also attempted to contact the conservative Eagle Forum's Court Watch. I did not receive any response from Court Watch's then national chair, Virginia Armstrong.

9. This chapter uses data from two interviews with Thomas Jipping, both of which

were conducted during the summer of 2002. The first was conducted in June by Nancy Scherer, who kindly allowed me to use the content of the interview for this analysis. The second I conducted in July.

10. Fewer groups on the right are represented because fewer groups on the right are consistently involved in lower court selection. However, it is not that conservative groups do not care about judicial selection; rather, groups on the right generally act as part of a coalition rather than individually. For example, the JSMP acts on behalf of more than 700 conservative grassroots organizations, but the vast majority of these groups do not participate on their own. Thus, as of 2002, Thomas Jipping was in many ways the voice of the right on the issue of judicial selection. Furthermore, at the time of the interviews, a Republican occupied the White House. Conservative groups were therefore acting in support of nominees, and they generally followed the lead of the White House. However, commentators noted that the early furor sparked by Justice David Souter's retirement announcement in May 2009 suggests a potential increase in the amount of conservative group activity on the issue of judicial selection, as well as an opportunity for Republicans and conservatives to regroup after losses during the 2008 election (Nagourney and Zeleny 2009; Wilson 2009).

11. Opposition inherently causes the administration and supportive senators to become involved as well, and these two groups usually take the lead in supporting the nomination. As the Jipping quotation underscores, the president and his administration have available to them numerous resources with which to fight for their nominees. As a result, groups spend much less of their own resources to help troubled nominees.

12. For example, media accounts reported that the AFJ found Michael Luttig's nomination during the 102nd Congress "troublesome," but the group decided not to formally contest his nomination (Dahl 1991). An article about his successful confirmation concluded, "Two liberal groups had questioned his credentials, but no material opposition surfaced to his nomination" (Hardin 1991).

13. Conservative groups interviewed in May 2009 in conjunction with the pending Supreme Court vacancy stated that a strong fight against the eventual Democratic nominee, even though the success of such a battle was unlikely given a Democratic Senate, would help to increase fundraising and aid the broader conservative movement. As one conservative fundraiser, Richard Viguerie, explained, "It's an immense opportunity to build the conservative movement and identify the troops out there. It's a massive teaching moment for America" (quoted in Savage 2009).

14. Not surprisingly, this type of strategic maneuvering almost always emerges when a Supreme Court vacancy arises. Groups—and senators—will warn the president that he will face a fight unless the concerns of crucial constituencies are acknowledged and respected. As a result, presidents engage in strategic selection decisions in an attempt to forestall such fights (Nemacheck 2008a). For further discussion, see chapter 1.

15. One formal source of information is the Judiciary Committee questionnaire each nominee must complete. Judges must provide copies of all opinions they have written, both published and unpublished; the published opinions are also easily accessible to the public. Law professors publish articles and books outlining their views on different issues, and they must also provide copies of any published works to the committee; again, these publications are generally easily accessible. Finally, all nominees must produce copies of any publications or public speeches they have given.

16. Prost was the lead nominations counsel under Hatch, and she was easily confirmed in committee and on the floor. Shedd's road to confirmation is discussed in more detail in chapter 6.

17. Arlen Specter is a moderate senator from Pennsylvania who often provided a bipartisan swing vote on the Judiciary Committee. He was elected to the Senate in 1980 as a Republican. On April 28, 2009, Specter announced he was switching his party affiliation to the Democratic Party and would run for reelection in 2010 as a Democrat (Hulse and Nagourney 2009).

18. "Grass-tops" lobbying denotes lobbying by prominent individuals and key decision makers. In this case, Senator Arlen Specter himself lobbied certain members of the Judiciary Committee extensively (most notably Joseph Biden, with whom Specter rode the Member train every day), and also brought in prominent Pennsylvanians to lobby key Democrats. Grassroots lobbying, on the other hand, involves communications and lobbying by members of the broader public. The emphasis of grassroots lobbying tends to be on the quantity of responses received by members of Congress, while the emphasis of grass-tops lobbying is on the quality of those drafted to lobby and their ability to sway particular members.

19. See, e.g., Jipping (2000b) concerning the confirmations of Richard Paez and Marsha Berzon; see also the Traditional Values Coalition special two-page report, "The Ninth Circuit Court Must be Split!" available at www.traditionalvalues.org/pdf_files/NinthCircuitCourt0404.pdf.

20. Durham withdrew within four months of her nomination for personal and family reasons.

21. Over Clinton's two terms, his group opposed approximately a dozen lower court nominees.

22. However, Gandy also acknowledged, "I guess the opposite argument is if you put all of your effort into one, and let the other five go, then you might actually beat one. And, instead, if you do a scattershot effort across the six, all six might get in" (2002). But she was still unsure of "how to make the choice" among "bad" nominees: "How do you say to women in the Fifth Circuit, 'We're going to let this bad person come to you because we're too busy trying to keep a different bad person off the Fourth Circuit or the Sixth Circuit'? I just think that you have to do what you can to fight them all" (Gandy 2002).

23. This quote is doubly interesting in that Jipping was talking about the decision to oppose nominees, but the group and its grassroots activists were actually discussing whether to rally in support of a nominee. Thus, while grassroots members need to be convinced that a nominee is in fact problematic on the issue of interest, grassroots members may also need to be persuaded that a nominee deserves support. In the case of George W. Bush's nominees who ran into opposition, membership group leaders had to convince their activists that they should expend their personal time and resources to help confirm the nominee.

24. Senator Charles Schumer convened a Judiciary Committee hearing on June 26, 2001, to explore the issue of ideological opposition to judges, titled "Judicial Nominations 2001: Should Ideology Matter?" Schumer argued that senators should openly vet a nominee's ideological positions, for otherwise senators would engage in "an escalating war of 'gotcha' politics." Opponents argue that discussing ideology openly will lead to

asking nominees about how they will rule in particular cases, and the creation of judicial litmus tests (Pilon 2002).

25. Eleanor Acheson was assistant attorney general for the Office of Policy Development during Clinton's two terms and was in charge of the Department of Justice's efforts on judicial nominations for the Clinton administration.

6 WHITHER NOMINEES?

1. Orrin Hatch, Statement on Amendment No. 3040, "The Fair Treatment of Presidential Judicial Nominees," March 21, 2002, *Congressional Record* S2201–S2204, at S2203.

2. Senator Grassley, quoted in a press statement put out by the Senate Judiciary Committee Republicans, "Democrats Continue to Block Judicial Nominees," on July 17, 2008, available at http://specter.senate.gov/public/index.cfm?FuseAction=NewsRoom .NewsReleasesanD.C.ontentRecord_id=32338467-d939-894f-0d41-3e6ff10f2175.

3. See, e.g., Levey's blog post on July 14, 2008, available at http://www.committee forjustice.org/blog/blog_archive/2008_07_01_archive.html.

4. See " 'He Is Latino': Why Dems Borked Estrada, in Their Own Words," Review and Outlook, *Wall Street Journal*, November 15, 2003; and "Memos of Special Interest on Hill," *Washington Times*, November 15, 2003.

5. Not surprisingly, beyond the question of whether the staffer who leaked the memos committed a crime (Lewis 2004), debate raged over whether Democrats followed the suggestions given to them as well as whether the Democrats themselves were guilty of racism (in response to a memo that suggested groups viewed Miguel Estrada as "especially dangerous," given his lack of a record and his Latino heritage) or of tampering with a legal case (in response to a memo that reported Elaine Jones, then president of the NAACP Legal Defense Fund, suggested a vote on Judge Julia Gibbons's nomination to the Sixth Circuit be delayed until after that court had decided the two affirmative action cases against the University of Michigan). For dueling views on the scope of this conflict, see, on the right, Hillyer (2004) and Kirkpatrick (2004), and on the left, Lithwick (2003).

6. An alternative is to use whether the nominee received a hearing or committee vote as the dependent variable. The concern is that it is difficult to accurately track the factors we know influence these activities but are not publicly discussed, such as when problems are found during the FBI's investigation. Since information in the FBI file is confidential, committee members historically refrain from publicly acknowledging when such problems derail a nomination. The dispute that arose during the George H. W. Bush administration over committee access to nominees' FBI files stemmed from a leak of information from Clarence Thomas's file during his confirmation hearings; this issue is discussed in chapter 3. The use of votes rather than a binary measure also allows us to more fully determine the impact of each potential influence. Thus, the statistical analysis may in fact underestimate the actual impact of informal group activities on the fate of a nomination. However, by limiting the analysis to the influence of group opposition on committee votes, we can have more confidence in the final results.

7. Duration analysis examines what factors influence how long it takes a nominee to be successfully confirmed. Since the vast majority of lower court nominees are eventually confirmed, scholars argue duration analysis, rather than a more typical outcome-

oriented analysis, more accurately reflects the reality of the lower court confirmation process. Most of these studies do not distinguish between nominees who are defeated in committee or on the floor and nominees who simply fail to move successfully through the process. Scherer, Bartels, and Steigerwalt (2008) specifically study the influence of informal interest group activity on confirmation durations and whether or not the nominee was successfully confirmed, and find group objections are the leading predictor of both increased confirmation durations and the increased likelihood of a failed confirmation. However, I am interested here in whether interest group objections persuade a senator to vote no on a particular nomination, even if the nomination is ultimately confirmed. As a result, the proper unit of analysis for this investigation is senators' votes rather than the time to confirmation.

8. The cautious language used here is not because a nomination may be defeated on the Senate floor but because the nomination may not ever receive a final confirmation vote. The effect of these types of scheduling decisions on confirmation outcomes is discussed in chapter 3.

9. National interest groups are defined as those with a national constituency. Two national groups had to oppose the nominee to ensure that only nominees facing sizable opposition were included in the analysis as opposed, rather than nominees who were only opposed by a single, rogue group; there was only one nominee who faced interest group opposition from only one group and so was not counted as opposed in the analysis. Finally, umbrella groups were counted as a single group, even though they technically speak for numerous groups. This coding decision means that even nominees opposed by an umbrella group needed to be publicly opposed by at least one other national group to be counted as opposed for the purposes of this study.

10. There were three instances in which nominees had back-to-back committee votes. In all three instances the nomination failed on the first vote, and the second vote was to send the nomination to the floor either without a recommendation or with a negative recommendation. In two of these instances the second vote was successful, and the nomination was sent to the floor; only one of these nominees, Daniel Manion, was confirmed.

11. However, Scherer (2003) argues that senators reject these interest group cues at their peril, as groups may then mobilize their members against those senators who confirm nominees the group finds "egregious."

12. Robert Katzmann, Maryanne Barry, and Charles Wilson all received one no vote each, while Sonia Sotomayor received two no votes and Merrick Garland received four no votes.

13. The issue concerned the vacancy created by Judge Stephen Trott's retirement from the Ninth Circuit. When Trott was appointed to the Ninth Circuit, he lived in California and had practiced extensively in California; he was also nominated to fill the seat of a retiring judge from California. However, Trott moved his chamber to Idaho during his tenure on the Ninth Circuit, and Bush (43) argued the seat had now become an "Idaho" seat.

14. Obviously, strong home-state support always helps a nominee. However, the important point here is not just that the nominee has home-state support but also that a connection to the Senate Judiciary Committee taps into the unique role of collegiality and reciprocity in the Senate. While the norm of reciprocity in the Senate overall has de-

creased over time (Sinclair 1989), Judiciary Committee staff highlighted its importance to the committee, especially given the length of time many of its members have served together. As highlighted in chapter 5, interest group leaders recognize the importance of these same factors when considering the benefits and deterrents to launching a fight against a particular nominee.

15. For more information about the American Bar Association's ratings, see chapter 3.

16. See chapter 3 for further discussion of the influence of scheduling decisions on confirmation outcomes.

17. Alternatively, we could simply measure whether the nominee was passed out of committee. However, given the small number of defeated nominees, we would learn little from this analysis. By examining the number of no votes each nominee received, we can better determine which factors lead to opposition as well as the degree to which they influence the amount of opposition a nominee encounters.

18. Raymond Kethledge was the only former Judiciary Committee staffer included in this analysis who did not receive a committee vote. He was nominated late in 2006. However, he was then renominated during the 110th Congress (the results of which are not included in this study) and was confirmed unanimously in committee and on the Senate floor.

19. All of the variables tested in this second model measure political factors that characterize the temporal political environment for each nominee but that also characterize the political environment of each Congress under study. I have assigned each case within a given Congress the same score on each of these variables. I am therefore using what could be considered aggregate-level data, but my analysis is proceeding on the individual case level. As a result, for those aggregate-level variables that are found to be significant using tobit, we must be cautious as to whether the null hypothesis has actually been rejected. I use tobit here, however, because of its overall robustness, ease of interpretability, and the problem that any aggregate-level analysis will be based on an extremely small *n*, which would also bias the results. These same cautions also apply to the results of Model 3, discussed below.

20. Senate Rule XXII provides the only mechanism for suspending debate on the Senate floor. Technically, once a senator is granted recognition on the Senate floor, he or she may speak for as long as he or she wishes. Invoking cloture ensures the measure will be brought to a vote but does not necessarily determine when; before 1979, senators could potentially conduct "post-cloture filibusters," since senators were limited to one hour of debate each, but this one-hour limit did not apply to the introduction of amendments or procedural matters; senators could thus control far more than their one-hour time limit by reading amendments, calling for votes on them, or calling for quorum calls. In 1979 the Senate amended Rule XXII to impose an overarching 100-hour limit on the consideration of the measure; each senator was still limited to speaking for no more than one hour. This ceiling was subsequently dropped to thirty hours in 1985. However, to ensure all senators are afforded the opportunity to express their opinion on the measure, the amended Rule XXII also stipulates that "any Senator who has not used or yielded at least ten minutes, is, if he seeks recognition, guaranteed up to ten minutes, inclusive, to speak only." The Senate may vote on a nondebatable motion, again by three-fifths majority, to increase the thirty-hour time limit. The Senate can also limit

post-cloture consideration to less than thirty hours or agree by unanimous consent to let this time period run even when the Senate is not technically in session. For additional information on the mechanics of cloture and filibusters, see Beth and Bach (2003).

21. In an ironic twist, Senate Republicans voted against cloture on one of George W. Bush's foreign aid bills in October 2001 to try to force the majority Democrats to confirm Bush's judicial choices more quickly. As of that date, and following both the September 11th attacks and the Capitol Hill anthrax scare, 110 vacancies existed on the federal bench (Biskupic 2001b).

22. This led to a rather odd event in which the Republican majority scheduled a thirty-hour all night talkathon to protest the Democrats' filibusters. Thus, to showcase these "hidden" filibusters, the Republican majority staged a filibuster to actually shut down the Senate (Lewis 2003).

23. As a CRS report explains, the "nuclear" or "constitutional" option requires changing the Senate rules in a manner not consistent with the Senate's "normal" rules of procedure (Palmer 2005, 3). There are thus multiple mechanisms by which the goal of the nuclear option—confirming judicial nominations with only majority support—could be achieved. The report describes four possible mechanisms. Two would occur on opening day when the Senate adopts its rules for the congressional term, and when debate exists about whether the rules from the previous Congress carry over until the adoption of the rules for the new Congress. Two would arise during the congressional term and involve the presiding officer declaring the supermajority requirement for cloture unconstitutional, either for cloture in general or for all nominations, or even for just judicial nominations.

CONCLUSION

1. National Organization for Women press release of statement by NOW President Kim Gandy, May 23, 2002, "Judiciary Committee Vote Insults Women; NOW Vows Campaign in Full Senate," available at http://www.now.org/press/05-02/05-23.html. In an interview with the author, Gandy revealed she had received calls from both Senator Biden and Senator Edwards to explain their votes in favor of Smith, as both these senators planned to court NOW's members during the 2004 presidential primaries (Gandy 2002).

2. In many ways, the "new" confirmation politics emerged when Obama explicated his requirement that his choice to fill the Souter vacancy possess "empathy" and recognize that "justice isn't about some abstract legal theory. It is also about how our laws affect the daily realities of people's lives" (quoted in Slevin 2009). This criterion drew criticism as Republicans accused Obama of wanting to select judges who had sympathy for certain groups and would not necessarily put the law first (Slevin 2009). Obama announced his nomination of Judge Sotomayor on May 26, 2009. Sotomayor almost immediately drew criticism from conservative commentators and groups for remarks that suggested she might rely too heavily on her particular ethnic background when making decisions (Lochhead 2009). She was also criticized by opponents of affirmative action for joining a Second Circuit opinion, *Ricci v. DeStefano* (530 F.3d 87 [2008]), which dismissed a reverse discrimination claim filed against New Haven, Connecticut (Long 2009). A group of white firefighters sued New Haven for throwing out the results of a promotion test because of concerns that the results—in which no African American

candidate was eligible for promotion—would trigger a "disparate impact" claim against the city under Title VII of the Civil Rights Act. This line of attack gained steam when the U.S. Supreme Court reversed the Second Circuit's decision on a 5–4 vote on June 29, 2009, thirteen days before Sotomayor's confirmation hearings were scheduled to begin (*Ricci v. DeStefano,* No. 07-1428).

BIBLIOGRAPHY

Abraham, Henry J. 1999. *Justices, Presidents, and Senators: A History of the U.S. Supreme Court Appointments from Washington to Clinton.* 4th ed. New York: Rowman and Littlefield.

Abrams, Jim. 2000. "Senate Approves Two Controversial Judges." Associated Press, March 9.

Acheson, Eleanor. 2002. Interview by the author. Tape recording. August 6. Washington, DC.

Ackerman, Bruce A. 1988. "Transformative Appointments." *Harvard Law Review* 101: 1164–84.

Allison, Garland W. 1996. "Delay in Senate Confirmation of Federal Judicial Nominees." *Judicature* 80:8–15.

Alter, Alison B., and Leslie Moscow McGranahan. 2000. "Reexamining the Filibuster and Proposal Powers in the Senate." *Legislative Studies Quarterly* 25:259–84.

American Bar Association. 2007. *Standing Committee on the Federal Judiciary: What It Is and How It Works.* http://www.abanet.org/scfedjud/home.html.

Aron, Nan. 2002. Interview by the author. Tape recording. July 9. Washington, DC.

Associated Press. 1997. "Revolt Aims at Activist Judges." *Deseret News,* March 6. http://archive.deseretnews.com/archive/547178/REVOLT-AIMS-AT-ACTIVIST-JUDGES.html.

Austen-Smith, David. 1993. "Information and Influence: Lobbying for Agendas and Votes." *American Journal of Political Science* 37:799–833.

Austen-Smith, David, and John R. Wright. 1994. "Counteractive Lobbying." *American Journal of Political Science* 38:25–44.

———. 1996. "Theory and Evidence for Counteractive Lobbying." *American Journal of Political Science* 40:543–64.

Austin, Peter C., Michael Escobar, and Jacek A. Kopec. 2000. "The Use of the Tobit Model for Analyzing Measures of Health Status." *Quality of Life Research* 9:901–10.

Bailey, Michael A., and Forrest Maltzman. 2008. "Does Legal Doctrine Matter? Unpacking Law and Policy Preferences on the U.S. Supreme Court." *American Political Science Review* 102:369–84.

Barrett, Barbara. 2007. "Bush Drops Push for Boyle: No Renomination to Appeals

Bench." *News Observer,* January 10. http://www.newsobserver.com/114/story/530799 .html.

Bartels, Brandon. 2009. "The Constraining Capacity of Legal Doctrine on the U.S. Supreme Court." *American Political Science Review* 103:474–95.

Baum, Lawrence A. 1977. "Policy Goals in Judicial Gatekeeping: A Proximity Model of Discretionary Jurisdiction." *American Journal of Political Science* 21:13–35.

———. 2008. *American Courts: Process and Policy.* 6th ed. Boston: Wadsworth.

Baumgartner, Frank R., and Beth L. Leech. 1996. "The Multiple Ambiguities of 'Counteractive Lobbying.'" *American Journal of Political Science* 40:521–42.

Bell, Lauren Cohen. 2002a. *Warring Factions: Interest Groups, Money, and the New Politics of Senate Confirmation.* Columbus: Ohio State University Press.

———. 2002b. "Senatorial Discourtesy: The Senate's Use of Delay to Shape the Federal Judiciary." *Political Research Quarterly* 55:589–607.

Berg, Linda. 2003. "Saving the Courts Crucial to Women's Rights." *National NOW Times,* Spring 2003. http://www.now.org/nnt/spring2003/index.html.

Berkson, Larry C., and Susan B. Carbon. 1980. *The United States Circuit Judge Nominating Commission: Its Members, Procedures and Candidates.* Chicago: American Judicature Society.

Beth, Richard S. 2002. *Cloture Attempts on Nominations.* CRS Report RS20801 (December 11). Washington, DC: Congressional Research Service.

Beth, Richard S., and Stanley Bach. 2003. *Filibusters and Cloture in the Senate.* CRS Report RL30360 (March 28). Washington, DC: Congressional Research Service.

Beth, Richard S., and Betsy Palmer. 2005. *Cloture Attempts on Nominations.* CRS Report RL32878 (April 22). Washington, DC: Congressional Research Service.

Binder, Sarah A. 2001. "The Senate as a Black Hole? Lessons Learned from the Judicial Appointments Experience." In *Innocent Until Nominated: The Breakdown of the Presidential Appointments Process,* ed. G. Calvin Mackenzie, 173–95. Washington, DC: Brookings Institution Press.

———. 2007. "Where Do Institutions Come From? Exploring the Origins of the Senate Blue Slip." *Studies in American Political Development* 21:1–15.

Binder, Sarah A., and Forrest Maltzman. 2002. "Senatorial Delay in Confirming Federal Judges, 1947–1998." *American Journal of Political Science* 46:190–99.

———. 2004. "The Limits of Senatorial Courtesy." *Legislative Studies Quarterly* 29:5–22.

Binder, Sarah A., and Thomas E. Mann. 1995. "Slaying the Dinosaur: The Case for Reforming the Senate Filibuster." *The Brookings Review* 13:42–46.

Binder, Sarah A., and Steven S. Smith. 1996. *Politics or Principle? Filibustering in the United States Senate.* Washington, DC: Brookings Institution Press.

Biskupic, Joan. 1995. "Judging Size of Court." *Washington Post,* October 23, A19.

———. 2001a. "White House Makes Pitch for Conservative Judges." *USA Today,* May 18, A4.

———. 2001b. "GOP Slows Foreign Aid Bill to Speed Judicial Choices." *USA Today,* October 22, A4.

Bonneau, Chris W., and Melinda Gann Hall. 2003. "Predicting Challengers in State

Supreme Court Elections: Context and the Politics of Institutional Design." *Political Research Quarterly* 56:337–49.

Bork, Robert. 1990. *The Tempting of America: The Political Seduction of the Law.* New York: Touchstone Press.

Brace, Paul, and Melinda Gann Hall. 1995. "Studying Courts Comparatively: The View from the American States." *Political Research Quarterly* 48:5–29.

Bronner, Ethan. 1989a. *Battle for Justice: How the Bork Nomination Shook America.* New York: Norton.

———. 1989b. "ABA Role in Selection of Judges Questioned." *Boston Globe,* May 6, National Section, 3.

Burdette, Franklin L. 1940. *Filibustering in the Senate.* Princeton, NJ: Princeton University Press.

Burn, Timothy. 1996. "Dole Blasts Clinton's Judicial Appointments." United Press International, April 19.

Caldeira, Gregory A. 1989. "Commentary on Senate Confirmation of Supreme Court Justices: The Roles of Organized and Unorganized Interests." *Kentucky Law Journal* 77:531–38.

Caldeira, Gregory A., Marie Hojnacki, and John R. Wright. 2000. "The Lobbying Activities of Organized Interests in Federal Judicial Nominations." *Journal of Politics* 62:51–69.

Caldeira, Gregory A., and John R. Wright. 1988. "Organized Interests and Agenda Setting in the U.S. Supreme Court." *American Political Science Review* 82:1109–27.

———. 1990. "The Discuss List: Agenda Building in the Supreme Court." *Law and Society Review* 24:807–36.

———. 1995. "Lobbying for Justice: The Rise of Organized Interests in the Politics of Federal Judicial Nominations." In *Contemplating Courts,* ed. Lee Epstein, 44–71. Washington, DC: CQ Press.

———. 1998. "Lobbying for Justice: Organized Interests, Supreme Court Nominations, and United States Senate." *American Journal of Political Science* 42:499–523.

Cameron, Charles M., Albert D. Cover, and Jeffrey A. Segal. 1990. "Senate Voting on Supreme Court Nominees: A Neoinstitutional Model." *American Political Science Review* 84:525–34.

Campbell, Andrea C., Gary W. Cox, and Mathew D. McCubbins. 2002. "Agenda Power in the U.S. Senate, 1877–1986." In *Party, Process and Political Change in Congress: New Perspectives on the History of Congress,* ed. David W. Brady and Mathew D. McCubbins, 146–54. Stanford: Stanford University Press.

Carp, Robert A., and C. K. Rowland. 1983. *Policymaking and Politics in the Federal District Courts.* Knoxville: University of Tennessee Press.

Carp, Robert A., and Ronald Stidham. 1993. *Judicial Process in America.* 2nd ed. Washington, DC: CQ Press.

Carr, Thomas P., and Stanley Bach. 2002. *The Legislative Process on the Senate Floor: An Introduction.* CRS Report 96–548 GOV (November 8). Washington, DC: Congressional Research Service.

Carter, Stephen L. 1994. *The Confirmation Mess: Cleaning Up the Federal Appointments Process.* New York: Basic Books.

Cavendish, Elizabeth. 2002. Interview with the author. Tape recording. July 10. Washington, DC.

Chase, Harold W. 1972. *Federal Judges: The Appointing Process.* Minneapolis: University of Minnesota Press.

Cigler, Allan J., and Burdett A. Loomis. 1998. *Interest Group Politics.* 5th ed. Washington, DC: CQ Press.

Cohen, Lauren M. 1998. "Missing in Action: Interest Groups and Federal Judicial Appointments." *Judicature* 82:119–23.

Conservative Activist. 2002. Interview with the author. Tape recording. July. Washington, DC.

Corley, Pamela C., Amy Steigerwalt, and Artemus Ward. 2008. "Deciding to Agree: Explaining Consensual Behavior on the United States Supreme Court." Paper presented at the 2008 Midwest Political Science Association Annual Meeting, Chicago, April 3–6.

Dahl, David. 1991. "Judicial Nominee Has No Experience." *St. Petersburg Times,* May 14, A4.

Daniels, William J. 1978. "The Geographic Factor in Appointments to the United States Supreme Court: 1789–1976." *Western Political Quarterly* 31:226–37.

Davidson, Lee. 2003. "Utahns Play Key Roles in D.C." *Deseret News,* January 8, B1.

Davis, Christopher M. 2007. *Invoking Cloture in the Senate.* CRS Report 98–425 (June 4). Washington, DC: Congressional Research Service.

"Democrats Fight for Activist Judges, GOP Caves." 2000. *NewsMax.com,* August 30. http://www.newsmax.com/articles/?a=2000/8/28/223819.

Den Hartog, Chris, and Nathan W. Monroe. 2008. "The Value of Majority Status: The Effect of Jefford's Switch on Asset Prices of Republican and Democratic Firms." *Legislative Studies Quarterly* 33:63–84.

DeNardis, Lawrence. 1989. "The New Senate Filibuster: An Analysis of Filibustering and Gridlock in the U.S. Senate, 1977–1986." PhD diss., New York University.

Denning, Brannon P. 2001. "Reforming the New Confirmation Process: Replacing 'Despise and Resent' with 'Advice and Consent.'" *Administrative Law Review* 53:1–37.

———. 2002. "The Judicial Confirmation Process and the Blue Slip." *Judicature* 85: 218–27.

Denzau, Arthur T., and Michael C. Munger. 1986. "Legislators and Interest Groups: How Unorganized Interests Get Represented." *American Political Science Review* 80:89–106.

DeParle, Jason. 2005. "Nomination for Supreme Court Stirs Debate on Influence of Federalist Society." *New York Times,* August 1, A1.

Duff, James C. 2008. *Judicial Business of the United States Courts: 2008 Annual Report of the Director.* Washington, DC: Administrative Office of the U.S. Courts.

Epstein, Lee, and Jeffrey A. Segal. 2005. *Advice and Consent: The Politics of Judicial Appointments.* New York: Oxford University Press.

Evans, Will. 2006. "Controversial Bush Judge Broke Ethics Law." *Salon,* May 1. http://www.salon.com/news/feature/2006/05/01/boyle/.

Flemming, Roy B., Michael C. MacLeod, and Jeffrey Talbert. 1998. "Witnesses at the Confirmations? The Appearance of Organized Interests at Senate Hearings of Federal Judicial Appointments, 1945–1992." *Political Research Quarterly* 51:617–31.

Fenno, Richard F., Jr. 1973. *Congressmen in Committee.* Boston: Little, Brown.

Fisk, Catherine, and Erwin Chemerinsky. 1997. "The Filibuster." *Stanford Law Review* 49:181–243.

Fox News. 2009. "Specter's Defection Could Help Republicans Block a Nominee to Replace Souter." *FoxNews.com,* May 1. http://www.foxnews.com/politics/2009/05/01/specters-defection-help-republicans-block-souters-potential-replacement/.

Frank, John. 1991. *Clement Haynsworth, the Senate, and the Supreme Court.* Charlottesville: University Press of Virginia.

Gailmard, Sean, and Jeffrey A. Jenkins. 2007. "Negative Agenda Control in the Senate and House: Fingerprints of Majority Party Power." *Journal of Politics* 69: 689–700.

Gandy, Kim. 2002. Interview by the author. Tape recording. July 11. Washington, DC.

Gerhardt, Michael J. 2003. *The Federal Appointments Process: A Constitutional and Historical Analysis.* Durham, NC: Duke University Press.

Giachino, Renee. 2006. "Interview with Judge Charles Pickering." *Your Turn: Meeting Nonsense with Common Sense.* WEBY 1330 AM. Posted online March 23. http://www.cfif.org/htdocs/freedomline/current/in_our_opinion/Pickering.htm.

Giles, Micheal W., Virginia A. Hettinger, and Todd Peppers. 2001. "Picking Federal Judges: A Note on Policy and Partisan Selection Agendas." *Political Research Quarterly* 54:623–41.

Gilligan, Thomas W., and Keith Krehbiel. 1989. "Asymmetric Information and Legislative Rules with a Heterogeneous Committee." *American Journal of Political Science* 33: 459–90.

———. 1990. "The Organization of Informative Committees by a Rational Legislature." *American Journal of Political Science* 34:531–64.

Gittenstein, Mark. 1992. *Matters of Principle: An Insider's Account of America's Rejection of Robert Bork's Nomination to the Supreme Court.* New York: Simon and Schuster.

———. 2002. Interview by the author. Tape recording. June 25. Washington, DC.

Goings, Kenneth W. 1990. *The NAACP Comes of Age: The Defeat of Judge John J. Parker.* Bloomington: Indiana University Press.

Goldman, Sheldon. 1966. "Voting Behavior on the United States Courts of Appeals, 1961–1964." *American Political Science Review* 60:374–84.

———. 1975. "Voting Behavior on the U.S. Courts of Appeals Revisited." *American Political Science Review* 69:491–506.

———. 1989. "Reagan's Judicial Legacy: Completing the Puzzle and Summing Up." *Judicature* 72:318–30.

———. 1997. *Picking Federal Judges: Lower Court Selection from Roosevelt through Reagan.* New Haven, CT: Yale University Press.

Goldman, Sheldon, and Elliot Slotnick. 1999. "Clinton's Second Term Judiciary: Picking Judges under Fire." *Judicature* 82:264–84.

Goldman, Sheldon, Elliot Slotnick, Gerard Gryski, and Sara Schiavoni. 2005. "W. Bush's Judiciary: The First Term Record." *Judicature* 88:244–75.

Goldman, Sheldon, Elliot Slotnick, Gerard Gryski, and Gary Zuk. 2001. "Clinton's Judges: Summing up the Legacy." *Judicature* 84:228–54.

Goldman, Sheldon, Elliot Slotnick, Gerard Gryski, Gary Zuk, and Sara Schiavoni. 2003. "W. Bush Remaking the Judiciary: Like Father, Like Son?" *Judicature* 86:282–309.

Grassley, Charles E. 1990. "Reforming the Role of the ABA in Judicial Selection: Triumph of Hope over Experience?" In *Judicial Selection: Merit, Ideology and Politics,* ed. Henry Abraham. Washington, DC: National Legal Center for the Public Interest.

Greenberg, Dan. 1994. *Cutting Congress Down to Size: How a Part Time Congress Would Work.* Heritage Foundation Policy Paper. Washington, DC: U.S. Congress Assessment Project, November 2.

Greenberger, Robert S. 2001. "ABA Loses Major Role in Judge Screening." *Wall Street Journal,* March 23, B8.

Greenberger, Robert S., and David S. Cloud. 2001. "Bush to Weaken ABA Role on Nominees." *Wall Street Journal,* March 19, B11.

Greenhouse, Linda. 1987. "Court Vacancy Renews Debate on A.B.A. Role." *New York Times,* December 27, A24.

Grossman, Joel B. 1965. *Lawyers and Judges: The ABA and the Politics of Judicial Selection.* New York: John Wiley and Sons.

Grossman, Joel B., and Stephen L. Wasby. 1972. "The Senate and Supreme Court Nominations: Some Reflections." *Duke Law Journal* 1972:557–91.

Guliuzza, Frank, III, Daniel J. Reagan, and David M. Barrett. 1994. "The Senate Judiciary Committee and Supreme Court Nominees: Measuring the Dynamics of Confirmation Criteria." *Journal of Politics* 56:773–87.

Haire, Susan B., Martha Anne Humphries, and Donald R. Songer. 2001. "The Voting Behavior of Clinton's Courts of Appeals Appointees." *Judicature* 84:274–82.

Hall, Kermit. 1979. *The Politics of Justice: Lower Federal Judicial Selection and the Second Party System, 1829–61.* Lincoln: University of Nebraska Press.

Hall, Melinda Gann. 1992. "Electoral Politics and Strategic Voting in State Supreme Courts." *Journal of Politics* 54:427–46.

———. 2001. "State Supreme Courts in American Democracy: Probing the Myths of Judicial Reform." *American Political Science Review* 95:315–30.

Hardin, Peter. 1991. "Justice Official Headed for 4th Circuit Appeals Seat." *Richmond Times-Dispatch,* July 30, 5.

Harris, Joseph Pratt. 1952. "The Courtesy of the Senate." *Political Science Quarterly* 67:36–65.

———. 1953. *The Advice and Consent of the Senate: A Study of the Confirmation of Appointments by the United States Senate.* Berkeley and Los Angeles: University of California Press.

Hartley, Roger E., and Lisa M. Holmes. 1997. "Increasing Senate Scrutiny of Lower Federal Court Nominees." *Judicature* 80:274–78.

————. 2002. "The Increasing Senate Scrutiny of Lower Federal Court Nominees." *Political Science Quarterly* 117:259–78.

Hendershot, Marcus E. 2008. "From Consent to Advice and Consent: Cyclical Constraints within the District Court Appointment Process." *Political Research Quarterly,* first published December 24. doi:10.1177/1065912908329354.

Hight, Bruce. 2000. "Political Clock Ticks for Judge Nominee: As National Election Nears, Texas Senators Block El Paso Lawyer." *Austin American Statesman,* June 25, A1.

Hillyer, Quin. 2004. "Conservatives Vent: Memos Still Beg for More Scrutiny." *National Review Online,* February 17. http://www.nationalreview.com/comment/hillyer 200402170902.asp.

Hodder-Williams, Richard. 1988. "The Strange Story of Judge Robert Bork and a Vacancy on the U.S. Supreme Court." *Political Studies* 36:613–37.

Hojnacki, Marie, and David C. Kimball. 1999. "The Who and How of Organizations' Lobbying Strategies in Committee." *Journal of Politics* 61:999–1024.

Holland, Jesse J. 2001a. "Lawmaker Pulls Name from Consideration for Appeals Court Seat." *Associated Press,* May 26.

————. 2001b. "Dems Won't Rush on Some Judges: 32 Bush Nominees Await Hearings in Senate." *Associated Press,* November 12.

————. 2002. "Dems Take GOP Side on McCain Nominees: Arizona Senator Demands That Bush Appoint His Choice to the FEC." *Grand Rapids Press,* July 11, A9.

————. 2003. "3 Court Nominations Pushed to Senate Floor Vote." *Philadelphia Inquirer,* January 30, A9.

Holmes, Lisa M. 2007. "Presidential Strategy in the Judicial Appointment Process: 'Going Public' in Support of Nominees to the U.S. Courts of Appeals." *American Politics Research* 35:567–94.

————. 2008a. "Why 'Go Public'? Presidential Use of Nominees to the U.S. Courts of Appeals." *Presidential Studies Quarterly* 38:110–22.

————. 2008b. "The Implications of Politicization in the Lower Federal Court Appointment Process." Paper presented at the 2008 American Political Science Association Annual Meeting, Boston, August 28–31.

Hoppin, Jason. 2003. "Senate Puts Fight over Judges on Display." *The Recorder,* November 14. http://www.law.com/jsp/article.jsp?id=1068651190108#.

Horn, Dan. 2003. "Political Divide Sparks Disorder in the Courts: 6th Circuit Court's Spats Lift Veil, and Picture Isn't Pretty." *Cincinnati Enquirer,* June 22, A1.

Howard, J. Woodford, Jr. 1981. *Courts of Appeals in the Federal Judicial System: A Study of the Second, Fifth and District of Columbia Circuits.* Princeton, NJ: Princeton University Press.

Howard, Robert M., and Scott E. Graves. 2009. *Justice Takes a Recess: Judicial Appointments from George Washington to George W. Bush.* Lanham, MD: Lexington Books.

Howlett, Debbie. 2001. "At Lawyers' Gathering, Ashcroft Defends Vetting Decision." *USA Today,* August 8, A4.

Hudson, Audrey. 2001. "Democrats Want ABA to Vet Judges; Will Put Holds on Confirmations Until Legal Group's Checks Are Completed." *Washington Times,* March 28, A4.

Hulse, Carl, and Neil A. Lewis. 2005. "Senators Wrangle as Panel Approves Judicial Nominee." *New York Times,* May 13, A18.

Hulse, Carl, and Adam Nagourney. 2009. "Specter Switches Parties; More Heft for Democrats." *New York Times,* April 29, A1.

Hurt, Charles. 2005. "Reid Cites FBI Files on Judicial Pick." *Washington Times,* May 13, A1.

Jacobi, Tonja. 2005. "The Senatorial Courtesy Game: Explaining the Norm of Informal Vetoes in 'Advice and Consent' Nominations." *Legislative Studies Quarterly* 30: 193–217.

Jipping, Thomas L. 2000. "Will Republicans Fight as Hard as the Democrats Did?" October 9. http://www.enterstageright.com/archive/articles/1000judges.htm.

———. 2002a. Interview by Nancy Scherer. Tape recording. June 6. Washington, D.C.

———. 2002b. Interview by the author. Tape recording. July. Washington, DC.

Johnson, Timothy R., and Jason M. Roberts. 2004. "Presidential Capital and the Supreme Court Confirmation Process." *Journal of Politics* 66:663–83.

Kahn, Michael. 1995. "The Appointment of a Supreme Court Justice: A Political Process from Beginning to End." *Presidential Studies Quarterly* 25:25–41.

Kernell, Samuel. 1997. *Going Public: New Strategies of Presidential Leadership.* 3rd ed. Washington, DC: CQ Press.

King, John. 2004. "Pickering Appointment Angers Democrats: Bush Bypasses Senate, Picks Judge for Appellate Bench." *CNN.com,* January 17. http://www.cnn.com/2004/ALLPOLITICS/01/17/bush.pickering/index.html.

Kingdon, John W. 1989. *Congressmen's Voting Decisions.* 3rd ed. Ann Arbor: University of Michigan Press.

Kirkpatrick, Melanie. 2004. "Memogate: Why Won't the Senate GOP Stand Up to Democratic Judiciary Committee Shenanigans?" (editorial). *Wall Street Journal,* March 5, A14.

Koppel, Nathan. 2000. "5th Circuit Nomination Rejected Because of Experience Level." *Texas Lawyer,* May 15, 1.

Krehbiel, Keith. 1991. *Information and Legislative Organization.* Ann Arbor: University of Michigan Press.

Kuhnhenn, James. 2002. "McCain Roars Back: This Time Taking on Corporate Greed." *Philadelphia Inquirer,* July 15, A1.

LaMarche, Gara. 2001. "Senate Confirmations: How Should We Judge Judges?" *Los Angeles Times,* July 15, M2.

Langer, Laura. 2002. *Judicial Review in State Supreme Courts: A Comparative Study.* Albany, NY: SUNY Press.

Lazarus, Jeffrey, and Amy Steigerwalt. 2009. "Different Houses: The Distribution of Earmarks in the U.S. House and Senate." *Legislative Studies Quarterly* 34:347–73.

Leahy, Patrick. 2001. "Judicial, Justice Department Nominees." Senate Judiciary Committee, Statement submitted for the public record, October 4.

Lewis, Neil A. 1998. "Clinton Agrees to G.O.P. Deal on Judgeships." *New York Times,* May 5, A1.

————. 2001. "A Conservative Legal Group Thrives in Bush's Washington." *New York Times,* April 18, A1.

————. 2002. "Democrats Reject Bush Pick in Battle over Court Balance." *New York Times,* September 6, A1.

————. 2003. "Angered by Filibusters on Nominees, Republicans Stage Their Own Protest." *New York Times,* November 13, A2.

————. 2004. "Report Finds Republican Aides Spied on Democrats." *New York Times,* March 5, A14.

————. 2006. "Senator Removes His Block on Federal Court Nominee." *New York Times,* December 19, A21.

Lichtblau, Eric. 2002. "Debate Club's 'Secret Handshakes' Turn into Public Grins." *New York Times,* November 17, A26.

Lichtman, Judith. 1990. "Public Interest Groups and the Bork Nomination." *Northwestern University Law Review* 84:978–79.

Lindgren, James T. 2001. "Examining the American Bar Association's Ratings of Nominees to the U.S. Courts of Appeals for Political Bias, 1989–2000." *Journal of Law and Politics* 17:1–40.

Liptak, Adam. 2004. "A Judge Appointed by Bush after Impasse in Senate Retires." *New York Times,* December 10, A22.

Lithwick, Dahlia. 2004. "Memogate: The Judiciary Committee Computer Scandal Is One Gnarly Sausage." *Slate,* February 19. http://www.slate.com/id/2095770/.

Lochhead, Carolyn. 2009. "Right Calls Sotomayor Racist over Line in Talk." *San Francisco Chronicle,* May 29, A1.

Long, Wendy. 2009. "Bench Memos: Sotomayor for the Court." *National Review Online,* May 26. http://bench.nationalreview.com/post/?q=OTU0NGI5MTFjYWI0 MWQ2ZGFlMWY5NjBjMzY2YWQyZTI=/.

Lovrich, Nicholas P., Jr., and Charles H. Sheldon. 1983. "Voters in Contested, Nonpartisan Judicial Elections: A Responsible Electorate or a Problematic Public?" *Political Research Quarterly* 36:241–56.

Mackenzie, G. Calvin, and Michael Hafken. 2002. *Scandal Proof: Do Ethics Laws Make Government Ethical?* Washington, DC: Brookings Institution Press.

Maltese, John Anthony. 1995. *The Selling of Supreme Court Nominees.* Baltimore: Johns Hopkins University Press.

Maltzman, Forrest, and Sarah A. Binder. 2000. "A Nomination for Change in the Senate: Process for Confirming Judicial Appointees in Desperate Need for Reform." *Roll Call,* June 19.

Martinek, Wendy L., Mark Kemper, and Steven R. Van Winkle. 2002. "To Advise and Consent: The Senate and Lower Federal Court Nominations, 1977–1998." *Journal of Politics* 64:337–61.

Massaro, John. 1990. *Supremely Political: The Role of Ideology and Presidential Management in Unsuccessful Supreme Court Nominations.* Albany, NY: SUNY Press.

Massey, Calvin R. 1991. "Getting There: A Brief History of the Politics of Supreme Court Appointments." *Hastings Constitutional Law Quarterly* 19:1–16.

Massie, Tajuana D., Thomas G. Hansford, and Donald R. Songer. 2004. "The Timing of Presidential Nominations to the Lower Federal Courts." *Political Research Quarterly* 57:145–54.

McCarty, Nolan, and Rose Razaghian. 1999. "Advice and Consent: Senate Responses to Executive Branch Nominations 1885–1996." *American Journal of Political Science* 43: 1122–43.

McConnell, Mitch. 2009. "McConnell Statement on Justice Souter, Upcoming Vacancy." Press Release from the Office of Senator Mitch McConnell, May 1. http://mcconnell .senate.gov/record.cfm?id=312391andstart=1.

McDonald, Forrest. 1994. *The American Presidency: An Intellectual History.* Lawrence: University Press of Kansas.

McFeeley, Neil D. 1987. *Appointment of Judges: The Johnson Presidency.* Austin: University of Texas Press.

McQueen, M. P. 1992. "Senate Delays Hispanic Nomination." *Newsday,* July 4, 10.

Metzenbaum, Howard. 2002. Interview by the author. Tape recording. June 26. Washington, DC.

Moran, Terence. 1987. "Battle Over Judges Brews in the Senate: Democrats Beef Up Investigations with More Staff and Money." *Legal Times,* January 26, 1.

Murphy, Bruce A. 1988. *Fortas: The Rise and Ruin of a Supreme Court Justice.* New York: William Morrow.

Murphy, Walter F. 1964. *Elements of Judicial Strategy.* Chicago: University of Chicago Press.

Myers, William G., III. 1990. "The Role of Special Interest Groups in the Supreme Court Nomination of Robert Bork." *Hastings Constitutional Law Quarterly* 17: 399–419.

Nagourney, Adam, and Jeff Zeleny. 2009. "Washington Prepares for Fight over Any Nominee." *New York Times,* May 2, A10.

Neas, Ralph. 2002. Interview by the author. Tape recording. August 6. Washington, DC.

Neff, Alan. 1981. *The United States District Judge Nominating Commissions: Their Members, Procedures and Candidates.* Chicago: American Judicature Society.

Nemacheck, Christine L. 2008a. *Strategic Selection: Presidential Nomination of Supreme Court Justices from Herbert Hoover through George W. Bush.* Charlottesville: University of Virginia Press.

———. 2008b. "Designated Justice: The Effects of Senate Delay on United States Courts of Appeals' Decisions." Paper presented at the 2008 American Political Science Association Annual Meeting, Boston, August 28–31.

New York Times. 2005. "Editorial: It Depends on What 'Member' Means." *New York Times,* July 26, A16.

NewsHour. 2000. "GOP Presidential Primary Debate." *NewsHour with Jim Lehrer,* January 7. Transcript. http://www.pbs.org/newshour/bb/politics/jan-june00/gop_ debate_1-7.html.

Nichols, Mike. 1991. "Judicial Vacancies Swell Backlog." *Milwaukee Journal,* December 11, B4.

Nixon, David C., and David L. Goss. 2001. "Confirmation Delay for Vacancies on the Circuit Courts of Appeals." *American Politics Research* 29:246–74.

O'Brien, David M. 1988. *Judicial Roulette: Report of the Twentieth Century Fund Task Force on Judicial Selection.* New York: Priority Press.

Oleszek, Walter J. 1996. *Congressional Procedures and the Policy Process.* 4th ed. Washington, DC: CQ Press.

———. 2008. *Senate Policy on "Holds": Action in the 110th Congress.* CRS Report RL34255 (March 14). Washington, DC: Congressional Research Service.

Ornstein, Norman J. 1999. "Extortion Is Legal in the Senate: It's Called 'The Hold.'" *Roll Call,* July 29, 1–7.

Overby, L. Marvin, Beth M. Henschen, Michael H. Walsh, and Julie Strauss. 1992. "Courting Constituents? An Analysis of the Senate Confirmation Vote on Justice Clarence Thomas." *American Political Science Review* 86:997–1003.

Palmer, Betsy. 2005. *Changing Senate Rules: The "Constitutional" or "Nuclear" Option.* CRS Report RL32684 (April 5). Washington, DC: Congressional Research Service.

Perine, Keith. 2003. "Both Parties Find Political Benefit from Battle over Judicial Nominees." *Congressional Quarterly Weekly Report,* October 4, 2431.

Pertschuk, Michael, and Wendy Schaetzel. 1989. *The People Rising: The Campaign against the Bork Nomination.* New York: Thunder's Mouth Press.

Pickering, Charles W., Sr. 2006. "Bench Repair: Op-ed." *Washington Times,* March 26, B1.

Pilon, Roger. 2002. "Bench Politics: Senate Stalls on Judges Who Would Uphold the Constitution." *Legal Times,* January 21.

Poole, Keith T., and Howard Rosenthal. 1998. "Estimating a Basic Space from a Set of Issue Scales." *American Journal of Political Science* 42:954–93.

Posner, Richard A. 1987. "What Am I, a Potted Plant? The Case against Strict Constructionism." *New Republic,* September 28, 23.

Provine, Doris Marie. 1980. *Case Selection in the United States Supreme Court.* Chicago: University of Chicago Press.

Raum, Tom. 1999. "Lott among Those Now Holding Up Holdbrooke." Associated Press, July 7.

Rehnquist, William. 2002. *2001 Year-End Report on the Federal Judiciary.* http://www.supremecourtus.gov/publicinfo/year-end/2001year-endreport.html.

"Rehnquist Battle Set, But Is Scalia's Role Overlooked?" 1986. *Seattle Times,* September 7, A3.

Renzin, Lee. 1999. "Advice, Consent and Inaction: How the Courts Can Require the Senate to Vote on Judicial Nominations." *Judicature* 82:166–75.

Robinson, Jeffrey. 2002. Interview by the author. Tape recording. June 17. Washington, DC.

Roger, K. Lowe. 1996. "Senate Compromise May Allow Confirmation of Federal Judges." *Columbus Dispatch,* July 14, B3.

Rosen, Jeffrey. 2009. "The Stealth Justice." *New York Times,* May 2, A21.

Rowland, C. K., and Robert A. Carp. 1996. *Politics and Judgment in Federal District Courts.* Lawrence: University Press of Kansas.

Rowland, C. K., Robert A. Carp, and Ronald A. Stidham. 1984. "Judges' Policy Choices and the Value Basis of Judicial Appointments: A Comparison of Support for Criminal Defendants among Nixon, Johnson, and Kennedy Appointments to the Federal District Courts." *Journal of Politics* 46:886–902.

Ruckman, P. S., Jr. 1993. "The Supreme Court, Critical Nominations, and the Senate Confirmation Process." *Journal of Politics* 55:793–805.

Rutkus, Denis Steven, and Maureen Bearden. 2009. *Nominations to Article III Lower Courts by President George W. Bush During the 110th Congress.* CRS Report RL33953 (February 18). Washington, DC: Congressional Research Service.

Saks, Michael J., and Neil Vidmar. 2001. "A Flawed Search for Bias in the American Bar Association's Ratings of Prospective Judicial Nominees: A Critique of the Lindgren Study." *Journal of Law and Politics* 17:219–55.

Sammon, Bill. 2002. "Bush Marshals Backers for Pickering." *Washington Times,* March 7, A3.

Sanbonmatsu, Kira. 2002. *Democrats, Republicans, and the Politics of Women's Place.* Ann Arbor: University of Michigan Press.

Saturno, James V. 2003. *How Measures Are Brought to the Senate Floor: A Brief Introduction.* CRS Report RS20668 (July 18). Washington, DC: Congressional Research Service.

Savage, Charlie. 2005. "GOP Rift Looms over High Court Nominations: Some Want Evangelicals to Keep Quiet During Fight." *Boston Globe,* June 26, A1.

———. 2009. "Conservative Map Strategies on Court." *New York Times,* May 17, A1.

Savage, David G. 2001. "Bush's Judicial Nominees Go 28 for 80 in the Senate." *Los Angeles Times,* December 31, A12.

———. 2002. "GOP Gets Delay on Court Nominee." *Los Angeles Times,* March 8. http://articles.latimes.com/2002/mar/08/news/mn-31787.

Scalia, Antonin. 1996. "A Theory of Constitutional Interpretation." Speech given at the Catholic University of America, Washington, DC, October 18. http://web.archive.org/web/19980119172058/www.courttv.com/library/rights/scalia.html

Scherer, Nancy. 2000. "Are Clinton's Judges 'Old' Democrats or 'New' Democrats?" *Judicature* 84:150–54.

———. 2001. "Who Drives the Ideological Makeup of the Lower Federal Courts in a Divided Government?" *Law and Society Review* 35:191–218.

———. 2003. "The Judicial Confirmation Process: Mobilizing Elites, Mobilizing Masses." *Judicature* 86:240–50.

———. 2005. *Scoring Points: Politicians, Political Activists, and the Lower Federal Court Appointment Process.* Stanford, CA: Stanford University Press.

Scherer, Nancy, Brandon Bartels, and Amy Steigerwalt. 2008. "Sounding the Fire Alarm: The Role of Interest Groups in the Lower Court Confirmation Process." *Journal of Politics* 70:1026–39.

Scherer, Nancy, and Banks Miller. 2009. "The Federalist Society's Influence on the Federal Judiciary." *Political Research Quarterly* 62:366–78.

Schlozman, Kay Lehman, and John T. Tierney. 1986. *Organized Interests and American Democracy.* New York: Harper and Row.

Seckora, Melissa. 2001. "Courting Prejudice: The ABA's Just Another Liberal Interest Group." *National Review Online,* March 21. http://www.nationalreview.com/nr_com ment/nr_comment032101b.shtml.

Segal, Jeffrey. 1987. "Senate Confirmation of Supreme Court Justices: Partisan and Institutional Politics." *Journal of Politics* 49:998–1015.

Segal, Jeffrey A., Charles M. Cameron, and Albert D. Cover. 1992. "A Spatial Model of Roll Call Voting: Senators, Constituents, Presidents, and Interest Groups in Supreme Court Confirmations." *American Journal of Political Science* 36:96–121.

Segal, Jeffrey A., Albert D. Cover, and Charles M. Cameron. 1989. "The Role of Ideology in Senate Confirmation of Supreme Court Justices." *Kentucky Law Journal* 77: 485–507.

Segal, Jeffrey A., and Harold J. Spaeth. 1986. "If a Supreme Court Vacancy Occurs, Will the Senate Confirm a Reagan Nominee?" *Judicature* 69:186–90.

———. 1993. *The Supreme Court and the Attitudinal Model.* New York: Cambridge University Press.

———. 2002. *The Supreme Court and the Attitudinal Model Revisited.* New York: Cambridge University Press.

Shapiro, Martin. 1990. "Interest Groups and Supreme Court Appointments." *Northwestern University Law Review* 84:935–61.

Shipan, Charles R., and Megan L. Shannon. 2003. "Delaying Justice(s): A Duration Analysis of Supreme Court Confirmation." *American Journal of Political Science* 47: 654–68.

Shogan, Robert. 1972. *A Question of Judgment: The Fortas Case and the Struggle for the Supreme Court.* Indianapolis: Bobbs-Merrill.

Silverstein, Mark. 1994. *Judicious Choices: The New Politics of Supreme Court Confirmations.* New York: Norton.

Sinclair, Barbara. 1989. *The Transformation of the U.S. Senate.* Baltimore: Johns Hopkins University Press.

Slevin, Peter. 2009. "Obama Makes Empathy a Requirement for Court." *Washington Post,* May 13, A3.

Slotnick, Elliot E. 1980a. "Reforms in Judicial Selection: Will They Affect the Senate's Role? (Part One)." *Judicature* 64:60–73.

———. 1980b. "Reforms in Judicial Selection: Will They Affect the Senate's Role? (Part Two)." *Judicature* 64:115–31.

———. 1984. "Judicial Selection Systems and Nomination Outcomes: Does the Process Make a Difference?" *American Politics Research* 12:225–40.

Slotnick, Elliot E., and Sheldon Goldman. 1998. "Congress and the Courts: A Case of Casting." In *Great Theatre: The American Congress in the 1990s,* ed. Herbert F. Weisberg and Samuel C. Patterson, 197–223. New York: Cambridge University Press.

Sollenberger, Mitchel A. 2003. *The Blue-Slip Process in the Senate Committee on the Judiciary: Background, Issues and Options.* CRS Report RS21674 (November 21). Washington, DC: Congressional Research Service.

Songer, Donald R. 1982. "The Policy Consequences of Senate Involvement in the Selection of Judges in the United States Courts of Appeals." *Western Political Quarterly* 35:107–19.

Star-Ledger. 2009. "Justice David Souter Remained Unpredictable" (editorial). *Star Ledger,* May 3. http://blog.nj.com/njv_editorial_page/2009/05/souter.html.

Steigerwalt, Amy. 2004. "The Four Tracks to Confirmation." Paper presented at the 2004 Annual Meeting of the Midwest Political Science Association, Chicago.

Stern, Seth. 2009. "Latino Lawmakers Call for Latino Justice." *CQ Politics,* May 1. http:// blogs.cqpolitics.com/legal_beat/2009/05/latino-lawmakers-call-for-lati.html.

Stolberg, Sheryl Gay. 2003. "Battle over Judgeship Tests Congressman's Loyalties to People and Party." *New York Times,* March 15, A14.

Strauss, Peter L. 1987. "One Hundred Fifty Cases Per Year: Some Implications of the Supreme Court's Limited Resources for Judicial Review of Agency Action." *Columbia Law Review* 87:1093–136.

Stuart, Reginald. 1987. "Bork Backers: ABA Ratings Are 'Political.'" *Philadelphia Daily News,* September 22, 6.

Tarr, G. Alan, and Mary Cornelia Aldis Porter. 1990. *State Supreme Courts in State and Nation.* New Haven, CT: Yale University Press.

Tetreault, Steve. 2001. "State's Senators Work Together Picking Judges." *Las Vegas Review Journal,* May 26, B1.

Thomas, Jennifer S. 1994. "Republicans to Whittle House Committee Staffs." *St. Petersburg Times,* December 19, A1.

Thomas, Ken. 2008. "Bush Nominates Michigan Appellate Judge to 6th Circuit Slot." *Grand Rapids Press,* April 16. http://blog.mlive.com/grpress/2008/04/bush_nomi nates_michigan_appell.html.

Thompson, Jake. 2006. "Congress Lacking Frugality?" *Omaha World Herald,* July 3, A1.

Thurman, James N. 1999. "What's behind Another Ambassador Delay?" *Christian Science Monitor,* November 1, 2.

Updegrave, Walter L. 1992. "What Congress Really Costs You." *Money Magazine,* August 1.

Verba, Sidney. 1993. "The 1993 James Madison Award Lecture: The Voice of the People." *PS: Political Science and Politics,* December, 677–86.

Vieira, Norman, and Leonard Gross. 1998. *Supreme Court Appointments: Judge Bork and the Politicization of Senate Confirmations.* Carbondale: Southern Illinois University Press.

Vining, Richard L., Jr., Amy Steigerwalt, and Susan Navarro Smelcer. 2009. "Bias and the Bar: Evaluating the ABA Ratings of Federal Judicial Nominees." Paper presented at the 2009 Annual Meeting of the Midwest Political Science Association, Chicago, April 2–5.

Volokh, Eugene. 2001. "Our Flaw? We're Just Not Liberals." *Washington Post,* June 3, B3.

Wagner, John. 1992. "Four Women Caught in Judgeship Fight." *Washington Post,* June 23, A19.

Wall Street Journal. 1999. "Stroke of the Pen" (editorial). *Wall Street Journal,* December 22, A18.

Washington Post. 1999. "A Shameful Performance" (editorial). *Washington Post,* October 6, A32.

Watson, George, and John Stookey. 1995. *Shaping America: The Politics of Supreme Court Appointments.* New York: HarperCollins.

Watson, Richard L., Jr. 1963. "The Defeat of Judge Parker: A Study in Pressure Groups and Politics." *Mississippi Valley Historical Review* 50:213–34.

Whittington, Keith E. 2001. *Constitutional Interpretation: Textual Meaning, Original Intent and Judicial Review.* Lawrence: University of Kansas Press.

Wilson, Reid. 2009. "Conservatives Gear Up for High Court Fight." *The Hill,* May 1. http://thehill.com/leading-the-news/conservatives-gear-up-for-high-court-fight-2009-05-01.html.

Wright, John R. 1996. *Interest Groups and Congress: Lobbying, Contributions and Influence.* Boston: Allyn and Bacon.

Yalof, David Alistair. 1999. *Pursuit of Justices: Presidential Politics and the Selection of Supreme Court Nominees.* Chicago: University of Chicago Press.

Yehle, Emily. 2009. "Congressional Budgets to Jump." *Roll Call,* March 2.

York, Byron. 2005. "Harry Reid Steps Over the Line—Again." *National Review Online,* May 13. http://www.nationalreview.com/york/york200505130859.asp.

Zuniga, Jo Ann. 2000. "Petitions Urge Senators to Back Latino for Judge." *Houston Chronicle,* August 2, A32.

INDEX

Concerned Women for America (*continued*)
124, 126, 133, 139–40, 146. *See also*
Jipping, Thomas
Conservative Activist, 127, 131, 137,
139, 141, 142
constituency concerns: for Judiciary Committee members, 107–9; for non–Judiciary Committee members, 109–10

delay: impact of, on nominees, 195–96;
increase in, 68–69; mechanisms of
or reasons for, 37–38, 69–74, 93,
214–15n15. *See also* holds; senatorial
courtesy
district courts: organization and structure
of, 3–4, 50
District of Columbia v. Heller, 15
Dole, Robert, use of holds by, 79
dual tracking, 181
Durham, Barbara, confirmation of, 135–36

Edwards, John, 63–64, 65, 192
Estrada, Miguel, confirmation of, 46,
139, 142, 152, 180–81

Federal Bureau of Investigation (FBI),
70–71, 98–99, 226n3, 231n6
Feinstein, Diane, 54, 62, 160
Female Nominees, 175
filibuster, 13–14, 38, 46, 54, 74, 76,
179–82, 217–18n37, 222n14. *See also*
cloture; Gang of Fourteen; nuclear
option
fire alarm theory, 17, 154–55, 162, 170,
172, 191
four tracks framework: description of,
17–18, 24–25, 29–30, 47, 187;
fluid nature of, 24–25, 39–40; noncontroversial track, 18–19, 30–33,
155, 187–88. *See also* holds; interest
groups; senatorial courtesy
Free Congress Foundation, 13
Frist, Bill, 181

Gandy, Kim, 128, 131, 132, 133, 135,
137–38, 141, 145, 234n1. *See also* National Organization for Women
Gang of Fourteen, 46, 64, 159, 181–82.
See also nuclear option
gender of nominee, effect of, 166–67,
172, 175–77
Gittenstein, Mark, 110–11
Gorton, Slade, 135–36
Grassley, Charles, use of holds by, 83,
151, 223n24, 224n33

Hatch, Orin, 54, 70, 72, 73, 99–100,
132, 136, 150–51, 152, 180–81,
215n18
Helms, Jesse, use of holds by, 36, 58–59,
63–64, 82
holds, 1–2, 19–20; description of, 38,
74, 75, 179, 216n23; determination
of, 200–201; examination of underlying intent, 87–91; history of, 67,
75; implications of, 91–93, 188–91;
media coverage of, 38–39, 76–77,
216n26; modern usage of, 84–87;
motivations for, 77–87; "revolving,"
76. *See also* delay; parliamentary procedures
home-state senator support, 132–34,
165–66, 219n10, 233–34n14. *See also*
patron; senatorial courtesy

ideology of nominees, 42–43, 130–32,
164–65, 170–72, 186, 205–6, 230–
31n24
information on nominees: formal
sources, 98–101; informal sources,
101; need for, from informal sources,
101, 104–7; need for, from interest
groups, 101, 103–5, 106–7; need
for, generally, 97–98, 191; nominee
sources, 98, 100, 227n7, 229n15. *See
also* interest groups: information role
interest groups: access and influence
based on type of group, 108–11;

Constitutionalism and Democracy